Population Economics

Tommy Bengtsson (Ed.)

Population, Economy, and Welfare in Sweden

Springer-Verlag
Berlin Heidelberg New York London Paris Tokyo
Hong Kong Barcelona Budapest

Associate Prof. Tommy Bengtsson
University of Lund
Department of Economic History
P.O.Box 70 83
S-22007 Lund
Sweden

ISBN 3-540-58423-4 Springer-Verlag Berlin Heidelberg New York Tokyo
ISBN 0-387-58423-4 Springer-Verlag New York Berlin Heidelberg Tokyo

42/2202-543210 - Printed on acid-free paper

Contents

The Authors:

Tommy Bengtsson, Associate Professor, Economic History, Lund University

Per Broomé, BA, Stockholm

Per Gunnar Edebalk, Associate Professor, School of Social Work, Lund University

Mats Johansson, Associate Professor, Expert Group on Regional and Urban Studies (ERU), Östersund

Agneta Kruse, Senior Lecturer, Economics, Lund University

Björn Lindgren, Professor, Community Health Sciences, Malmö, and Economics, Lund University

Christer Lundh, Associate Professor, Economic History, Lund University

Carl Hampus Lyttkens, Associate Professor, Community Health Sciences, Malmö, and Economics, Lund University

Christina Jonung, Lecturer, Economics, Lund University

Rolf Ohlsson, Professor, Economic History, Lund University

Inga Persson, Professor, Economics, Lund University

The book has been written as part of the research programme *The Aged and the Economy* at the School of Economics and Management, Lund University, with support from the Council for Social Research (SFR), Sweden.

Chapter 1

Introduction
Tommy Bengtsson

The Swedish welfare model of the 1960s and 1970s excited great interest among many other countries. Today it still is an ideal image for some but a warning for many others. The reason why opinion about the Swedish welfare model has changed is primarily Sweden's financial problems, which are associated with a badly financed and excessively large public sector. It is argued that the size of the budget deficit is a great problem in itself, but also, and perhaps more importantly, that the large public sector has negative effects on the entire economy since it lead to inefficient allocation of resources. A first step in order to solve these problems is to examine how they arose. The questions then are to what extent the large public sector which Sweden has today results from social entitlements which have come into existence since the 1960s, from the maturing of welfare systems decided upon earlier, from unfavourable demographic developments, or from economic stagnation, and how these factors are interlinked.

What is quite clear is that Sweden has had very low economic growth during the 1970s and 1980s compared with the preceding period. But so have many other industrial countries, without their having in consequence found themselves in difficulties as great as Sweden's. Therefore economic stagnation alone cannot explain Sweden's situation.

Have demographic developments, then, been specially inauspicious for Sweden? In an international perspective Sweden stands out as a country different from others in this respect. Sweden have the highest proportion of old people in the world, the highest proportion of cohabiting couples, the highest proportion of children born outside wedlock, and the highest proportion of refugees in relation to population. Sweden is among the countries with the highest average lifespan and the highest living standards, and also one of the industrial countries with the highest fertility despite the fact that we also have the highest female labour force participation rates. However, these peculiarities do not set us totally apart from other industrial countries in all these fields - they merely mean that developments were earlier or more extreme in Sweden and that this has quite serious implications for public sector expenditure.

As regards the development of the welfare system during the 1970s and 1980s, certain new entitlements did appear, including increased parental insurance and lower pensionable age. Nevertheless the main structure of the welfare system dates further back in time. In addition to individual and political rights its citizens received social rights or entitlements, and step by step these became more and more extensive, including rights to high compensation for lost income (for example during illness and unemployment).

The welfare ideology has its roots in late nineteenth-century industrial society. The first steps towards a welfare society were taken in the period around the turn of the century when legislation was enacted covering such matters as compensation for industrial injuries, state subsidies for the voluntary friendly society movement, and a national pension system. The latter in fact was the first pension system in the world to cover the entire population. On these questions there was a considerable measure of agreement between the great political parties, as was also the case on the majority of the sociopolitical issues on which decisions were taken subsequently.

At first, the evolution towards a welfare state did not proceed any faster in Sweden than in other West European countries. In 1960 public expenditure in Sweden formed 31 per cent of GDP, which was not unique but was somewhat lower than in France, Germany, Great Britain and Austria. By 1970 the proportion of GDP absorbed by public expenditure had risen to 43 per cent - only Holland had higher public expenditure - and during the 1970s Sweden took the top position in the expenditure league. In the 1980s Sweden not only retained but even increased its lead. Public expenditure today, including transfer payments, accounts for 75 per cent of GDP, which places Sweden in a unique position compared with other countries. Now a transfer payment is not a cost in itself. Nor is it certain that private solutions are better than public. The main point, rather, is that such a large part of incomes is channelled through the public sector and that the financing creates inefficiencies. Thus the cost of a high level of transfer payments results from inefficient allocation of resources.

When the welfare ideology burst into full bloom in the 1960s, social and economic developments were favourable. With the high birth figures of the second half of the 1940s it was believed that the population crisis of the 1930s was already past. The demographic transition was over and done with, and a future free of population disturbances now awaited. Nor was there any disquiet over economic trends. Total production was increasing by around 4 per cent a year, industry by 5-6 per cent. The 1960s were a golden age for Swedish households. It was then normal to be able to buy a telephone, TV, car etc. Social entitlements were being expanded in one area after another: child care, child allowances, education, education allowances, unemployment insurance, social welfare allowances, industrial injuries compensation, disability compensation, early retirement pensions, partial retirement pensions, housing allowances, supplementary pensions and so forth.

The underlying idea was that the individual should be able to live at a tolerable standard of living whether he or she was working or not, and that a pensioner should have almost the same standard which he had when working. This was to be accomplished by means of transfers, chiefly from wage-earners to other groups but also from high- and medium-income earners to low-income earners. The market economy was to be controlled, modified and supplemented so as to implement the distribution desired by the majority. In order to achieve the declared goal of guaranteeing all citizens a good standard of living, a healthy economy and an active state were required. The policy and the institutions which gradually emerged came to be called "the Swedish model" later on. The expression is not precise, and there is a handful of differing interpretations of the concept. The term really refers to the system of collective wage negotiations which came into use during the 1960s. Today it has a broader content and includes all the most important forms of state intervention in the economy for the purpose of implementing the transfers needed to create social justice.

One of the cornerstones of "the Swedish model" is a strong economy. Labour market policy is an important feature in this, and from the historic settlements arrived at between trade unions and employers during the 1930s and 1940s a new type of active labour market policy was formulated in the late 1940s and early 1950s. In order to create a mobile labour force capable of moving into expanding sectors of the economy, the assistance provided for the temporarily unemployed was very generous, and special allowances were given to make internal migration easier.

Another important feature of "the Swedish model" is the size of public consumption. Transfers of resources between individuals should not only take place as transfers of cash but also, and perhaps principally, through the consumption of public services. Most of these are produced today under local authority auspices, and in most municipalities the public sector is far and away the largest employer.

Even though the major part of the sociopolitical system was already fully developed by the 1960s, the great growth of public expenditure did not happen until the 1970s, and 1980s, and then as a result of the maturation of the systems and to demographic changes. The pension system is an example of this. Today pension benefits are bigger than pension contributions. The deficit is defrayed from pension funds and tax receipts. Under today's rules the gap is expected to widen in the future. Therefore a new pension system has seen the light of day. The new system on which the Riksdag (the Swedish parliament) has just resolved is characterised by more direct links between payments in and payments out, i e a reduction of redistribution effects. In many areas of the public sector the charging element of finance is being increased in order to improve efficiency and freedom of choice. This applies to health care, for example, in which charges have hitherto covered only a very small proportion of costs. The transfer system is also criticised for leading to a number of undesirable distortions of the economy. Voices are being heard calling for a return to the "minimal state", which probably cannot become all that small because of, among other things, the promises already made. Bearing in mind the intensive current debate concerning the financing of the welfare system, for example the new pension scheme, it is interesting to note that the financing of the predecessors of such schemes was not properly analysed and debated in advance but in some cases has came as an unpleasant surprise afterwards.

Sweden has experienced one long demographic cold shower because of the maturation of social welfare systems and the growing proportion of elderly, and other industrial countries are moving towards one as well. Another one is accordingly awaiting us within a relatively near future because some way into the twentyfirst century, the proportion of pensioners is going to increase further as the bulge of children born during the 1940s come up to retirement age. This certainly is one of the reasons why Sweden recently has adopted a reform of health and social care of the elderly and introduced a new pension system. Sweden has in some respects been a forerunner in the development of social entitlements. In a way it has also been a forerunner in terms of demographic trends. Is it now to become a forerunner in the discovery of new forms for developing and/or redefining the role of the welfare state?

There are certain areas which it is important to analyse in order to understand the changing role of the welfare state. One of these areas, analysed in this book, is that of population trends in Sweden in a long-term perspective - the so-called demographic transition. It is argued that it is not over and done with at all but still going on. Another area is that of women's economic status, where both the paid and unpaid work of women is analysed. The number of women in the labour force in relation to the total number of women of working age in Sweden today is almost the same as that of men. But women work fewer hours outside the home than men, though more inside the home. Another area which also impinges on the labour market is migration, both within the country and in relation to foreign countries. Internal short-distance migration has increased while long-distance has decreased. The former immigration of labour from abroad has turned into refugee immigration. Still another area of importance which is discussed in the book is the economic aspects of the elderly: their financial situation as well as the organisation of social and health care.

Altogether it is intended that these articles should give the foreign reader an insight into the way in which different social systems have emerged in Sweden during the twentieth century and what problems the country faces today in maintaining social security, problems that have come earlier and are more severe than in other countries. We hope that a reading of this book will not only lead to an increased understanding of what is going on in Sweden but may indicate what will happen in other industrial countries, too, thus showing what lessons can be learned from the Swedish experience.

Population and labour market

Sweden's transformation from an agricultural country with large-scale production of raw materials such as timber and ore to an industrial country occurred rather late - the industrial revolution came around 1870. It was not until the 1930s that industrial workers outnumbered those working in agriculture. Industrialisation transformed Sweden from a small, poor country on the margins of Europe to one of the richest countries in the world. According to *the classical view of the demographic transition*, the country's modernisation led first to a fall in mortality, then to a decrease in family size simultaneously with a substantial reduction of the variations in death and birth rates. This transition was considered to have been completed during the 1930s. The reason for the decrease of family size was partly an adaptation to reduced child mortality and partly an adaptation to the changes in economic conditions brought about by modernisation. With the rise of modern society the direct costs of raising children increased in consequence of factors such as compulsory education. The need for children as security in old age diminished, and so on. When family planning then became a social norm, family size decreased rapidly.

According to *Bengtsson and Ohlsson* (chapter 2) a great deal of this is a *misconception*. The decline in mortality which started at the end of the eighteenth century took place prior to the modernisation of the Swedish economy - before real wages rose. Accordingly there is no connection, during the *initial phase* of the decline in mortality, between that decline and the economy. However, better living standards (better food, better hygiene etc.) caused mortality to *continue falling* during the latter part of the 19th century instead of returning to a high level again as had happened before over the centuries.

The decline of fertility, on the other hand, is directly linked to the rise of modern society. It is true that fertility had gone up and down before as well, but with the emergence of the industrial society it went down for good. Nevertheless the demographic transition was not completed until the end of the 1930s according to the classical view. Such a view signifies that the costs of having children relative to the income from them did not change any more and that women's wages relative to men's were stable - in plain terms, that women's entry to the labour market was completed. However, birth rates did not remain stable at a low level after the transition was completed but varied in long waves. According to Bengtsson and Ohlsson, these waves cannot be explained in terms of changes in children's *direct costs* but by changes in the situation of women on the labour market, i.e. by changes in *indirect costs* of having children. The changes in women's working conditions take place in conjunction with structural changes in the economy. During the 1950s and 1960s, for example, the employment intensity of housewives increased, chiefly as a result of the growth of the public sector. The demand for this labour increased in consequence, among other things, of a reorientation of the care of old people. From 1950 onwards, old people were increasingly looked after in their own homes, and usually it was housewives who were employed by the hour for these tasks (see chapter 7 by Edebalk and Lindgren). Later on, when this labour supply reserve ran out in the early 1970s, home care had to be totally reorganised.

From the mid-1960s until the mid-1980s, birth rates fell continuously. This seems to be mainly the result of a gradual rise in the age at which mothers have their first children. And as long as the age rises the birth rate falls, other things being equal. The rise in the average age must be viewed in context with the rapid increase in the duration of women's education. With the expansion of the educational sector in the 60s and 70s women made good almost the whole of the educational lead which men had over them. At the same time wages were being more and more equalised between men and women. When the average age of the mother at the birth of the first child stopped rising, birth rates rose to a new level.

In *Jonung and Persson's* chapter an analysis is made of how the work situation and family situation of women changed during the twentieth century. Their main conclusion is that Sweden, in an international perspective, has become an outlier with regard to women's participation in the labour force *and* fertility rates. This is a result of economic developments in combination with a deliberate equality policy designed to make labour force participation and having children compatible for women, i.e. to increase the profitability of market work and at the same time reduce the costs of raising children. In this chapter, it is shown how the labour force participation rate, measured as the number of women with or looking for jobs outside the home in relation to the total number of women of working age, has gradually increased since the 1930s. In 1990 it was only 5 percentage points lower than men's, which for the 20-64 age group was 91 per cent - and today they are equal. However, women differ from men when it comes to the distribution of time between work inside and outside the home. The hours they work outside the home are fewer than men's and the hours inside it more, because of part-time working, parental leave, absence due to children's illness and so on. The increase in aggregate time worked on the labour market from the early 1960s to the present day has come from women, while men's time has fallen in a long-term perspective. The fact that men's labour force participation has diminished results from the shorter working week, longer holidays and lower labour force participation rates among younger and older men as a result of increased education and more early retirement. At the same time, women's education has increased and is now virtually the same as men's. A significant equalisation of wages has also taken place over the long term, although it has been interrupted during recent years, as shown elsewhere.

Increased female employment outside the home has meant that childbearing has decreased over the long term. However, this trend was interrupted in the middle of the 1980s, when the birth figures increased sharply. Fertility in recent years has been in the region of net reproduction, which is high compared with most other industrial countries. In this way Swedish women combine gainful employment with high childbearing. The prerequisite of this is a well-developed child care system and opportunities for absence from work when the children are small. This is facilitated by means of compensation to parents for lost earned income, and the Riksdag has recently approved a special "care allowance" (*vårdnadsbidrag*) which will make it easier for a parent to stay at home when the child is small. Although significant improvements for parents have been made lately, the first steps in this direction were taken much earlier. A law rendering it illegal to dismiss women on the ground of pregnancy, childbirth or marriage has been in force since 1939. In addition, the defrayal by central and local authorities of a substantial part of the costs of children - day care, schooling, school lunches, medical and dental care etc. - also dates back in time to the period around the Second World War.

The high labour force participation rates of women mean that most Swedish multi-person households today are dependent on two incomes. The emphasis of the tax system since 1971 has been on the individual, which means that married and cohabiting men and women are taxed separately. As the tax system is progressive this means that it is now more profitable for women to work outside the home than before while the opposite is the case for men.

Labour market and migration

An important feature of economic development since the war has been that the proportion of women gainfully employed has steadily increased. Today it has reached such a level that it cannot be expected to rise much more. A large proportion of the new jobs for women emerged in the public sector, especially within the health and social services. From the early 1960s onwards, the proportion engaged in the provision of services has risen while industry's share of the labour force has shrunk. A transition is taking place from the production of goods to the provision of services, and most of these services are provided by the public sector. Because the production of services takes place in the main in the "localities" where the consumers are to be found, this development has meant that it has become easier to get jobs outside the big city areas and industrial districts. The local authority itself, or the county hospital, is the biggest employer in most local authority districts. In many of the sparsely-populated local authority districts, moreover, the proportion of elderly people is very high in consequence of many years of net migration of younger people along with low birth rates, and it is for old people that a large proportion of public services are produced.

It is not merely job opportunities that have become more equally distributed regionally than when goods production dominated: differences in incomes have been evening out between the various parts of the country at the same time. An industrial worker today has practically the same wages regardless of where he or she works, whether in a big-city borough or in a sparsely-populated county. At the same time as living costs have been rising more rapidly in big-city areas than in the rest of the country, real wages have been becoming more even. The result, as *Bengtsson and Johansson* show in chapter 4, is that long-distance migratory movements diminished substantially from the early 1960s to the mid-1980s, when the ending of the long-term boom interrupted this development. However, there is nothing to suggest that this interruption is more than temporary.

It seems likely that the rise in the proportion of two-earner families would also help to moderate migratory movements, since it is not just one member of the family who has to find a job in the new locality but two. However, by comparing migrants of different ages, Bengtsson and Johansson find that the decrease was about equally large at those ages where lone persons predominate as at those where family migrations are in the majority. Therefore it is unlikely that the question of one or two incomes has any decisive effect on the changes in migratory behaviour.

An alternative explanation of the reduced long-distance migratory movements is that developments in information technology have made it possible to continue living at a place while working with the aid of computers, telefax and telephone. This has probably helped to reduce movements, but the big decline came long before the new technology had been developed. Therefore the latter cannot have had any crucial influence on the way migration evolved.

The reduction in long-distance migration in Sweden is not a unique Swedish phenomenon. On the contrary, the information available about such migration in other industrial countries points in the same direction. The causes seem to be the same, and this is probably in the highest degree an international phenomenon resulting from the actual process of transition to a post-industrial society.

Thus, one important feature of the labour market's development during the last 35 years has been that employment in the service sector has increased while that in the production of goods has decreased. Another is that the content of work has changed markedly. This results partly from the rise in the production of services but chiefly from the fact that work is organised differently from the way it was before - in goods and services production alike. Work now takes place to a much greater extent in work teams, and this requires different qualifications and also varies much more than before. The ability to cooperate and to take on new tasks has become more and more important. Heavily standardised jobs, as in the engineering and textile industries for instance, have largely melted away or been transformed into more skilled jobs. In the same way, highly specialised jobs in the public sector have largely disappeared.

During the golden years of the 1960s, when the economy was running at top speed, it was not only women working at home but immigrants as well who increased the labour force. Even in the 1930s, after the large-scale emigration to America had ebbed away, Sweden was already becoming the recipient of net immigration. Immigration increased further during the Second World War, consisting then mainly of people from neighbouring countries around the Baltic. The heavy demand for labour directly after the war stimulated further immigration, and Sweden now became a land of permanent net immigration. The immigrants were needed in industry, and as a rule the cultural gap was small. They therefore adapted quickly to Swedish society and furnished a valuable contribution to the country's economy. Gradually the immigration of labour from other countries increased, especially from southern Europe.

This situation lasted until the beginning of the 1970s. After that the picture altered completely. *Lundh and Ohlsson* present in chapter 5 an analysis of the way in which different factors interacted so that immigration policy and the content of immigration became totally transformed during the 1970s. Both the overall labour requirement and the need for competence changed rapidly. At the same time the turbulence in the world was forcing rich countries such as Sweden to open their doors to the immigration of refugees. The new immigrants had a completely different background from before. Immigration became more heterogeneous than it had been previously in terms both of the causes of immigration and of the education, language, religion and culture of immigrants. At the same time the labour market was changing. It became increasingly difficult for the new immigrants to find work. Unemployment among immigrants today is very high and hopes for its diminution are small.

Earlier studies have shown that the effects of immigration on the Swedish economy were for the most part propitious in the 1960s. The reason was that the immigrants were usually fit and of working age, so that their participation in employment was high. As regards the later wave of immigration, we do not know very much about the socioeconomic effects. What can be said, then, about future immigration? Only two things in fact. One is that it is highly improbable that Sweden will again experience a large labour requirement in the way it did throughout the postwar period up to the end of the 1960s. The second is that the international floods of refugees do not seem to be abating. Sweden's immigration policy, like that of other West European countries, was shaped during a period when we needed immigration, and it has changed very little since then. But reality has changed, and Sweden cannot isolate itself from it. The new situation therefore demands a new immigration policy to make immigration into something beneficial both to Sweden and to the immigrants themselves.

The elderly

The last three chapters deal with the economics of the elderly: old age pensions, social care and health care. Inasmuch as old people form such a large group of society it is something which concerns practically everybody. The sums which are disbursed via the state pension system are very large, forming about 12 per cent of GDP today compared with 5 per cent in 1970. Payments into the pension system currently absorb almost 20 per cent of total wages. Thus every fifth working hour goes to pay for old age pensions. Social welfare and health care of the elderly are very big business which require an efficiently organised and stable financing mechanism. The production of these services, most of which takes place under public auspices, provides a multitude of job opportunities. The elderly form a large proportion of the population and their consumption of goods and services constitutes a large market which influences the entire economy. Old people's consumption consists in large measure of locally produced services. The effect has been a wide regional diffusion of job opportunities, which has meant that the labour force has not needed to migrate in the same degree as before (see chapter 4). Thus the production of goods and services for pensioners has quite significant financial and organisational implications, including its great impact on the labour market.

The basis of pensioners' consumption is the state pension. This consists of a fixed component which is the same for all and a variable component which depends on previous income, and forms 70 per cent of pensioners' incomes. The rest comes from contractual pensions between the two sides of the labour market, private pension insurance and the return on private savings. The proportion deriving from pensioners' own work is negligible. The fixed component of the pension has its roots, as mentioned earlier, in the pension system established in 1913 as the first fully-comprehensive pensions system in the world. The pension system at its introduction was an ingredient of poor relief. The rate was low and insufficient to live on. It was improved gradually but it was not until after the Second World War that it became possible to subsist solely on the pension. With expanded local authority housing assistance, pensioners were no longer dependent on their own work, on social welfare assistance or on financial help from their children.

A variable pension, called ATP from the initials of its Swedish title (Allmän TjänstePension, General Supplementary Pension), began to be paid in 1964. The question was raised in the Riksdag as early as 1947 and after that was discussed by a number of committees of enquiry on pensions. With the aid of a single abstention by an opposition member, the government's proposal was voted through in 1959 by 115 votes to 114. The object was no longer for pensioners to have a tolerable living standard but that they should be able to continue living at about the standard which they had on retirement. The variable portion of the pension was designed as a pay-as-you-go system, i.e. as a distribution system, under which the payments out are taken from the current year's wage sum. As little unease was felt over its future financing when the system was introduced as there had been in 1913. There was more disquiet over the effects it would have on saving.

As *Kruse* shows (chapter 6), the Swedish system, in which disbursements were adjusted upwards in conformity with the consumer price index, would turn out to be sensitive to both changes in the age composition of the population and to economic growth. None of these problems was noticed at first. To begin with there was a delay before the system matured, secondly the additional inflow of paying workers was large, and thirdly economic growth was high. It was therefore to be thirty years before it was realised by the politicians that the system was not sustainable in the long run although it was already coming under criticism from Kruse and others in the late 70s. The object is to create a more direct relationship between payments in and out, and to relate pensions to the general trend of the standard of living - not to the trend of prices. A portion of the pension system will probably be designed as a funded system. But this will not solve the problems inherent in the fact that the fund is sensitive to growth and that the purchasing power of pensions therefore cannot be guaranteed. The reason is that the return on the funds is comes from the current year's production, like the contributions in a pay-as-you-go system. If matters go badly for Sweden the wage sum, and therefore the payments in, will be low, but at the same time the return on the fund will be low. In both systems, therefore, payments out will be dependent on economic growth, which is the idea behind the new system.

An important feature of the care of old people is concerned with daily supervision and accommodation. In the former peasant society the employer, the offspring and in the last resort the local authority had responsibility for the old. Society's responsibility was met by boarding out, auctioning off or "group rotation", and by institutions such as poorhouses and workhouses. No distinction of treatment was made between the aged, paupers, handicapped etc. Looking after old people was a heavy burden for many small and poor parishes. As industrialisation came to absorb an increasing proportion of the population, the parishes' problems increased. In industry, it was more difficult for the employer to find jobs for older workers than it had been in agriculture. In addition, the proportion of older people increased substantially in the closing years of the nineteenth century. The responsibility was shifted on to the children, and if they could not handle it the local authorities had to accept responsibility for the aged.

Edebalk and Lindgren show (chapter 7) that a distinction can be made between three phases in the care of old people. Around 1900, an institution called an "old people's home" became increasingly common. "Old people's homes" were reserved for the elderly, for whom they provided food, accommodation and care. In this way the care of old people had become separated from care of the poor, the handicapped and the sick. The pension reform of 1913 meant that pensioners got their own income, however small, and in 1918 a reform dealing with their accommodation was adopted. "Auctioning off" and "group rotation" were prohibited. The reform was aimed at improving institutional accommodation. Local authorities were made responsible for establishing old people's homes. During the 1930s special pensioners' housing was built at subsidised rents. This form signified a step away from institutional care of the aged.

The next phase began about 1950. The Riksdag had brought in a national pension sufficient large to live on some years earlier. At the same time a local government reform had been adopted with the aim of creating larger local authorities capable, *inter alia*, of taking greater responsibility for the aged. This enabled pensioners who were in good health to continue living in their own homes. "Living at home" in fact became the key words. Outside help was needed so as to be able to live at home longer. Normally this help had come from the children, but nowadays it was not always possible for them to give it. Families were much smaller than before. Urbanisation and uneven regional development meant that sometimes the children were living elsewhere.

An important initiative was launched by the Red Cross in Uppsala in 1950, when a home help service for old people was started up. This service was relatively cheap, became very popular with old people, and made it possible for them to remain at home much longer than they would otherwise have done. Those who worked in home care were often housewives employed by the hour. The system spread rapidly over the whole country but now under the auspices of local authorities.

This system assumed a new guise during the 1970s. The reserves of housewives who had formed the labour supply for the home help service were now exhausted. Staff were now employed on a permanent basis at monthly wages. They were trained, and were allotted increasingly skilled tasks. Their work became more taxing as the proportion of very old people requiring a great deal of care increased. The organisation became more and more complex, and costs soared.

The third phase has just started. In 1990 a new reform was enacted. Social care and long-term health care were brought under the same aegis - that of the local authorities. Formerly local authorities had been responsible for social care and the county council for health care. The reform is intended to create new forms of care of the elderly and thereby to increase its efficiency. It aims at competition between providers, freedom of choice for consumers, and privatisation. Too few years have passed for the reform to be evaluated. It has its apologists and its detractors.

The eldercare reform thus brought changes not merely in social care but also in health care, and these are discussed by *Broomé, Lindgren, Lyttkens and Ohlsson* in chapter 8. Health care of the elderly was formerly an integrated aspect of ordinary health care, under the aegis of the county councils. A county council is an independent regional organ possessing the right to tax individuals residing within its boundaries. The county councils made their appearance in 1862 and health care became one of their main tasks. The health care of old people is very costly and one of the objects of the eldercare reform was for it to be no longer possible for county councils to shift the costs on to local authorities by earlier discharge of patients to old people's homes. By placing both the social care and the long-term health care of old people under the same heading it was hoped also to achieve gains in general efficiency through increased flexibility.

The reason why the costs of health care for old people are high in Sweden is firstly that when people become old they get ill; secondly that there are a lot of them; and thirdly that the Swedes seem to have allowed their elderly to become more costly than they are in other countries. The costs of different types of health care have been reckoned up for every one-year age group. These calculations show that with practically all illnesses, costs rise rapidly with age. Thus they are particularly high for very old people. In so far as the proportion of people over 80 years of age continues to rise during the coming years, the demand for health care will also rise. In addition, the costs per head for the very old have risen during recent times because technical developments in health care have made it possible to treat complicated illnesses at higher and higher ages. Altogether, therefore, it may be expected that the costs of health care of old people will soar in the immediate future if the increased demand is to be satisfied and if efficiency cannot be raised. So, the pressure inherent in the problems of financing pensions, social care and health care for the elderly calls for a complete reorientation of the Swedish welfare model. In the final three chapters, the lessons learned from past experience and the new ideas now being developed and implemented are treated and discussed at full length.

To sum up, the Swedish welfare model of the 1960s and 1970s excited a great interest among many other countries and today is still an ideal for some but a warning for many others. The reason why opinion about the Swedish welfare model has changed, obviously, is the large budget deficits coupled with unprecedented high unemployment and low economic growth. It is argued that the large public sector has negative effects on the entire economy since it leads to inefficient allocation of resources. Part of the increase of the public sector is due to the maturation of welfare systems decided during the "golden years" of the 1960s or earlier, part to increase in benefit levels, and part due to an increased demographic pressure, in particular an ageing population. Some way into the twentyfirst century, the proportion of pensioners is going to increase further as the bulge of children born during the 1940s reach retirement ages which may have serious effects on the pensions system and on social and health care systems. Thus Sweden has experienced one demographic cold shower and another one looms within a relatively near future. The present financial problems and the demographic prospects explains why the entire concept of the welfare state is at present under lively debate and why some measures have already been taken within the field of pensions and social and health care of the elderly. Sweden has been something of a forerunner in the development of social entitlements and in terms of demographic trends. Is it now to become a forerunner in the discovery of new forms for developing and/or redefining the role of the welfare state?

Chapter 2

The Demographic Transition Revised
Tommy Bengtsson and Rolf Ohlsson

The theory of the demographic transition was long regarded as one of the most firmly-established of socio-economic theories. This theory was thought to explain how mortality and fertility were changed through the improvements in living standards and new labour conditions that followed the agricultural and industrial revolutions of the nineteenth century. The population changes were just as radical in their way as the economic changes, and "the vital revolution" was one of the terms suggested when the theory of demographic transition was being christened.[1] Gradually, however, the theory of the demographic revolution has come under severe criticism. But it still has a strong influence over our understanding both of how today's industrial countries have developed and of developments in those countries which just now are in the midst of such a process. The reason why the theory still survives despite all criticism is that there is a great need for a general theory of population trends during the transition from an agrarian to an industrial society and that no sensible alternative to the demographic transition theory has been presented.

What we shall try to do in this paper is to revise the theory of demographic transition and in doing so make use of the criticism to which it has been subjected. One of our most important findings is that the demographic transition started considerably later and went on for much longer than we formerly believed. We would even argue that it is still going on at the present time in today's industrial countries.

We further believe that this revision also makes possible a better understanding of the causes and consequences of the demographic processes currently in progress and the way in which these are bound up with economic and social events.

Former and present conditions of life

The great upheavals of the economic and social structure during the past two centuries have meant that the conditions of human life have been changed in a fashion that has no counterpart in history. Totally new products and services - inconceivable and impossible to predict for eighteenth-century man - have appeared as the result of swift and accelerating technological advance. The organisation, content and character of labour have been drastically altered. Towns have grown in

---

1 This emerged in the course of conversation with Kingsley Davies at Palo Alto in October 1992.

size and the countryside has been depopulated. At the same time improved communications have caused the contact network to expand and regional differences to be erased to a large extent. People have come closer together, with increasingly similar values as a result. Incomes and living standards have risen step by step, and the common resources have increasingly been devoted to the production and consumption of collective services such as child care, education, health and medical care, and care of the aged.[2]

These dramatic upheavals have brought the consequence that the life cycle and demographic behaviour of individuals present an appearance now which is quite different compared with 200 years ago. Family structure and family relationships have undergone radical changes as well.

In the old agrarian society children formed a large proportion of the population, while old people were relatively few. Thus, of Sweden's 1.7 million inhabitants in the mid-eighteenth century one third were under 15 years of age, while the proportion above age 65 formed only six per cent (see Diagram 2). In other words there were more than five times as many children as old people. This may be contrasted with the situation today. At the present time, out of a population of 8.6 million there are as many old people over age 65 as children under 15, but fairly soon the elderly will outnumber the children. On the other hand the proportion in the "active" 15-65 age group was about the same in 1750 as now. The big difference now, however, is that those of active age must provide the main support for the old, whereas their dependency burden in the eighteenth century consisted almost exclusively of children.[3]

The change in the proportion of older people has not happened gradually but more in the form of leaps. One such leap occurred during the later decades of the nineteenth century as a result of diminished mortality among the elderly but also because of diminished fertility and large-scale emigration to America. The big rise in the proportion of elderly took place considerably later, however - during the second half of the twentieth century. This rise resulted primarily from the fact that birth rates fell and that the number of younger people therefore did not increase as much as before, but declining mortality among older people also played a certain role. This applies especially to the increase of the proportion over 80 years of age during the most recent decades.

By far the largest proportion of children in Sweden in the middle of the eighteenth century were born to parents who lived in the country and tilled the soil. Those children who managed to survive into adulthood belonged to a privileged group - almost half of those born never attained the age of marriage. The first year of life, when one child in five died, was particularly problematical. But the other childhood years were filled with peril too, partly because of the smallpox epidemics and other plagues which regularly swept through the nation and hit children hardest, and partly because of inadequate food in combination with harvest failures.

Those children who survived had to earn their keep from an early age, and in

---

2 This chapter is a further elaboration of Bengsson and Ohlsson (1993) and Bengtsson (1992).
3 For a discussion of old age security in preindustrial Sweden see Bengtsson and Fridlizius (1994).

many cases that of their parents as well, by going into service as maids or farmhands. They would usually spend more than ten years in service before it was time to wed. By then they would have been servants to many employers, since custom stipulated only a short stay at each farm. In other words migration and mobility of labour were relatively high even in the old agrarian society.[4] The picture of a static and immobile Swedish agrarian society in the eighteenth century can therefore best be described as a myth.

A woman usually married at age 25 and a man when somewhat older, at 27. Marriage ages in the peasant-proprietor class were somewhat below those among the agrarian lower classes. Crop failures delayed marriages, so that the marriage age, both for men and women, would be even higher during such periods. For the eighteenth century agrarian lower class, marriage commonly formed the occasion for renting land from the crown or the nobility. The hope then was to be able ultimately to buy the farmstead and appurtenant land to hand down to one of the children. This, in principle, was one of the few chances of creating an assurance of being looked after when no longer capable of doing the heavy work on the farm. If possible the farm would be passed to one of the children when the parents were between 55 and 60 years of age.[5]

On average a married couple would produce six children. But there was also a relatively large group of men and women, something like 20%, who never married and thus did not have children. Of the six children in a family, scarcely five survived the first year of life. Three would reach adulthood. But it was far from certain that a couple who bore six children would be lucky enough to see a grownup son capable of taking over the farm or the tenancy.

The average life expectancy of boys born in Sweden in the middle of the eighteenth century was 35 years and of girls 38 years. But to use average life expectancy at birth as a demographic measure for describing the pattern of mortality during the eighteenth century is virtually meaningless. For almost half died during childhood, while those who managed to survive into adulthood could look forward to living to about age 60, by which time most of the siblings would already be dead. By then one or perhaps two grandchildren would have come into the world as well.

High mortality and the high marriage age meant that the probability of there being a male or female grandparent available to look after children was not particularly great. By the time the younger children were born, as a rule only one out of the four grandparents would still be alive. Surviving aunts and uncles were also few, and the parents were relatively old.[6]

Consequently, reality goes against the widespread romantic myth that the old agrarian society had an efficiently-functioning vertical family structure where people lived in some form of extended family in which the generations lived and worked together, with the children looked after by grandparents and the old cared for by the extended family.

---

4 See e g Bengtsson (1987) and Bengtsson (1989).

5 Information culled from the research project "Life events in a peasant society in transition", Department of Economic History, Lund University.

6 Johansen (1976).

The contrast between then and now could scarcely be greater. Children born today generally grow up in an urban environment with parents employed in the public sector or in the private production of services. Hard manual labour has largely vanished.

Broadly speaking, all the children born today achieve adulthood. The few deaths prior to age 25 can be ascribed almost entirely to traffic or other accidents. Even in middle age mortality is extremely low.

Entry to the labour market usually takes place in the 20s, after a period of education lasting 12-15 years and in many cases considerably longer. Cohabitation with a partner often commences at the same time as establishment on the labour market or shortly thereafter. There is then a delay of some years before marriage. Commencement of cohabitation usually takes place at a lower age than was the case in the eighteenth century. There is no longer a direct link today between family formation and work. Forming a family used to mean starting up a household, which would also constitute a base for the householder's own employment, whether this meant farm work or some craft.

A cohabiting or married couple of today will opt to have two children. Because so many of them are cohabiting, half of all children are born outside wedlock. The two children are usually born in quick succession, after which the mother returns to the labour market. The portion of the woman's adult life during which she is neither pregnant nor looking after small children has thus increased substantially. This means that she has the opportunity of working on the open labour market for considerably more years than would previously have been the case - an opportunity of which today she avails herself.

A boy in Sweden today can expect to live to 75 and a girl to 80 years of age if prevailing mortality patterns at different ages continue to apply. But if we assume that mortality at different ages continues to change in future in the same way as it has been doing for the past 50 years, then many of the children being born today are likely to reach age 100.

Family relationships too present an appearance quite different from those of the eighteenth century. In somewhat simplified terms they can be said to be becoming increasingly vertical, whereas those of the eighteenth century were horizontal. A child now has only one sibling. The number of cousins has fallen to between five and six. The parents are relatively young. The family often comprises four living generations. This changed family structure has also brought about changes in relations between the generations. Contrary to the general supposition, evolution towards a vertical family structure has brought increased dependency between the generations. Here again, reality goes against the myth that the modern society has diminished contact between the generations. Grandparents, who by this time have often left a life of industrial employment behind them, frequently help by lending a hand with their grandchildren. Each child is important to the survival of the family and is therefore much cherished. When the elderly reach the stage of needing care, a very large part of this function is discharged via the relatives. The growing numbers of elderly will probably lead increasingly to people's being forced to look after their elderly relatives themselves.[7]

However, to compensate for the reduced horizontal family structure, the social network outside the family has also become increasingly important, and will probably become even more so in future.

The reason why we can give a relatively good picture of the pattern of population conditions in the middle of the eighteenth century is that Sweden introduced modern population censuses at this time, being one of the first countries in the world to do so. This unique body of source material makes it possible for us to describe and analyse in some detail the drastic changes in the life cycle and demographic behaviour of the individual that took place in conjunction with Sweden's transformation from a poor agrarian society to a rich industrialised welfare state. This process of demographic change, which in Sweden's case went on from about 1800 to about 1930, is usually termed the demographic transition. All the industrial countries of the western world, and the recently industrialised countries of the third world as well, have undergone a similar experience. In fact it is only in parts of Africa and Southern Asia that those changes have not yet started in earnest. The demographic transition has manifested itself in different guises. The feature common to the countries where it is underway is that the conditions of life have been altered radically by increased living standards and life expectancy along with reduced family size.

Criticism of the theory of the demographic transition

The theory of the demographic transition was launched in the early 1940s.[8] The theory's interpreters considered that this model of explanation described the demographic transition from an agricultural to an industrial society, and also that it explained the transition's connection with the process of economic and social change in the nation. This claim was based primarily on the Swedish population statistics because of their early start and acknowledged high quality and reliability. The transition was broken down into phases, as shown in Diagram 1.

The first phase, i e the traditional agrarian society, is characterised by high mortality resulting from low living standards and recurrent epidemics. At the same time death rates fluctuated widely from year to year. In order that birth rates should be at least as high as average death rates but without exceeding the death rates too much either, social institutions and conventions were evolved, for example in the shape of established norms for the age at which people ought to marry, breast-feeding customs, birth control practices and so forth, which determined the level of birth rates.[9] The family was the unit on which both production and consumption were

---

7 Odén (1988) and Ohlsson, Broomé and Nilstun (1993).

8 The two scholars associated with the genesis of the theory are Kingsley Davies and Frank Notestein. Davies seems to have been first to use the phrase "demographic transition", see Davies (1945), Notestein (1945 and 1953).

9 We concur here in Douglass North's definition of the term institution as meaning firstly sundry contrivances such as departments of state or the church, secondly the regulatory

based in the traditional agrarian society, and it was frequently economically necessary to have many children. In this way a degree of slow population growth still took place - an average of about 0.5% per year in Sweden's case - although in occasional years death rates could be higher than birth rates.

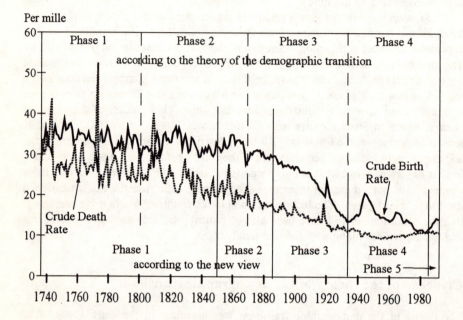

Diagram 1. Crude birth and death rates for Sweden 1736-1992.

The second phase was inaugurated when long-term mortality began to fall. This happened in Sweden about the year 1800. According to the theory of demographic transition, advances in industry and agriculture led to improvements in living conditions in a variety of ways. The population's diet improved both in quantity and in nutritional value, which increased resistance to disease. Housing and hygiene were improved, and there was better access to health care and medical treatment. Consequently mortality fell, especially among children, while at the same time the wide year-to-year variations in mortality began to subside. At first birth rates remained at the high levels of the first phase because the social norms and institutions which determined the level of births were slow to change. The result was a rise in population which accelerated as time went on. Sweden's population increased by an average of 0.7 - 0.8% per year during the nineteenth century, which meant that population numbers rose from 2.4 millions in 1800 to 5 millions in 1900 despite extensive emigration.

mechanisms of society in the form of constitutional law along with other laws and ordinances, down to unwritten rules such as table manners, honour and other human conventions or customs.

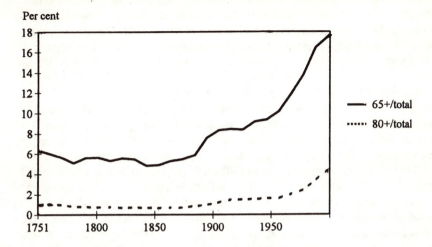

Diagram 2. Population in ages 65 years and above respectively 80 years and above in relation to total population 1751/55 1986/90.

The third phase commences when the long-term birth rates fall. In Sweden this occurred during the latter part of the nineteenth century. More precisely, the years around 1880 are usually cited as the time of the change. The overall birth rate itself began to fall some decades earlier but it was not until about 1880 that family size diminished. The latter was a consequence of the way changes in the social structure reduced the significance of the family as a production unit, developed a labour market for women outside the home, increased urbanisation, and nullified the economic advantages of large families. In conjunction with all this there were changes in norms and institutions which impinged on the view of how many children a family ought to have. A further argument is that because of lower child mortality, a woman did not need to bear as many children as before in order to get the desired number of surviving children. Population growth also abated in step with falling birth rates.

The demographic transition was then completed by a fourth and concluding phase in which birth rates stabilised at a level lying immediately above the death rates. Population growth was now low and year-to-year variations in mortality and fertility were quite small. The significance of the economic factors in explaining the level of and fluctuations in birth rates and mortality had played out its role. Thus the demographic transition from an agrarian to an industrial society was completed. According to the transition theory, this happened in Sweden's case around 1930.

The theory of the demographic transition has enjoyed great popularity and it has set its mark over a long period on our view of population trends and the economic and social factors which determined these. By degrees, however, it has been coming under wide-ranging criticism. There are many who argue that it cannot really be characterised as a theory in the true sense of the term but should mainly be regarded primarily as a generalisation. For gradually, as population trends in other countries have been reconstituted, it has been discovered that the demographic transition has followed quite different patterns. In France, mortality began to fall at the same time as in Sweden, i e in the early nineteenth century. But in contrast to Sweden, birth rates started going down at the same time. Consequently the second and third phases coincided. No substantial population growth corresponding to that in Sweden took place in France. In England, where mortality likewise began to fall early in the nineteenth century, birth rates were rising at the same time.[10] England therefore experienced a period of extremely high population growth.

One factor not touched on in the original transition theory is the extensive emigration from Europe during the second and especially third phases. The peak was reached in Sweden during the 1880s, but emigration was already gathering momentum prior to the middle of the century. Over the period between 1850 and 1930, 1 144 000 Swedes emigrated, most of them to the United States, which should be compared with Sweden's population of 3.5 million in 1850. Thus there are several ways in which the transition took place. Consequently the transition theory's pronouncements as regards sundry causal relations can be called into question. Criticisms focus on the actual groundwork of the theory, i e the demographic pattern prevailing prior to the transition, and also on the causes of declining mortality, the causes of declining birth rates, and the description of the situation after the transition. In other words they touch on every single aspect of the transition theory. Taking these criticisms as our starting point, we can then offer a new interpretation of the demographic transition.

The agrarian society - balance between high mortality and high fertility?

In order to believe in the explanatory value of the transition theory it is important to believe also that in the agrarian society preceding the demographic transition, mortality was always at a high level even if it varied widely from year to year. For in the first place, the fall in mortality is utilised in order to date the transition from the first to the second stage. If the mortality level is not stable in the first stage, it is scarcely possible to assert that the fall *must* be the start of something new. The fall in mortality could then equally well be an integral part of an old pattern with recurrent long-term up- and downswings of mortality. In the second place, a high average mortality level is an explanation of high birth rates. The only societies with high mortality which could survive in the long run were those which developed social and economic institutions and norms that encouraged relatively prolific childbearing.

As long as the theory was based on Swedish population data from 1750 onwards, there was nothing to necessitate calling into question the conception of high mortality in the first phase. However, studies made of population conditions in England, based on reconstitution of that country's population from 1541 to 1871, give us quite a different picture.[11] In England, the mortality level varied widely over time. For example, mortality increased over the span of a one hundred-year period from the end of the sixteenth century, then diminished again from the middle of the eighteenth

10 Schofield (1984).
11 Wrigley and Schofield (1981).

century. And the data, going back to 1722, available for Sweden from the period prior to the population censuses likewise show that the mortality level in the Swedish agrarian society was far from stable (see Diagram 1).[12]

Neither does there appear to be any link between mortality level and standard of living in England. In other words death rates varied independently of the movement of real wages. Consequently the causes suggested by the transition theory for the decline of mortality during the second phase of the demographic transition can also be called into question. It may further be questioned whether high mortality really did cause the old agrarian society to develop institutions and norms (e g that a woman should bear as many children as it pleased God to bring her) designed to keep fertility at a high level, and whether these norms and institutions stand out as important explanations of the length of time it took for fertility to diminish despite the fact that mortality had fallen much earlier.

The primary indication from the results of the English studies is that the norms and institutions which controlled birth rates in both the long and the short run were sensitive to economic changes. Marriages were the principal governing factor in this connection. When times became harder fewer people got married and the marriage age rose simultaneously. The new research results thus overthrow completely the basic assumptions of the theory of demographic transition. The mortality level was not stable, and it was births, not deaths, which were influenced by the long-term trend of the economy. Consequently both the dating of the shift from the first to the second stage and the causes of the transition itself can be called into question. The Swedish studies which brought demographic and economic links during the eighteenth century under scrutiny likewise point in the same direction.[13] Births and marriages were considerably more sensitive to changes in the economy, both long- and short-term, than mortality.[14] Population changes were determined more often by economic incentives than by social norms.

The decline in mortality

The reason why mortality decreased during the second phase, according to the theory of demographic transition, is that the general power of resistance to disease rose in consequence of improvements in living standards and food supply following from advances in agriculture. The living standard argument, including the role of potatoes, has been the subject of lively debate in both international and Swedish research. The argument has many supporters but it has also been called into question. A counter-argument in the Swedish case has been that the standard of living first began to rise in the middle of the nineteenth century but that the fall in mortality began much

---

12 The only data to have survived for the period 1722 to 1735 are for nine counties and the city of Stockholm. The data refer to the whole country from 1736 onwards. Details of the size of population have been computed backwards in time from 1749 to 1722 on the assumption that foreign net migration was nil. See Bengtsson (1992).

13 Principally Fridlizius (1984).

14 Principally Bengtsson (1993) and Galloway (1988).

earlier, as early as the end of the eighteenth century in fact.[15] Moreover, the decline started almost simultaneously in different parts of Sweden, independently of economic and social structure and independently of when the revolutionary agricultural reforms were implemented. It seems as though mortality began to decline in different countries at approximately the same time. On the other hand the economic growth process started at quite different points in time. Consequently improved nutrition can scarcely explain the *initial* decline in mortality, whether in Sweden or on the Continent. It must be stressed at this point that this initial decline in mortality consisted mainly of falling infant and child mortality (see Diagrams 1 and 3).

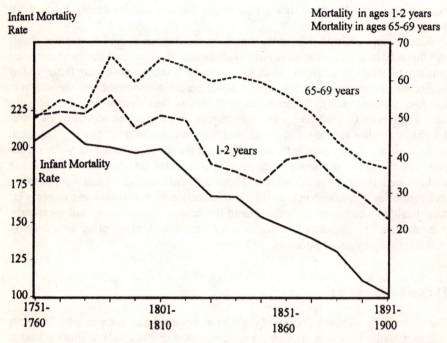

Diagram 3. Infant mortality, child mortality in ages 1-2 years and adult mortality in ages 65-69 years 1751/60 - 1890/1900. In per mille.

Changed breast-feeding practices have been adduced as the principal cause of the decline in infant mortality. A study based on the analysis of infant mortality in a number of parishes, primarily in northern Sweden, has shown that the breast-feeding campaigns which were waged by provincial doctors and nurses were successful and that they played a vital role in the survival of more children.[16] However, the breast-feeding campaigns started after mortality had begun to diminish and therefore cannot

---

15 Fridlizius (1984) who in this and other works analyses mortality in different age groups and from different illnesses.
16 Brändström (1984).

explain the initial fall. Moreover, that changed breast-feeding practices should be the principal explanation seems implausible since mortality also decreased in the districts where no breast-feeding campaigns were waged.

The significance of climatic changes (temperature, precipitation etc) has also been debated. Northern Europe was dominated during the latter part of the eighteenth century by a climate which brought a lowering of average temperatures. The climate did not improve until after 1810, when a period of more maritime character commenced. Thus the initial fall in mortality started at a moment which was inauspicious from a climatic standpoint. Therefore the changed climate can scarcely have had any positive effect on the chances of survival until perhaps after 1810.

It has also been argued that it was medical progress which led to the decrease of mortality in the early nineteenth century. In this connection special emphasis has been laid on the significance of smallpox vaccination for the fall in child mortality. But here too a counter-argument has been adduced to the effect that smallpox vaccination had was of no significance at all in the initial fall in child mortality because the fall started before the vaccinations. There are also contemporary sources which allege that vaccination was not effective.

It has been questioned whether medical factors were of any importance at all in the decline of mortality which started in the early nineteenth century and then continued until our own day. A study of mortality trends in England and Wales suggests that medical advances had no effect before the 1930s when antibiotics made their breakthrough.[17] The exception is diphtheria, which began to be treated with antitoxins around the year 1900 at the same time as mortality was diminishing. However, this disease was not sufficiently common for its treatment to be capable of influencing the overall death rates appreciably. A modern American study even contends that medical factors can explain only 3.5% of the decline of mortality in the United States since 1900. The study asserts, moreover, that this is an upper limit for the significance of medical factors. A similar Swedish study, which has not been made yet, would probably produce a lower figure as its outcome, because the fall in mortality was even more accentuated in Sweden than in the United States. One might ask at this point how the myth of the great importance of medical progress and of doctors in the decline of mortality has been able to survive as long as it has done and still does.

Another explanation which has been propounded for the initial decrease of mortality is that the balance between micro-organisms and man has shifted in favour of man. This changed balance may have resulted from some diminution of the virulence of parasites, from natural selection of people with high resistance having taken place, or from an increase of general powers of resistance. There is much to suggest that the decline in mortality prior to vaccination was the consequence primarily of *the virulence of the parasites having diminished*, with reduced mortality from smallpox as a result. By virtue of smallpox having become less common, its consequential maladies also diminished. The birth cohorts which escaped smallpox therefore became healthier and developed better immunity defences.

One problem with the virulence theory is that it can only be verified indirectly or

---

17 McKeown and Record (1962), McKeown (1976).

through the elimination of other conceivable explanations. The reason is that changes in the explanatory variable, i e in the virulence of parasites, are not susceptible to measurement, unlike the other types of explanations (better nutrition, vaccination, changed breast-feeding practices etc).

If the virulence explanation is the most important one here, it also becomes possible to explain why repeated rises and falls of the mortality level were experienced by the agrarian society prior to the demographic transition. The decline of mortality after about 1800 will then not appear as something new but as an element in an old pattern. Then the question that presents itself instead will be why mortality did not rise again later on in the nineteenth century as it had always done previously after a decline. Consequently the new phenomenon is not the decline in mortality but the rise that did not happen.

"Peace, vaccine and potatoes", the Tegnérian phrase of 1833 summing up the causes of the decline of mortality in Sweden, bears many resemblances to the basic explanations offered by the transition theory. The phrase contains a grain of truth but even so should be regarded as the embodiment of a myth. The decline in mortality began before the end of the Napoleonic Wars; vaccine and medical progress played a very marginal role; and improvements in living standards (potatoes) cannot explain the first phase of the steep fall in mortality because they did not come until later.

The fall in mortality was not the start of something new but the end of something old. The new did not happen until later on in the nineteenth century, when general improvements in conditions of life, in the form of better diet, better housing, improved hygiene, better child care and better sanitary systems in the towns, caused mortality not to increase again as it had probably always done before following a period of low mortality. It should also be observed that the path followed by Swedish mortality was not unique. There are strong resemblances between what happened in Sweden and what happened in other west European countries such as England and France, and Norway and Denmark as well.[18]

The decline in fertility

The shift from the second to the third stage of the demographic transition took place when birth rates began to decrease over the long term. According to the transition theory, fertility, like mortality, is influenced by the modernisation of the economy. The economic advantages of small families disappear. The time-delay results from the fact that fertility is governed by norms and institutions which are sluggish of movement.

The crude birth rate in Sweden began to decline after about 1880. Actually there was a fairly sharp fall in the crude birth rate during the 1860s, probably as a result of a harsh economic situation, but it went up again during the 1870s. From the beginning of the 1880s onwards, however, it fell continuously for a long time. Diagram 4, which shows fertility at different ages, gives a more detailed picture of how the decline proceeded. From the early 1880s onwards, childbirths among women

---

18 See Bengtsson (1992).

over 30 years of age fell sharply. In the 25-29 years age group they fell slightly and among women under 25 years they increased. It was not until the 1910s that fertility diminished among younger women. The reason for the rise in fertility of young women was that more of them were marrying at younger ages. This is usually interpreted to mean that during the initial decline young married women bore children in accordance with the traditional pattern but that they ceased to bring children into the world once they had reached some particular desired number. But the ensuing families deferred childbearing and increased the time-intervals between the children. Only then was family planning fully in place. This interpretation is correct as far as it goes but it is not the whole truth. In order to understand the decline in fertility more completely, every age cohort of women must be charted throughout its entire fertile period.

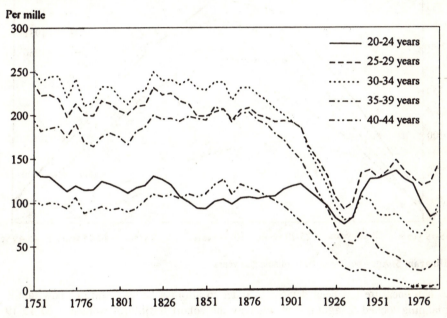

Diagram 4. Age-specific fertility rates 1751/55 - 1986/90.

Diagram 5 shows the fertility at different ages for slected years. The curves shows that fertility went down only slighly during the 125-year period between 1751 and 1876. The shape of the curves indicates that family planning was uncommon during this period. From the end of the nineteenth century onwards fertility was decreasing rapidly and the fertility pattern from then on bears the typical hallmarks of modern family planning. The differences between the curve for the 20th century and those for the middle of the 19th century and earlier can be said to be a measure of the extent of family planning.

Family planning may mean that parents deliberately defer the birth of the first child ("delaying"), that they increase the birth intervals ("spacing"), or that they cease childbearing sooner ("stopping"). As has already been remarked, the curves for age-specific fertility (Diagram 4) give the impression that stopping came first, then spacing and delaying. This would mean that the young women in question did not avail themselves of the job opportunities which industrialisation and commercialisation provided during the second half of the nineteenth century, especially after the industrial revolution which is usually dated at 1870. Instead, they bore children in the traditional way until they reached the desired number, when their fertility diminished rapidly.

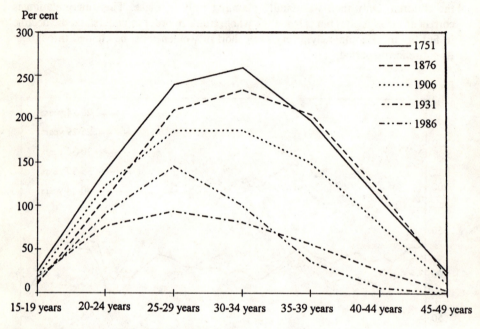

Diagram 5. Age-specific fertility in selected years.

A new measure has been devised in order to afford a better picture of how family planning looked. Diagram 6 shows how the cohort fertility of women aged 15-19 years from 1881 to 1911 diverges from that of women aged 15-19 in 1861. Cohort means that we are following a certain group over time. Thus we are not comparing age-specific fertility rates at a given time period any longer. We presume that those aged 15-19 in 1861 did not use family planning to any major extent. This group is used as a base group. The fertility for the other cohorts are then divided by the fertility of the base group. In order to cope with the fact that the marriage age was changing, the curves have then been indexed so that all cohorts have the same fertility at ages 15-19 as the 1851 girls in this age group. The curves in Diagram 6 show how large a share of the decline that took place at ages 20-24 years, 25-29 years and so on given that they all started at the same fertility rate in ages 15-19 years. Thus the curves shows the proportion of fertility regulation taking place in each age group. The similarities between the curves are striking. Thus indepentent of how much the women who are entering into the fertile ages from 1881 onwards are lowering their total fertility, they spread the regulation of their fertility over their fertiliy age period proportionally. Family planning meant primarily a decrease of fertility at the most fertile ages. Even at the outset, Swedish women were bearing fewer children than was biologically possible. Even at the outset, fertility was at least limited if not planned. The conclusion therefore is that spacing was common but that the other forms of family planning were common as well. Certain differences, although minor, can be discerned over time. Those who were 15-19 years of age in 1881/85 to 1891/95 shifted a bit towards stopping while their younger sisters and children shifted somewhat towards delaying. Thus we are able to establich a typical pattern of fertility regulation from which only minor deviations shows up.

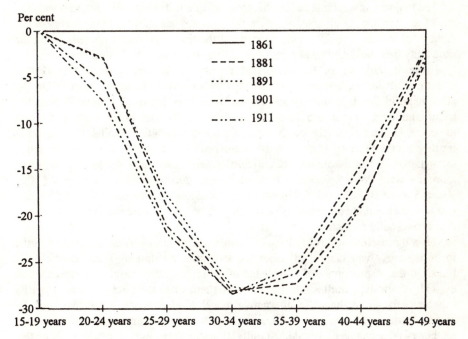

Diagram 6. Proportion of fertility regulation by age with age-specific fertility in 1861 defined as unregulated fertility.

What we can establish is that it was not only family size that came to be adapted to conform to the new conditions prevailing during the latter part of the nineteenth century but that the timing of childbearing was influenced too. This indicates an adaptation to the new labour market opportunities which opened for women during this period - an intepretation that makes more sense than earlier ones. The fact that the fertility decline started in the towns and continued in the countryside for some decades is consistent with this interpretation.

The proportion of children born outside wedlock in Sweden in the early nineteenth century was about 5 per cent, just as in the neighbouring countries.[19] This proportion then increased steadily during the century to reached a maximum of about 10 per cent during the 1880s. It then stabilised, but rose again during the 1920s. This rise can be regarded as a result of society's accepting children born outside wedlock in a quite different way from before. To a large extent these were the children of affianced couples. Even so it can be argued that these children were unwanted. Therefore this can be regarded as a sign that the methods of controlling fertility were relatively ineffective. That the view taken of marriage was changing prior to the great decline in fertility is quite clear, however.

The majority of explanations of the great decline in fertility are bound up with the rise of modern society, directly or indirectly. This applies likewise to the theory of the demographic transition. The early versions of the transition theory also discussed the possibility that the decline was a result of falling infant and child mortality.

However, analyses of the decline of fertility in Europe show that in certain countries the decline had not been preceded by any fall in child mortality.[20] On the other hand in Sweden, Norway and Denmark, the decline of child mortality started about a hundred years before the decline of fertility. The time-delay makes it difficult to believe in any causal relation. Another argument which tells against the decline of fertility having been an adaptation to diminished child mortality is that it was much too massive. In fact the number of childbirths went down from 4-5 to 2 while infant mortality went down by about 10 per cent units during the 19th century, i.e. that about .5 more children per family survived. Consequently the time-delay in Sweden was too great and the decline too drastic for it to be linked more than marginally with diminished child mortality.

Thus the decline of fertility has been explained primarily as an *adaptation* to the modern society which emerged from the industrial revolution. The explanation is based on the assumption that knowledge of effective contraceptive measures already existed previously. Families then began to use them when there was reason, primarily economic, for using them. An alternative model of explanation is the theory of declining births as an *innovation*.[21] Dissemination of information about contraceptive methods and a changed attitude to family planning form important elements of this model of explanation.

Quite likely there is no cause for making any sharp distinction between adaptation and innovation theory. Few would assert that the decline of fertility was independent of socioeconomic changes, at least in a general sense. But the question still is whether some innovative process did not form an important element of the decline.

A fundamental question at this point is whether methods of family planning were well known before the decline of fertility. There is much to suggest that this was the case. One may refer to the great regional disparities in fertility which existed prior to

---

19 Bengtsson (1992).

20 Van de Walle, F in Coale and Cotts Watkins (1986).

21 See Carlsson (1967) for a discussion of the relevance of adjustment and innovation theories for Sweden.

1880, as well as to the differences between town and country and between different social classes. However, regional and social disparities in fertility may well result from factors quite other than family planning, such as differences in breast-feeding practices.

Fertility age-patterns in Sweden prior to the great decline of fertility, however, deviate somewhat from what is typical of populations where family planning is entirely absent, which suggests that part of the population did apply some type of family planning. However, the deviation is small, and it is also stable from 1750 to the end of the nineteenth century, which must be interpreted as meaning that family planning was uncommon prior to the decline of fertility. Analyses of age-specific fertility in countries adjacent to Sweden give the same result.

In a large-scale study of the decline of fertility in various European countries, the hypothesis that family planning started when the society had reached certain threshold values in terms of economic structure, health, education etc was taken as a starting point. In other words it was assumed that the decline in fertility was a process of adaptation. But the result was quite otherwise. It was found that decline started at about the same time in several European countries. The conclusion drawn was that three conditions must be satisfied: (1) control of fertility must be a socially acceptable form of conduct and be present as an alternative in the family's deliberate planning, (2) to limit family size must be considered beneficial, and (3) effective methods of such planning must be available.[22] The conclusion which has dominated subsequent research is that the socioeconomic motivation (2) was changed in the long run by the emergence of modern society but that the actual timing of the decline was determined by the fact that family planning became socially acceptable (1), possibly in combination with knowledge of effective methods of contraception becoming more widespread (3).

Another way of expressing it would be to say that the modernisation of society towards the end of the nineteenth century causing a situation of economic choice to emerge. For the first time it became a feasible option to refrain from begetting children in order to improve one's economic and social situation. The great emigration, which broadly coincided in time with the decline of fertility, can be regarded in principle as a manifestation of the same modernisation process. Considerably more options became available than before. To emigrate or to beget fewer children presented themselves as new and feasible alternatives.

However, there is a certain amount of uncertainty about why the great decline in fertility started during the last two decades of the nineteenth century. The labour movement's rapid emergence and rise, embodying the values and spirit of a new age, may be cited as important innovative factors to explain the timing. The feminist movement and the entry of the suffragettes into the arena brought a questioning of women's traditional role. In 1880 Knut Wicksell delivered the first neo-Malthusian lecture in Sweden, then published a number of papers on the subject during the 1880s. The massive increase of population was regarded as the root of all poverty and voluntary restriction of childbearing as the only solution to the problem. New types of contraceptive devices were being introduced as well. For example, new condoms

---

22 Coale and Cotts Watkins (1986).

made of rubber were being manufactured instead of the earlier ones made of animal gut. Diffusion of information increased in general, e g through the rise of daily newspapers.

But these innovative factors, which in many cases remained as principal explanations of the decline in fertility, must not be exaggerated. The most important driving force still consisted of the desire of people to have fewer children, and in this the modernisation of society and the radically changed economic situation of families were the primary underlying causes.

The industrial society - new population balance with low mortality and low fertility?

After 1880, fertility diminished rapidly. The steep decline of fertility constitutes the demographic transition's third phase, which can be said to have ended in the 1930s. In somewhat simplified terms, the drastic decline in fertility can be viewed as a consequence of the falling incomes and rising costs which the decision to beget another child would entail for the parents. The pecuniary benefits of having children (as risk insurance against possible death of the man, as pension insurance and as a supplementary source of income in the form of child labour) diminished with the rise of the welfare state and technological and organisational changes in the economy. At the same time the costs involved in having children were rising by virtue of e g the expansion of the educational system, women's entry into the labour market and increasing urbanisation. It may be expressed thus: that families acted rationally in economic terms as a response to changes in the economic conditions of bringing children into the world.

At this point one may wonder at the speed of the demographic adaptation to the changed economic conditions. Over a 50-year period, family size gradually fell from an average of six children per married women to an average of two. This rapid adaptation took place in an environment where propaganda for the use of contraceptive devices was prohibited, where religion, with its negative attitude to child limitation, still had some hold over people's values, and in which the existing contraceptive devices were not of particularly good quality.

It may be worth while to take note here of the view of the population situation of the 1920s recorded for posterity by the Myrdals in *"Kris i befolkningsfrågan"* (The Population Crisis). The low birth rates of the 1920s and early 1930s were ascribed primarily to overcrowding, depression, high unemployment and general destitution, which was later used as an argument in favour of far-reaching social reforms. Regarded from the perspective of modern population economic theory the Myrdals' analysis presents a relatively crude appearance in which no clear distinction is made between structural and cyclical patterns of events. As we have seen above, the low birth rates must be regarded primarily as an adaptation to the rise of modern society and to the changed economic conditions with respect to the utility and costs of having many children.

According to the transition theory, fertility stabilised after about 1930 at a level immediately above the death rates. However, we can state that this was not the case.

Even though the norm of two children per family has prevailed all through the twentieth century, fertility has still varied fairly widely around this norm. Contrary to what the transition theory asserts, moreover, there is much to suggest that variations in fertility can be attributed mainly to economic factors.

Thus the deviations from the long-term trend of fertility tie in principally with what happened on the women's labour market and to some extent what happened on the labour market for young people, although other factors were obviously at work as well. When the labour market was good and relative wages (women's wages relative to men's) were high, childbearing was deferred, and vice versa. The following patterns can be discerned. During the 1910s and 1920s, fertility declined steeply at the same time as women's relative wages were increasing sharply. In the early 1930s there was a clear reversal inasmuch as fertility began to rise while women's relative wages were moving simultaneously in a negative direction. A new turning point can be discerned at the end of the 1940s, when relative wages again rose at the same time as fertility was falling. Both relative wages and fertility then remained unchanged for most of the 1950s. After 1964 fertility fell while relative wages rose simultaneously. There is much to indicate that the rise in childbirths after 1984 was associated to a certain extent with a relative wage for women that had worsened.

As is evident, the parallelism between women's relative wages and childbirths, with reversals occurring more or less simultaneously, is surprisingly good. In this connection it also ought to be pointed out that the fact that such a strong link exists between fertility and relative wages over time suggests that the economic factors determined fertility. If the causality had gone in the other direction, i e from fertility to economic factors, then a rise in fertility could have been accompanied by a fall in the female labour supply and thus by a rise in relative wages. But what we observe is the opposite.

These different phases of childbirths and movements of relative wages can in turn be related, with certain modifications, to periods of structural transformation and structural rationalisation. Thus the Swedish economy after the industrial revolution is distinguished by a pattern in which 40-50 year periods of varying characters are marked off by structural crises. The latter struck in the early 1890s, in the early 1930s and during the 1970s. Each and every one of the periods thus demarcated consisted of two phases, one of structural transformation and one of structural rationalisation. During the transformation phase the economic structure was renewed through the diffusion of innovation, rapidly increased investment, and large-scale investment in buildings compared with investment in machinery, especially in industry. Furthermore, the expansion took place largely on the home market. The rationalisation phase showed the opposite characteristics. The new elements introduced during the transformation phase were now established and had become vested interests, which inhibited tendencies towards renewal.

Periods which are characterised by rapid and extensive structural transformation have a special investment pattern with considerable new enterprise and production of new goods, a situation less propitious for women on the labour market. The background to this is that the labour market situation during transformation periods is favourable mainly to groups such as engineers and trained workers. The proportion of women in these groups, historically speaking, has been small. During periods when structural rationalisation predominates, conditions on the labour market are different. Rationalisation includes efforts to reduce the cost of production through standardisation and automation. In this way the demand for labour tends to be shifted, relatively speaking, towards less qualified labour, i e towards women. It can also be shown that women's wages have risen during periods when rationalisation was dominant, but have been stationary or declining during transformation phases.

The 1910s and 1920s display here the typical hallmarks of a period of structural rationalisation with vigorous efforts to reduce production costs through standardisation and automation. What this mainly involved was an increased need for assembly-line working and less skilled labour. If it is also borne in mind that in the uncertain economic conditions which prevailed during the 1920s, firms were not specially inclined to employ a labour force one of whose characteristics was that its wage at the beginning of its period of employment generally exceeded the value of the marginal product - i e young people. This, in combination with an increased supply of young workers, may explain why the labour market position worsened for young people. According to Easterlin's fertility model, in which there is a positive correlation between the numbers of children born to young people and their (i e young people's) relative wages compared with older people, this ought to have led to reduced fertility.

The 1930s and 1940s can be characterised as a period of structural change quite different from earlier decades, with expansion generally being marked by a large number of new establishments, and with a growing proportion of industrial investment consisting of new plant. Scope was thereby created for new jobs at the lower levels, i e for young people, with relative wages of young people rising as a result, and so rising fertility. Again, the labour market situation was specially favourable to highly-trained workers, technicians, engineers etc, while the changed alignment of production made demand for unskilled labour (women) relatively low.

The 1950s can be characterised as mainly a transitional period, with comparatively small changes in relative wages of both women and young people. The fertility of older women continued to fall simultaneously with a gradual improvement of their labour market situation. On the other hand we find the fertility of young women rising, which is more difficult to explain in terms of labour market factors. But it is possible that the extremely high economic growth during this period, the "golden" years of Swedish economic history, resulted in a classical "income" effect, i e a feeling on the part of individuals, generated by the prevailing prosperity and independent of other factors, that they could afford to have several children.

The period after 1964 can be characterised as the most intensive phase of rationalisation in Sweden's economic development, with women's relative wages rising steeply. A massive rush into the education system was also going on at the same time. This combination resulted in a very pronounced decline in the fertility *of all* age groups (see diagram 4).

After 1983 fertility rose again, partly as an automatic reaction to the earlier steep decline. It is also probable that the rise was linked with a deterioration of the situation of women on the labour market. However, the rather strong link between economic factors and childbearing which we have been able to establish was not as strong from this point on as it had been formerly, principally as a result of the expansion of public child care services, of parents' insurance, and of the recent marked improvement in women's relative situation on the education front compared with that of men. The link between labour market and childbearing will probably become even weaker in future. It is possible that we shall then enter a fifth phase of the demographic transition.

One important element of the fourth phase has been large-scale immigration. Thus immigrants have also played an important role in childbearing in Sweden. However, this factor must not be exaggerated. Foreign citizens form about 5% of Sweden's population and account for 10% of childbirths in the country. However, this higher level of births is explained mainly by the fact that immigrants are over-represented at childbearing ages and that more of them are married or cohabiting. If the childbirths to foreign married or cohabiting women of a specific age are examined it is usually found that they bear somewhat *fewer* children than Swedish women. For all that there are variations depending on nationality. But even women who have come to Sweden from cultures with high fertility adapt themselves very quickly to the Swedish birth pattern. In this connection it is interesting to discover a very rapid adaptation in both directions. When Swedish women have increased their childbearing, the foreign women have done the same. When Swedish women's fertility has gone down, so has that of foreign women.

A revision of the theory of demographic transition

In our opinion, *the theory of the demographic transition* has a limited explanatory value. What we should like instead is to sum up the demographic transition in its relation to Sweden's transformation from an agrarian to a post-industrial society, as follows. During the first phase, which extended as far as the middle of the nineteenth century, the mortality level varied between different periods fairly independently of economic factors. Fertility was somewhat more stable, although in essence it was more dependent on economic factors than mortality was. This meant that population growth varied from period to period. Moreover birth rates and death rates, especially the latter, varied widely year to year, which led to population decrease in occasional years. During the second phase, which began in the middle of the nineteenth century and continued until its end, the standard of living increased in consequence mainly of improvements in agricultural productivity. The old mortality pattern was broken as a result of better nutritional standards. Mortality no longer returned to the same high levels as before but subsided gradually while at the same time the wide annual variations diminished and later on ceased almost completely. The new economic conditions changed the circumstances of households. When family planning little by little became socially accepted the numbers of offspring diminished swiftly. This constituted the third phase, which started during the closing decades of the nineteenth century and can be said to have ended in the 1930s. Because of the time-delay between declining mortality and declining fertility, the population grew substantially. The great emigration formed an integrated part of this phase. Finally, fertility in the fourth phase varied around the two-child norm in long waves, with mortality continuing to fall at the same time. The varying birth rates can be ascribed chiefly to changes on the women's labour market. This again brought periods of varying population growth, but at a much lower level than prior to the demographic transition.

It is possible that we are now moving into a fifth phase in which fertility will stabilise around the two-child norm and where economic factors play a smaller role in determining the timing of childbearing. A further important element in the fifth phase will probably be a substantial decrease in the mortality of the very old. Thus we find mortality over the age of 80 to have fallen steeply since the Second World War, some of the most important underlying factors being the pension reform of 1948, a decided improvement of the living standards of the very oldest people, and the introduction of antibiotics, all of which has enabled the very old to survive influenza and colds in quite a different fashion from before.

We are gradually moving, then, towards a population structure which can best be likened to an up-ended rectangle, with far-reaching consequences for health care, pensions and so forth. Only when this phase arrives will it be possible to say that the demographic transition has been concluded.

REFERENCES

Bengtsson T (1987) Migration och löner. Tillämpning av Todaros migrationsteori på 1800-talets svenska urbanisering. Ekonomisk-historiska vingslag, Lund.

Bengtsson T (1989) Migration, Wages, and Urbanisation in 19th Century Sweden, in Hayami A, de Vries, J, van der Woude, A (eds.) Urbanisation and Population Dynamics in History. Oxford.

Bengtsson T (1992) Den demografiska utvecklingen i de nordiska länderna. Lund Paper in Economic History, No 15.

Bengtsson T (1993) A Re-Interpretation of Population Trends and Cycles in England, France and Sweden, 1751-1860, Histoire & Mesure, VIII-1/2, 1993.

Bengtsson T, Fridlizius G (1994) Public Intergenerational Transfers as Old-Age Pension Systems: An Historical Interlude? in Ermisch J, Saito O (eds) The Family, the Market and the State. Oxford University Press. Paper presented at an IUSSP conference in Sendai City 1988.

Bengtsson T, Fridlizius G, Ohlsson R (eds) (1984) Pre-Industrial Population Change - The Mortality Decline and Short-Term Population Movements. Lund.

Bengtsson T, Ohlsson R (1993) Sveriges befolkning - myter och verklighet. Äventyret Sverige - En ekonomisk och social historia. Stockholm.

Brändström A (1984) De kärlekslösa mödrarna, Umeå.

Carlsson G (1967) The Decline of Fertility: Innovation or Adjustment Process. Population Studies, Vol XX, No 2.

Coale A J, Cotts Watkins S (1986) The Decline of Fertility in Europe. Princeton.

Davis K (1945) The world demographic transition. Annals of American Academy of Political and Social Sciences, 237:1-11.

Fridlizius G (1984) The Mortality Decline in the First Phase of the Demographic Transition: Swedish Experiences, in Bengtsson T, Fridlizius G, Ohlsson R (eds).

Galloway P (1988) Basic Patterns in Annual Variations in Fertility, Nuptiality, Mortality, and Prices in Pre-Industrial Europe. Population Studies, vol 42.

Johansen H C (1976) The Position of the Old in the Rural Household in Traditional Society. Scandinavian Economic History Review, 76:2, p 129-142.

McKeown T, Record R G (1962) Reasons for the decline in mortality in England and Wales during hte nineteenth century. Population Studies, vol XVI, p 94-122.

McKeown T (1976) The modern rice of population. London.

Notestein F W (1945) Population - the long view, in Schult T W (ed.) Food for the World. Chicago.

Notestein F W(1953) Economic Problems of Population Change, in Proceedings of the Eight International Conference of Agriculture. London.

Odén B (1988) Vem hade makt och inflytande i ett äldre samhälle - de gamla eller de unga? Gerontologia 1/88.

Ohlsson, Broomé, Nilstun (1993) Operation sjukvård. Stockholm.

Schofield R (1984) Population Growth in the Century after 1750: the Role of Mortality Decline, in Bengtsson T, Fridlizius G, Ohlsson R (eds) (1984).

Van de Walle F (1986) Infant Mortality and the European Demographic Transition, in Coale A J, Cotts Watkins S (1986).

Wrigley E A, Schofield R S (1981) The Population History of England 1541-1871 - A Reconstruction. London.

Chapter 3

Combining Market Work and Family

Christina Jonung and Inga Persson

Introduction

In an international perspective, Sweden had by 1990 come to look like something of an outlier with regard to women's participation in market work *and* fertility rates. The female labour force participation rate for women aged 20-64 amounted to about 86 per cent. This was only about 5 percentage points lower than the male participation rate and it was the highest female participation rate among the industrialised countries. High participation rates did not, however, keep women from having babies. The (period-based) fertility rate decreased from the mid-1960s onwards, but after 1983 it started to increase again.[1] At around 2.1 per mille by 1990, it surpassed the fertility rates of most other European countries. Clearly, Swedish women were having it both - combining market work with having and raising a family.

In this chapter we will first trace how Sweden came to end up in this position, with a focus on developments since the mid-1960s. We will look at how changes in the economy, and welfare programmes and policies of various kinds, combined to change and transform the time allocation patterns of Swedish women and, also, those of Swedish men. As a result, by 1990 the two-earner family had become the dominant mode of family organisation. Then we will look at the outcome and consequences of these developments, focusing first on the position of Swedish women in the labour market and then on family patterns and family life.

Historical background

Looked at in a longer historical perspective Sweden does not stand out as a country with exceptionally high rates of female labour force participation. The female labour force (as a percentage of the total female population) remained fairly stable at about

---

1 Chapter 2 gives a detailed account of the development of fertility rates in Sweden. Swedish fertility developments are also discussed in Hoem (1993) and Meisaari-Polsa & Söderström (1993a).

30 per cent from the mid-1800s and up until the 1930s.[2] But then, after a certain downturn during the 1930s and the early 1940s, a continuous increase took place over the following decades. However, as late as in 1960, the Swedish rate remained comparable to that of several other countries. While the Swedish participation rate (as a percentage of the female population aged 15-64) reached 51 per cent in 1960, the corresponding rate for Denmark was 44 per cent, for France 47 per cent, for Germany 49 per cent and for the UK 49 per cent.[3] It was not until then that the rapid increase took off which over the coming decades was to take Sweden to its 1990 outlier position. Other countries also experienced upward trends in female participation during these decades, but the increase often started later and was less strong than in Sweden (and Denmark).[4]

The relatively stable female participation rate up to the 1930s meant that women's share of the Swedish labour force also remained relatively stable.[5] However, this picture of stability hides a story of significant changes over time. The *composition* of the female workforce changed in terms of both economic structure (employment status, sectors of employment, occupations) and demographic structure (age, marital status). Work in agriculture and in domestic services was replaced by work in industry and in trade and other services. Status as unpaid family worker was replaced by employee status. To begin with unmarried women dominated the female labour force, both because there were so many of them and because their participation rate was much higher than for married women, and also increased over time.[6] After 1930 changes took place in the demographic structure of the female population. The age-distribution changed towards higher ages, there was a marked increase in the marriage frequency, and marriages took place at younger ages. In this way women over 40, the majority of them married, came to dominate in the female population of productive age. This change in the composition of the female population in combination with a gradually increasing participation rate among married women (to start with particularly among young, married women without children and then among older, married women) meant that the proportion of married women and the share of older women increased in the female workforce. In 1963, the first official Swedish Labour Force Survey reported a female participation rate of 49 per cent.[7] Married women had a labour force participation rate of 44 per cent and accounted for 57 per cent of the female workforce. Market work among mothers of small children was not uncommon. Thirty-eight per cent of Swedish women with children under 7 years old

---

2 Pott-Buter (1993) p. 21. Silenstam (1970) and Jonung (1982) give lower figures (about 20 per cent) for the earlier census years, probably because of differences when it comes to the inclusion of unpaid female family workers. See also the discussion in Nyberg (1989).

3 Pott-Buter (1993) p. 28.

4 See also OECD (1988).

5 Pott-Buter (1993) p. 33.

6 About one-fifth of Swedish women never married and almost half of the female population of productive ages was unmarried during the first decades of the 20th century. In 1930 59 per cent of unmarried women as compared to only about 8 per cent of married women belonged to the labour force. (Jonung 1982 p. 302.)

7 SCB (1974).

(the Swedish school-starting age) belonged to the labour force, which meant that they comprised 14 per cent of the female workforce. This proportion was to increase rapidly during the coming years.

The evolution of women's market work

The past three decades have undoubtedly involved thoroughgoing and dramatic changes in the lives of, and division of labour between, Swedish women and men. The changes involve time spent at work, time spent at home, the organisation of the care of children, the sick and the elderly, the organisation of working life, as well as the conditions and the financing surrounding the combination of home work and market work. Nevertheless, as will be shown below, at the beginning of the 1990s there still remains a substantial specialisation between men and women both between home work and market work and in the type of work they do. A narrow focus on labour force participation rates tends to obscure other important changes in the organisation of work.

Between 1963 and 1990 the labour force participation rate of Swedish women aged 20-64 grew from 54 to 86 per cent.[8] This meant that at the beginning of the 1990s there remained only a 5 percentage points difference from the participation rate of Swedish men aged 20-64 at about 91 per cent. During the same period the labour force participation rates of men decreased a few percentage points, chiefly due to reduced labour force participation among the younger and older age groups. See Table 1.

The inflow of women to the labour market has varied somewhat over the three decades. Women supplied the whole of the net addition to the labour force during the 1960s and 1970s. A majority of the women added to the labour force were married. During the 1960s the number of women on the labour market rose mainly as a result of population growth. In the early 1960s the labour force participation rate varied over the business cycle, but since 1967 the female participation rate has steadily climbed upwards. This upward climb was broken, however, by the severe recession that hit the Swedish economy in the 1990s.

The rise in the number of women on the labour market during the past two and a half decades can be traced primarily to an increased propensity to work among women. The 1970s were especially characterised by the rapid rise in the labour force participation rate of mothers of young children, which started around 1968. In 1983 the labour force participation rate of women with children under 7 years of age had become as high as 82 per cent.

---

8 The figures and tables in this paper are based on the yearly averages of the Labour Force Surveys, a monthly survey of the Swedish population, aged 16-74 years. A person is classified as in the labour force if he/she has worked 1 hour or more during the survey week, is temporarily absent from work or has been actively looking for a job.

Table 1. Labour Force Participation Rates and At-work rates, 20-64 Years of Age,
1963-1988 (per cent).

	Labour Force Participation Rates			At-work rates		
Year	Men	Women	Women with children 0-6	Men	Women	Women with children 0-6
1963	93.2	54.0	37.9	84.9	46.8	34.2
1968	91.3	56.7	41.8	80.5	48.3	30.4
1973	89.9	63.9	53.8	77.5	52.5	39.1
1978	90.6	73.5	68.7	75.9	58.5	48.7
1983	90.2	80.6	82.0	75.4	62.8	54.0
1988	90.0	84.7	85.8*	76.3	64.1	55.9*
1990	90.6	85.5	86.9*	77.2	66.4	53.4*
1993	85.5	81.1	81.3*	67.0	60.7	49.7*

* Women 16-64 Years of Age
Source: Swedish Labour Force Surveys, Statistics Sweden.

Thus, by the end of the 1970s it could already be said of Swedish women that they no longer chose between market work and home work. Paid market work was now no longer a spare time activity compared with household work, something to keep women busy while awaiting marriage and children or a forced undertaking for family support reasons. Work in the market had become a self-evident part of the life of adult women, even during periods with small children.

The labour force participation rate for women continued to rise during the 1980s but at a slower pace. Women still supplied the major proportion, but no longer the whole, of the net increase to the labour force. The proportion of mothers among the inflow was lower than their proportion of the existing labour force.

In total, slightly more than one million persons were added to the labour force between 1963 and 1990. Out of these, somewhat more than 80 per cent were women.

The result of the developments described above is a changed lifetime pattern of work for women. Traditionally, women's labour force participation has varied with age since age is related to marriage and childbearing. In Sweden before 1960, and even today in countries with low female participation rates, the rate of labour force participation reaches a maximum at ages 20-25 with decreasing levels thereafter.[9] Diagram 1 shows the participation rates of Swedish women in different age-groups 1963-88. The curves for 1963 and 1973 have the typical two-peaked pattern, one peak before the ages of childbearing and one after. The rise of the curves over time shows that all age groups except the youngest have increased their labour force

9 OECD (1988).

participation. The increase started among women over 35 years old. The increase among women aged 25-35 did not take place until after 1968.

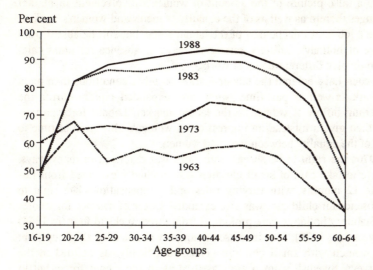

Diagram 1. Labour force participation rates for women in different age-groups 1963-88.

By the end of the 1970s the decrease in the labour force participation rates connected with childbearing had virtually disappeared. One decade later the participation rate was roughly the same, around 90 per cent, among Swedish women in all the age groups between 25 and 55 years old. This means that the two-peaked pattern has disappeared for Swedish women and that their labour force participation pattern by age now looks very much like that of Swedish men, with a broad plateau. The labour force participation pattern by age for men (not shown here) displays very little change over the same period, except for decreases in the oldest and the youngest age groups.

A cohort analysis shows that at every age except the youngest, each cohort of Swedish women has had a higher labour force participation rate than the one preceding it.[10] The large cohorts born around the middle and end of the 1940s were the first that tried to combine children and market work, and simultaneously work both in market and non-market production. The youngest cohorts of Swedish women show no signs of exits from the labour force during childbearing ages.

As a consequence of the developments described above the composition of the Swedish labour force has changed significantly during the postwar period, not only in terms of the proportion of women, but also in terms of the background of these women. In 1963 women accounted for 36 per cent of the Swedish labour force. By 1990 their proportion was all of 48 per cent; at least 60 per cent of the women in the labour force were married or cohabiting, about 45 per cent of the women in the labour force had children under 17, and about 20 per cent children under 7 years of age.

---

10 Jonung and Persson (1990) p. 30.

The labour force participation rates show that Swedish women have developed a firm and continuous attachment to the labour market all through the life-cycle. They do, however, give a false picture of the amount of women's involvement in market work and the changes therein as well as of the equality of men's and women's work. It is possible to have a job, and thus be part of the labour force, but still be absent from work, e.g. because of holidays, military service or leave of absence for child care. Different jobs also involve different hours of work.

Women in Sweden have entered the labour market on other conditions than men. Absences from work as well as part-time work have expanded rapidly during the decades with a strong inflow of women to the labour market. Labour force participation rates will then give a misleading impression of women's allocation of time to market work and of the equality between men and women.

During the 1970s the right to be absent from work was extended in many ways. Paid parental leave to take care of small children was gradually extended from initially 6 months to 12 months, with varying rules and compensation. The right to unpaid leave of absence for child care was also extended. Leave of absence for studies was introduced. Statutory holidays were prolonged from three weeks to four (in 1965) and then to five weeks (in 1978). This increased temporary absence for all groups, but in particular for women with small children. Thus, statistically, as defined in the Labour Force Surveys, Swedish women are classified as in the labour force, but in reality many are on temporary leave from market work, looking after their children.

The importance of this phenomenon, and its uneven distribution between women and men, can be illustrated by the *at-work rates.* The at-work rate measures the persons who actually are active in market work during an average week of the year as a percentage of the total population in the group in question.[11,12] The at-work rates reveal that the change in women's market work has been far less than indicated by the labour force participation rates. While the difference between the labour force participation rates of men and women amounted to only about 5 percentage points in 1990, the difference between their at-work rates amounted to 11 percentage points (see Table 1). While the labour force participation rate of women with children under seven years old was about 86 per cent, their at-work rate was only 53 per cent (see Table 1).

Clearly then, there is still a very marked division of labour between Swedish men and women, with women undertaking a much larger proportion of reproductive non-

---

11 Temporary absence in the Labour Force Surveys means an absence with a duration of at least one week.

12 It means that the labour force participation rate will be adjusted downward by the proportion of the population that is temporarily absent from work, but also by the proportion of the population that is unemployed. This means that variations in the rate will occur due to business cycles. (This is illustrated in Table 1 by the drastic fall in the at-work-rates for both men and women between 1990 and 1993; the decrease in the at-work-rate for mothers with small children between 1988 and 1990, on the other hand, is due to an extension of the parental leave.) But since our focus is on long-run trends and since the difference in unemployment rates between men and women was not large in Sweden during this period we deem this to be of minor importance for our conclusions.

market work than men. However, it should be pointed out that even if it is still mainly Swedish women who adapt their labour supply to the birth and rearing of children, their situation today is very different from that of earlier cohorts of women. A low participation in market work because of parental leave is very different from a low participation resulting from departure from the labour force. Firstly, women keep their employment and belong to the labour force, which means that they have a job to return to after their temporary absences from market work. Secondly, they receive direct financial compensation (inclusive of occupational pension rights) via the parental insurance system for part of their non-market work.

If we are interested in the extent to which women have really transferred their time to market work and how the time allocation between men and women has changed over time, the analysis should focus directly on the development of *actual hours of market work* for men and women. In addition to the growth of temporary absences, the increase in labour force participation rates has been accompanied by a growth in part-time work during most of the period studied. During the period 1970-80 75 per cent of the employment growth for Swedish women was part-time. The proportion of part-time workers among female employees increased sharply, from 38 per cent in 1970 to 47 per cent in 1982, when a maximum was reached.[13] The 1980s, however, witnessed increased hours of work and in 1990 the part-time proportion was back at 38 per cent.

The combined effect of changes in labour force participation, absenteeism and working hours is captured by what we call the *market-hours rate*.[14] This measures the total number of hours actually worked in the market per week for a given population group, divided by the total size of that population group.

Table 2 reports the results of calculations of the development of the market-hours rate for Swedish women and Swedish men respectively during the period 1963-88.[15] Looking at women aged 20-64, it turns out that the large increase in the labour force participation rate of women between 1963 and 1988 resulted in an increase in the average number of hours in actual market work per woman in this population group of about six hours. Surprisingly enough, about half of this increase took place during the 1980s, a period with rather slow increase of labour force participation rates. Between 1963 and 1973 there was very little change in the actual hours of market work per woman. The increased market hours arising from increased female labour force participation during this period were offset by shorter weekly working hours and increased temporary absence from market work among women. The increase in the labour force participation rate from 63.9 per cent in 1973 to 80.6 per cent in 1983 (see Table 1) resulted in a net transfer of actual market hours amounting to only about three hours per woman 20-64 years old. Thus there is no direct correspondence

---

13 Sundström (1987) and (1992).

14 Other measures that would reflect the same thing are actual hours worked per person per year (used by OECD 1991, but not calculated separately for men and women) or a full-time equivalent at-work-rate. See also the discussion in Hakim (1993).

15 See Jonung and Persson (1993) for a more detailed presentation of the calculations of the evolution during the period 1963-88.

between increases in labour force participation rates and increases in actual market work.

Contrary to the conventional picture, a focus on the allocation of time to the market reveals that during the period studied there was as much, or more, of a revolution taking place in male labour supply. The male market-hours rate decreased from 39.6 hours in 1963 to 31.9 hours in 1988. In other words, Swedish men transferred about 8 hours per person from market work to activities outside the market during those years. Most of the decrease took place between 1963 and 1973. Shorter weekly working hours, longer vacations and decreased labour force partici- pation rates among younger and older men (due to longer education and early retirement, respectively) meant that men's market hours on average decreased by about 22 per cent between 1963 and 1983. However, between 1983 and 1988 there was a net transfer of hours per man back to market work again.

Table 2. Market-hours rate[a], 20-64 years of age 1963-1988 (hours).

Year	Men	Women	Total population
1963	39.6	16.4	27.5
1968	35.7	15.9	25.2
1973	32.3	16.6	23.7
1978	31.0	18.0	23.8
1983	30.7	19.8	24.0
1988	31.9	22.2	25.8
1963-88	-7.7	+5.8	-1.7

a) Number of hours actually worked per week per person in a given population group.
Source: Own calculations based on the Swedish Labour Force Surveys.

What has taken place in Sweden since the 1960s is thus very much a *redistribution of market work* between men and women, with men moving time out of the market and women moving time into the market. The increase in women's proportion of actual market work, an increase from 29 per cent in 1963 to 41 per cent in 1988, was thus the result not only of increases in female labour supply but to an even larger extent reflected decreases in male labour supply. The 1980s, however, differ in this respect. It is the only decade when men as well as women increased their labour supply.

The age-patterns of these transfers and redistributions of market hours are shown in Diagram 2 (women) and Diagram 3 (men). The female age-profiles show that the age-profiles for actual hours worked, in contrast to the labour force participation rates, again display the traditional two peaks, one at age 20-24 and one at age 45-54. The hours profile thus reveals that women's pattern of work is still to a substantial degree adapted to the birth and rearing of children. However, the number of actual hours worked has increased over time for all age-groups above 24 years old. The largest increases between 1963-88, about 8 hours per week and woman, took place in the age-groups 35-54 years old. The largest transfer in terms of hours has actually occurred in the 1980s. Thus while the 1970s involved a revolution with respect to labour force participation rates, the 1980s, seemingly less dramatic, involved something similar with respect to hours actually worked.

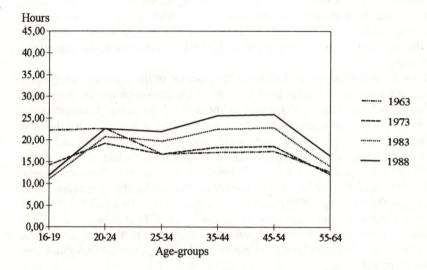

Diagram 2. Market-hours-rate for Women in Different Age-groups 1963-1988.

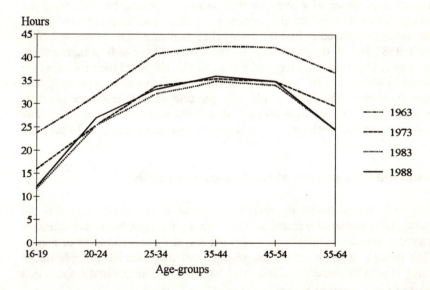

Diagram 3. Market-hours-rate for Men in Different Age-groups 1963-88.

The number of hours actually worked per man decreased in all age-groups between 1963 and 1988. The decreases were largest, about 7 hours per man and week, between 1963 and 1973. Between 1983 and 1988 the decrease was reversed or halted for all age-groups. For men aged 25-54 the market-hours rate increased by about 1.0-1.5 hours between 1983 and 1988. The labour force participation rates convey a static picture of men's labour supply. But the market hours-rates reveal that men have significantly reduced the proportion of time they devote to market work, even in their middle age. However, in contrast to the female market-hours rate profile, the male one has only one peak, at ages 35-44, and thus shows no adjustment to childrearing.

In Table 2 we also show calculations of the outcome of the changes taking place in the allocation of time to market work in terms of the market-hours rate per person in the total population (men and women) in the Swedish economy. It confirms the picture that a redistribution has taken place in that the market hours rate for the total age-group 20-54 (men and women) was roughly unchanged between 1963 and 1988. In addition, our calculations show that there has been a marked change in the allocation of time to market work over the life-cycle. Market work has increasingly become concentrated in ages 35-54. The market-hours rates for the age-groups 35-44 and 45-54 (for the total population) were in fact higher in 1988 than in 1963, i.e. men and women *combined* spent more time in the market in 1988 than in 1963.[16] Thus the combined work load of household work and market work for men as well as women in these ages, which also are periods of childrearing, remains heavy and may even have increased.

The changes in the distribution of market work between men and women described above also transformed Swedish families into two-earner ones and reduced the economic dependence of women on their husbands. Nermo has calculated the proportion of households where the woman received a specific proportion of her financial resources (defined as half the household's total earnings) via her husband's earnings in 1981 and 1991 respectively. In 1981 about 13 per cent of married/ co-habiting women 18-60 years old received almost all (85-100 %) of their resources via their husband's earnings.[17] In 1991 that proportion had decreased to 3 per cent. The proportion of women that received only 5-24 per cent of their resources via their husband's earnings increased from 26 per cent in 1981 to 34 per cent in 1991. The proportion of households with roughly equal earnings increased from 9 to 13 per cent.

Factors behind the growth of the two-earner family

According to economic theory the division of labour in the family, and thus the labour force participation of women, is determined by the household's evaluation of the advantages and disadvantages of housework and the gains and costs of market work. The family's decision on the use of time will then depend not only on its preferences (e.g. with respect to child-care) but also on the husband's and wife's

---

16 Jonung and Persson (1990) p. 36.
17 Nermo (1994) p. 175.

respective income opportunities in the labour market, their respective productivity in household work (which is influenced e.g. by the existence and number of children) and the price and availability of market substitutes for housework. The net advantages of specialisation within the household will also be affected by the probability of divorce.

Fertility, on the other hand, is determined, according to economic theory, by the and benefits and costs of children. The costs of children comprise monetary outlays as well as the opportunity cost of the carers' time. Theory would thus predict a negative relation between women's labour force participation and fertility, since a large number of children increases the value of housework and reduces labour force participation and vice versa; good opportunities for women in the labour market and a high labour force participation will increase the price of children and reduce fertility. Seemingly then, there is a contradiction in the Swedish development that has resulted in high fertility as well as high labour force participation. Our answer to this puzzle is that economic developments in combination with a deliberate equality policy has served to make labour force participation and having children compatible for women, i.e. to increase the profitability of market work and at the same time reduce the costs of having children.[18]

Equal opportunity policy

The design of Swedish family policy and equal opportunity policy with its emphasis on the possibility of combining market work and having a family dates back to the pronatalist debates of the 1930s.[19] Instead of introducing marriage bars for women's work as in many other countries, Sweden in 1939 passed an act which made it unlawful to dismiss a woman because of pregnancy, childbirth or marriage. Women were also allowed 12 weeks of absence due to childbirth and women below a certain income level were given a minor cash benefit. The legislation was the outcome of concern over the low birth rates in Sweden in the 1930s. The argument, put forward by the Myrdals in their famous book "Kris i befolkningsfrågan", was that a pronatalist policy should be based on financial support to families with children and on the protection of working women, so that they could afford to marry and have children.[20] From then on, the equal opportunity debate in Sweden came to be framed not only as an issue of women's right to work but as *working* women's (and later on men's) right to marry, have children and have time to spend with their children.

During the 1950s the emphasis was still on women's two roles - as a mother and as a market worker. Women should be able to choose one or the other, or both, without serious economic consequences for the family. The typical life-cycle would be the one with two peaks, one before and one after the child-rearing years. Policy

---

18 This is also the conclusion reached by Sundström and Stafford (1992).

19 Recent articles describing Swedish family policy in greater detail are Gustafsson (1993), Meisaari-Polsa and Söderström (1993b), Sundström (1991) and Sundström and Stafford (1992).

20 Myrdal and Myrdal (1934).

should encourage young women to get an education, facilitate their return to the labour market and assist women with children financially. Universal cash allowances for children directed to mothers were introduced in 1948 and they still remain an important part of Swedish family policy. As early as 1945 the right to leave in connection with childbirth was extended to six months. In 1954 the leave was linked to the health insurance system, with a certain level of remuneration being paid for three months. From 1962 compensation was paid for six months.

In the beginning of the 1960s there was a reaction against this so-called "conditional liberation of women", under which women were allowed to work only on condition that they also assumed the full responsibility for the family and adjusted their work in the market accordingly. The analysis and debate that followed propounded the view that the conflict between family and work was a problem not only for women, but for men as well. Any efforts towards equality between men and women required that men's social role also be changed.

These lines of thought eventually gained a great influence on Swedish policy. In a report to the United Nations in 1968 the goals of Swedish equal opportunity policy were formulated in a way that remains valid today. "The aim of a *long term* programme for women must be that every individual, irrespective of sex, shall have the same practical opportunities, not only for education and employment, but also, in principle, the same responsibility for the upbringing of the children and the upkeep of the home".[21] Two principles, which since then have formed the basis for Swedish equal opportunity policy, are brought out in the report:

1) Equality requires economic independence for men and women, i.e. that each one is able to support him/herself *and* share the responsibility for the economic support of the children.
2) Equality requires changing the role of both men and women and that legislation is such that the same rules apply regardless of sex.

From these principles it follows that Swedish equal opportunity policy has been characterised; firstly by a focus on *market work* (economic independence); secondly by a focus on *equality* - the similarity between men and women; thirdly by a focus on the *individual* - not the family. Women's issues have mainly been concerned with women in their role as wage-earners. Equality between the sexes has also often been advocated as a question of efficient use of resources and not only as a matter of justice. Until the last few years, it has not been regarded as an issue of power relations at all.

Labour market policies

The 1970s mark the beginning of a purposeful equal opportunity policy in Sweden. This policy was part of an overall economic policy that strongly emphasised full employment. Its primary aim was to stimulate and facilitate market work for women,

---

21 The Status of Women in Sweden (1968) p. 5.

not only for equality reasons but also as a means to supply labour to the Swedish labour market. In the mid-1960s labour shortages were predicted, and the policy of encouraging women's market work was a deliberate preferred choice to the alternative of a guest worker policy.

In Sweden home-working women wanting a job, also those looking for part-time employment, have been counted among the unemployed and have been eligible for labour market policies. In the 1970s, besides large-scale labour market policy measures available for both men and women, several projects specifically aimed at women were initiated; intensified service at the public employment agencies, wage subsidies, projects to assist women in non-traditional occupations etc.

On the other hand, policy action and legislation directed at the demand side of the labour market and employer behaviour came late in Sweden. A law against discrimination by sex was introduced as late as 1980. In the 1980s, in public debate as well as policies, greater attention than during earlier decades has been paid to women's career opportunities and affirmative action type measures.

Tax and social security policy

An example of the emphasis on the individual as a basis for equal opportunity policy is the development of tax policy. In 1971 Sweden introduced separate taxation for spouses. Before then the system was one of joint taxation, with a minor deduction for working women to compensate for the loss of house work, and a separate tax scale for married and single women. The system discouraged market work by women, since women's earnings were hit by high marginal tax rates. This effect was intensified as progressivity increased over time.

With a system of separate taxation a family can lower its total taxes by equalising market income between the spouses. The combination of separate taxation and high progressivity in Sweden has provided a strong incentive for married women's market work since family income has often been increased more by a secondary worker's additional net income per hour than by overtime work of the primary worker.[22] On the other hand, a high progressivity may have discouraged women from full-time work and made investments in a career show a low economic return.

A tax reform in 1991 reduced marginal tax rates and the differential between the husband's and wife's marginal tax. Often they will now encounter the same rate, and the incentive to redistribute work from the high income earner to the low income earner will be reduced. In addition value-added taxes were introduced, or raised, on substitutes for work at home such as e.g. restaurant meals and haircuts. On the other hand, lower marginal tax rates in general on market work may give stronger

---

22 Gustafsson (1992) and Gustafsson and Bruyn-Hundt (1991) study the tax incentives for women's work in the Netherlands, Sweden and West Germany and find the Swedish system to be most conducive to women's market work. OECD (1990) compares the result for a family's take-home-pay of increasing the primary earner's income and of having a secondary earner in 18 OECD countries and finds the latter strategy to be most rewarding in Sweden.

incentives for Swedish women (as well as for Swedish men) to work full-time and to pursue career ambitions.

An additional incentive towards women's market work has come from the Swedish social security system. The emphasis on the individual and on market work and economic independence has here resulted in a system where women's benefits mainly derive from, and are related to the size of, their own market earnings.[23]

Time and money costs of children

Swedish family policies subsidise the monetary costs as well as the time costs of having children. The policies relating to child care make evident the emphasis of equal opportunity policy on employment for women. Many subsidies are benefits in kind such as schooling, school lunches, health care, dental care and various leisure time activities that are available gratis to all children. The general child allowance is also paid for all children until 16 years of age and for all older children if they are in secondary schooling, regardless of the income or the employment of the parent(s).

Other benefits, however, and those that have been introduced or expanded during the 1970s and 1980s, are dependent on the employment status of the parent(s). An example is public child care. Swedish children start school at seven years of age. School lunch is included in the school day but school hours are short during the first three years. That leaves many years during which various forms of child care have to be found by employed parents. In 1965 only 3 per cent of children under school age had access to public, subsidised child care. At that time an extensive programme for local authority care was initiated. Today slightly more than half of all pre-schoolers are in public care. In 1993 a law was passed which, starting in 1995, will hold the local authorities responsible for making child care (public or private) available to all parents who demand it for children over one and under 12 years old.

Almost every child less than one year old is cared for at home by either of its parents. Public child care for pre-schoolers is provided in two forms: in a day care centre or in a private home by a "day mother" employed and paid by the local authority. 62 per cent of all children 1-6 years old are in public care, 2 per cent in private paid care and 36 per cent are cared for full-time by their parents. Care, especially at day care centres, has been quite costly (due to a high personnel/child ratio, high material standards and a relatively high wage), but parents pay only about 10 per cent of the actual cost. Since supply has fallen short of demand during most of the period, the large subsidy involved has been a source of income inequality among Swedish families with children. Families that have not been lucky enough to get a place in public care receive no subsidy for day care and cannot deduct their child care costs. This has led them to use "tax-free" child care; by relatives, by co-operative arrangements with friends, by "black market" day mothers, or by the parents themselves.

---

23 For a description of the Swedish pension system and its implications for women, see Ståhlberg (1994).

Another policy has been to make it easier for families to adapt their working hours to family life. Part-time work has been very popular among Swedish women and has gradually been extended within all areas of work and all occupations, including even the professions. All statutory social benefits apply also to part-time work, and negotiated benefits extend at least to part-time work above 16 hours per week. Note, however, that part-time work among Swedish women in general is long part-time work of around 30 hours per week.

Parental leave has been a cornerstone of family policy and equal opportunity policy. In 1974 maternity leave was transformed into parental leave, available for fathers as well as mothers. The leave has successively been extended and today (1994) Swedish parents have the right to 15 months of paid parental leave of absence in connection with childbirth. For 12 months the parent on leave can get a 90 per cent compensation for loss of earnings and for 3 months a per diem grant. The use of the paid leave is very flexible. It can be proportioned between parents as they see fit, be used full-time or part-time and be spread out over a period of eight years. In addition, parents have the legal right to (unpaid) leave of absence from work for 18 full months and the legal right to reduce working hours to 75 per cent of full-time until the child is eight. The regulations thus provide parents with generous opportunities to organise their work life and home life as they see fit and to get income compensation for most of the reduced working time. In addition, when marginal tax rates were high it did not cost very much, for example, to take 75 per cent paid parental leave plus 25 per cent unpaid leave and in that way spread the fully paid leave over 16 months.

Parental leave has been used mainly by mothers. Only about 9 per cent of the number of compensated days were claimed by fathers in 1992. However, as many as 40 per cent of married or cohabiting men use some leave, with an average of around 50 days, during the child's first year. The limited utilisation of the parental leave by fathers has led to proposals, not yet accepted by Parliament, that 30 days of the leave should be reserved exclusively for fathers.

Other benefits in the parental insurance scheme are more popular among fathers. Each father is entitled to 10 days of paid leave in connection with childbirth, and 82 per cent of fathers availed themselves of this opportunity in 1992. Since 1979 parents are also allowed to stay home to take care of sick children on the same conditions as when they are sick themselves. In 1992 men constituted 41 per cent of those who used this benefit and they accounted for 34 per cent of the total number of days utilised by parents.

Altogether the conditions of Swedish working life, the legal rights provided by the parental insurance system and the provision of public child care have developed in a manner which stimulates and enables two-earner families to combine work with a life with children. In addition, the benefits provided by parental leave provide a strong incentive for young women to establish themselves in the labour market before having children.

Lone parents

The vast majority of Swedish children under 18 years of age, around 80 per cent, live with both of their biological parents (for pre-schoolers the proportion is about 90 per cent). Slightly above 12 per cent live in single parent households - most of these are single mothers. The attitude towards single mothers has been the same as towards women in general - to support women's employment. E.g. single parents have been given preferential treatment in public child care with faster access and lower fees. Single mothers in Sweden fare better financially compared with two-parent families than in other countries. Part of the explanation is the existence of public benefits, such as a government-run maintenance advance system for child support (in effect since 1937) and housing subsidies. The latter are means-tested, but still reach roughly 80 per cent of single mothers. Nevertheless Gustafsson argues that the basic reason for the relatively favourable standard of living of single mothers in Sweden is that they have fairly good jobs, and that this in turn results from a policy aimed at employment for all women, married and single.[24]

Public sector growth

The policies described above facilitated the entry of women to the labour market. But such policies would have been of minor importance had there not been a steadily rising demand for the female workforce. This demand has emanated from the public sector in the form of jobs in the areas of education, health care and social care. In fact, since 1950 all employment growth in Sweden has been in public sector jobs, most of them with local authorities. Almost 90 per cent of the expansion in female employment during recent decades has emanated from local authorities. More than half of all the women in the Swedish labour market have public bodies, mostly local authorities, as their employer.

In a way one could say that women's work in the home has been socialised by the local authorities. But this disregards the revolutionary changes that have taken place in many of these services. In the same way as the industrial revolution generated growth and created new products through new techniques and methods of production, the service revolution has created new and qualitatively different services as a response to the demands of a modern society within areas such as education, medicine, social security etc.

Wages

The profitability of market work for Swedish women was increased by the policies described above. But the profitability of their market work was also strongly enhanced as a result of the development of wages during the period. Despite the great inflow of

---

24 Gustafsson (1994).

women to the labour market, women's real wages increased during most of the period and their wages also rose significantly in relation to men's wages.

Empirical evidence

Hitherto we have described a number of economic changes and policies that according to economic theory should have acted as a stimulus to women's market work. To what extent have such effects been confirmed by empirical studies? Several studies have analysed the evolution of women's labour force participation and hours of work during the 1960s and 1970s.[25] All have found the explanation of women's increased labour supply to be that the profitability of market work has increased relative to that of work in the home. The main factors behind the increased profitability have been the increase in women's real market wages, and the increase in women's wages relative to those of men. In addition, the studies stress the incentives towards sharing of market work and two-earner families provided by the tax system.

According to Sundström, the increased proportion of part-time workers in the female labour force during this period was mainly (i.e. about 65 per cent) due to increased labour force participation among groups of women who already had a high propensity to work part-time (married women with pre-school children and with low to average educational attainment).[26] But the *propensity* to work part-time increased as well, which Sundström ascribes to increased marginal tax rates for full-time workers in combination with the extension of statutory rights for parents to work part-time.

Until now, the factors behind the development of labour supply during the 1980s have been empirically less well researched.[27] But Sundström, Sundström & Stafford (1992) and others have drawn attention to the role of tax reforms that decreased the marginal tax rates and increased the profitability of additional market hours and full-time work.[28] Econometric studies have shown the labour supply of Swedish women to be more responsive than that of Swedish men to such changes in the profitability of market work.[29]

Probably developments during the 1980s can also be seen as a continuation of the forces that drew women into the labour force during the preceding decades. The women who at that time found it profitable to belong to the labour force during their years with small children had now become middle-aged with older children and less demanding domestic duties. They were then likely (particularly considering the tax reforms) to find it profitable to increase their hours of work and cash in on their earlier investments in continued participation in the labour force. To this can be

---

25 Gustafsson and Jacobsson (1984), Tegle (1985), Burtless (1987), Sundström (1987), Gustafsson (1992) and Gustafsson and Stafford (1992).

26 Sundström (1987).

27 The results of several empirical studies evaluating the labour supply effects of the big 1991 tax reform are due to appear in 1995.

28 Sundström (1991) and (1992).

29 See e.g. Blomquist and Hansson-Brusewitz (1990).

added that the proportion of women with small children decreased and the proportion of women with higher education increased in the female labour force of the 1980s. This should also have served to increase hours of work among women. Finally for younger women, small children may have had less of a restraining effect on labour supply during the 1980s than during the preceding decades primarily because of the increased availability of child care.[30] This picture of the 1980s is largely confirmed by Sundström.[31]

What about fertility and the costs of children? A demographic expert states that: "Public policies probably have a much stronger influence on women's labour force participation than on their childbearing, at least in Sweden."[32] The effects on fertility may very well be smaller, but will still be there. Completed cohort fertility has hovered at around the same 2.0 per mille level for the cohorts born between the mid-1930s and the mid-1940s. As to the *pattern* of fertility, about 88 per cent of Swedish women give birth to at least one child. Of these women about 82 per cent go on to have a second child and almost 40 per cent of these mothers in turn also have a third child. Childlessness is thus not very common and the two-children norm is strong and dominant. Thus there is no sign in Sweden of the growing popularity of childless or one-child families that demographers have recorded in central and southern Europe, and no evidence for a substantial increase in permanent childlessness.[33] It is hard not to suspect that the deliberate efforts to reduce the costs of children, particularly to their mothers, and to make market work and children compatible, have played some role in this, even if direct empirical corroboration is hard to achieve.[34] It is easier to provide empirical evidence that policies and policy design have affected the timing and spacing of births in Sweden.[35]

The outcome for women

Above we have described Swedish family policy and equal opportunity policy as being aimed at making work in the market compatible with having a family. The policy must be deemed successful in this respect. Women today generally participate in the market sector as well as in the home. There is a great flexibility in working hours and in the way work can be organised over time and proportioned between parents. The cost of children is subsidised in terms both of money and time. Swedish fathers have and take the opportunity to participate in the care of their children to a larger extent than fathers in other countries. Lone parents are better off financially

30 Gustafsson and Stafford (1992) found female labour supply to be positively affected by the availability of child care.
31 Sundström (1992).
32 Hoem (1993) p. 30.
33 Hoem (1993) p. 26.
34 See also the discussion and evaluation in Sundström and Stafford (1992).
35 See Hoem (1993). This provides another example of the responsiveness of Swedish fertility patterns to economic factors, discussed in chapter 2.

relative to the rest of the population than in other countries. Swedish families seem to have responded by giving birth to more children than in other countries.

But has the policy been equally successful in other respects? What effects have these kinds of policies had for example on the labour market position of women? We will consider the results with respect to occupational segregation and women's wages. Finally, we will also briefly consider what has happened to family life.

Occupational segregation

It is often expected that a country with a high participation of women in the labour market will also display a low occupational segregation by sex. However, the analysis above has revealed that women's entry to the labour market in Sweden has been the result of efforts to combine family life and market work. Rising labour force participation rates will thus mean a rising proportion of women who divide their commitments between the home and the market. Women entering the labour market will be looking for occupations offering working conditions compatible with family life, which may be easier to find within traditional female areas. In addition, a larger number of women in the labour force will of itself increase the demand for services in typical female occupations; e.g. child care or old age care. Thus there are several reasons to expect occupational segregation by sex to persist rather than decline.

Occupational segregation in Sweden follows the traditional pattern: women are concentrated in a limited number of occupations and the labour market is divided into male and female occupations. As remarked above, the entry of women to the labour market has to a considerable extent been a response to a growing demand for female labour, stemming primarily from the public sector and areas of work which traditionally have been the domain of women: education, health and sick care, and social welfare. The 1960s saw a growth of clerical work for women, but in later decades occupations within health and sick care and social work have been the most expansive. In the 1990 census one-fourth of the female labour force was classified in occupations within the latter occupational area. It may also be noted that no less than 88 per cent of the employees in this field are women. The second most important area for women, consisting of occupations within administrative and clerical work, held one fifth of the female labour force. Manufacturing has been a declining area for women, in terms of both numbers and relative importance. Only 7 per cent of the female labour force works here. Manufacturing, although declining for men as well, is still the most important occupational area for men, accounting for one third of the male labour force. Work in technology, natural and social sciences, etc., which includes a lot of the professions in this area, ranks second (16 per cent).

A study of individual occupations reveals that during the period studied women have broken into virtually every area of the labour force. Since 1978, when military service was opened to women, there are no longer any occupations without women. The same is true for men since 1975, when the first men were found as dental assistants and midwives. Nevertheless, there is a great concentration of women in certain occupations. Although women are entering male professions and more occupations are becoming integrated, three-fourths of the female workforce still work in occupations where women constitute more than 60 per cent. The five most common occupations (out of about 300) for women in 1990 were nurses' aid, general secretarial work, sales worker, children's nurse and home care assistant (caring for old persons in their homes). The five occupations together formed almost 30 per cent of the female labour force. With the exception of sales representative, which is a popular occupation among men as well, over 90 per cent of those employed in these occupations are women.

Women have made substantial inroads into many of the learned professions formerly dominated by men. This is especially noticeable in the legal professions, among veterinarians, biologists, chemists, doctors and dentists. Some occupations, e.g. psychologist and social administration, have become feminised. However, engineering is still a male preserve, with only a small percentage of women. Women have shown little interest in taking up blue-collar work, but are quickly moving into male-dominated service-oriented occupations, such as railway clerks, postmen and postal clerks, customs officers and police officers.

A common way to summarise the extent of segregation and measure the change over time is with the aid of a segregation index. The dissimilarity index has the advantage of being easy to interpret.[36] It can be understood as the proportion of women in the labour force that has to change occupation in order to make the distribution of women across occupations identical to that of men. Since the measure is symmetrical it can alternatively be interpreted as the proportion of men in the labour force that would have to change occupation to have the same occupational distribution as women. Calculations of this measure show that there is a high but clearly falling level of occupational segregation by sex in Sweden.[37] Whereas in 1960 75 per cent of the female labour force would have to switch occupations to attain the male distribution, in 1990 the corresponding figure was 65 per cent. The rate of change has been about the same for the three decades studied. Structural changes in the size of occupations have served both to increase and decrease segregation. The fall in segregation has mainly been due to a changed composition of occupations: men moving into women's occupations and women moving into men's occupations. In particular women have moved into male professional occupations requiring a high level of education. In choosing between blue-collar work and lower level health, service and clerical work, women have remained in the female occupations.

At the current rate it will take no less than about 100-150 years before the Swedish labour market is integrated. Moreover, our discussion has been concerned with horizontal segregation, i.e. the distribution across occupations, and not vertical segregation, i.e. the distribution across levels of employment or positions within

---

36 The dissimilarity index is calculated as $D_t = \frac{1}{2}\sum_{i=1}^{n}|m_{it} - f_{it}|$, where m_{it} and f_{it} designates the percentage proportion of the male and female labour force respectively employed in occupation i in year t.

37 The calculations, presentation of the method and data used are found in Jonung (1984) and Jonung (1993). The figure for 1990 is calculated on the new standard of occupational classification.

occupations. Women's progress into the professions is encouraging, but does not tell us how women fare relative to men in these professions. One way to shed some light on this is to study the development of wages.

Wage differentials

The 1960s and 1970s in Sweden were characterised by declining wage differentials between women and men in all sectors of the economy and for different groups of workers. Between 1973 and 1982 the female/male wage ratio (for full-time workers) increased from 84 per cent to 91 per cent for industrial workers, from 63 per cent to 73 per cent for white-collar employees within industry, from 81 per cent to 90 per cent for central government employees and from 74 per cent to 86 per cent for local authority employees. However, during the 1980s the increase in these wage ratios was reversed or halted.

To begin with, a significant factor behind the decline in the wage differential was that Swedish women increased their educational level and work-experience. But towards the mid-1980s only a minor part (about 10 per cent) of the wage differential that remained between men and women reflected differences in their human capital variables.[38] According to Blau, differences in human capital variables between men and women no longer accounted for a major part of the female/male wage differential in either Sweden or the United States.[39] That the wage differential by sex was smaller in Sweden than in the United States was mainly the result of the fact that the overall Swedish wage distribution was much more compressed than that of the United States. In terms of their ranking in the male wage distribution relative to men with the same labour market characteristics, Swedish women fared no better than American women.

A recent study provides further evidence of what happened to the male/female wage ratio between 1968 and 1991.[40] The observed (non-standardised) male/female wage ratio decreased from 137 per cent in 1968 to 129 per cent in 1974 and to 120 per cent in 1981. By 1991 it had increased to 121 per cent again. After taking into account differences in education and work-experience between men and women (and, within parentheses, also social class and sector of the economy) the male/female wage ratio changed from 130 per cent (127 per cent) in 1968, to 123 per cent (120 per cent) in 1974 and to 115 per cent (112 per cent) in 1981. In 1991 the standardised wage ratio had increased to 119 per cent (113 per cent). What seems to have happened during the 1980s is that the wage premiums paid for education and work-experience, which were about the same for women and men in 1968 and 1974, started to diverge and by 1991 were significantly lower for Swedish women than for Swedish men. During the 1980s women were penalised for their over-representation in the public sector, since this sector lost out in relative wages. Recent wage changes thus give cause for concern. It could be that the strong occupational segregation, and the fact

---

38 Löfström (1989).
39 Blau (1993).
40 le Grand (1994).

that vertical segregation and affirmative action measures have not been emphasised until recently in Swedish equal opportunity policy, are now being reflected in wage developments. Recent studies of female/male wage differentials within occupations requiring academic training reveal differences in positions and career advancement between men and women within these occupations to be the major factor behind existing wage differentials.[41]

Family patterns and family life

The period since the 1960s of rapid change in women's market work and economic independence has also been marked by significant changes in Swedish family patterns. For one thing, the marriage frequency has decreased. Whereas in 1960 about 80 per cent of women and men aged 30-49 years were married, by 1990 that proportion was only slightly over 60 per cent.[42] However, at the same time co-habitation outside wedlock has become more common. Consequently, in 1990 75 per cent of the Swedish population aged 30-49 years was either married *or* cohabiting, which was only somewhat less than the (estimated) proportion in 1950.[43] Living together as a couple is thus still by far the most common "family pattern" in Sweden during these "middle" years of the life-cycle.

The overwhelming majority of Swedish children are born to parents who are either married or cohabiting.[44] The tendency for women to postpone their first birth to older ages, which in the Swedish case has probably been enhanced by the replacement rules of parental leave insurance, also means that most children in Sweden today are born to mothers who are fairly well established in the labour market.[45] The mothers thus normally have a basis for helping to provide for their children financially, either as one of a two-earner couple or, if it so turns out, as a single mother.

Although living as a couple remains the dominant family pattern, these "families" are much less stable than they used to be. In 1960 0.5 per cent of existing marriages were dissolved. But during the course of the 1960s and 1970s the frequency increased, particularly when changes occurred in divorce legislation in the mid-1970s. Since then it has remained at about 1.1-1.2 per cent per year. Of the 1960 marriages about 1 in 10 had been dissolved after 10 years, of the 1970 marriages

---

41 SACO (1992).

42 Gähler (1994).

43 In 1950 the proportion that was married was 78 per cent. The proportion that was cohabiting in 1950 is not known, but could at most be estimated to have been 6 per cent (which was the proportion in 1975 when it was first recorded separately). This gives an upper estimate of 84 per cent for the proportion married or cohabiting in 1950. See Gähler (1994).

44 More than 90 per cent of all Swedish children under 3 years live with both biological parents (Sundström 1991:174).

45 See Hoem (1993). The first-birth rates generally fell at all ages below 30 from the mid-1960s through the early 1980s, but showed a mild recovery after 1984. The average age of first-time mothers rose from 24.4 years in 1974 to 26.7 years in 1987 (Sundström 1991:174).

about 1.8 in 10 and of the 1980 marriages about 2.4 in 10.[46] Separation is more common among cohabiting than among married couples; according to an estimate for 1986, three times more common (independently of the number of children). Thus, a larger proportion of both children and adults than in earlier cohorts have experienced, or will at some point during their lifetime experience, separation or divorce.[47] However, it should be pointed out that in spite of these developments almost 8 out of 10 children born in the early 1970s have grown up with both of their biological parents.

In the mid-1980s, 78 per cent of children aged below 17 years lived with their original parents, 11 per cent lived with a single mother, 2 per cent with a single father and 9 per cent with a restructured family.[48] As we have seen, in most cases the children would have a mother doing significant amounts of market work and a father with more time available outside the market than earlier generations of fathers. Time budget data (see Table 3) allow us to look inside the families and get a picture of how non-market work is shared between women and men.

In the early 1990s Swedish men aged 20-64 years devoted on average 41 hours per week to market work (incl. travel to work) and 20 hours per week to non-market work.[49] Swedish women devoted 27¼ hours per week to market work and 33¼ hours per week to non-market work. Clearly, men were still specialising in market work and women in non-market work. Time-allocation patterns by sex, as revealed by Table 3, are significantly affected by the presence of children. The costs of (particularly small) children in terms of reduced hours of market work are born by women, who consequently also take care of most of the non-market work. The male provider role still prevails, with men with (particularly older) children taking on more market-hours, although by 1990 they also were doing significant amounts of non-market work, particularly when their children were small. Thus the goal of "equal sharing" is far from having been achieved. But this does not mean that there has not been any change over time. According to Nermo, Swedish cohabiting men increased their time devoted to housework from 2.2 hours per week in 1974 to 4.1 hours in 1981 and 4.8 hours in 1991.[50] Swedish cohabiting women decreased their time devoted to housework from 31.9 hours per week in 1974, to 26.6 hours in 1981 and 18.7 hours in 1991. Thus the total time allocated to housework by the households was greatly reduced, which helped to make women's and men's total (market plus non-market) work-load roughly the same (see Table 3).

---

46 Gähler (1994) p. 64.
47 The welfare consequences for Swedish men, women and children of experiencing divorce or separation have recently been investigated by Gähler (1994), using panel data.
48 Meisaari-Polsa and Söderström (1993b).
49 SCB (1992).
50 Nermo (1994).

Table 3. Average time (hours and minutes per week) spent in different activities

	Cohabiting with youngest child 0-6 years	Cohabiting with youngest child 7-18 years	Cohabiting, 25-44 no children
MEN			
Market work	44.39	46.53	41.58
Non-market work	25.53	20.00	19.55
of which			
Housework	6.44	6.15	6.53
Repairs	4.23	5.24	5.35
Care of own children	8.15	1.36	0.08
WOMEN			
Market work	19.05	32.52	33.06
Non-market work	49.43	33.00	24.46
of which			
Housework	20.24	18.26	14.03
Repairs	1.44	2.36	3.17
Care of own children	19.01	3.38	0.02
SINGLE MOTHERS			
Market work	24.53	34.28	
Non-market work	39.44	30.43	
of which			
Housework	15.07	15.57	
Repairs	1.30	2.07	
Care of own children	14.22	4.11	

Source: SCB (1992)

What could the future bring?

The situation of the Swedish economy has changed radically since the peak of the business cycle in 1990. After a long period in the late 1980s with an overheated economy characterised by strong internal demand, money and credit expansion, extremely low unemployment, high labour force participation rates, increasing hours of work, rapidly rising wages, low productivity growth and high inflationary pressure, Sweden moved into a deep and severe business slump. Open unemployment, which was 1.5 per cent in 1990, climbed to an unprecedented level of 8 per cent in 1993. To this can be added another 7 per cent placed under labour market policy measures and not reflected in the unemployment statistics. A financial and banking crisis and high real interest rates caused severe problems in the credit markets. The fiscal budget position deteriorated rapidly. The result was three years of negative growth.

The recession has also led to a reduction in the labour force participation rates of women as well as men (see Table 1). For the first time since 1967 women's labour force participation rate has fallen and the fall is no less than 4 percentage points in 3 years. The effect on at-work rates is of course much stronger, since these encompass the effect of unemployment. Women's at-work rates are back where they were around 1980.

These developments have led to an intensified analysis and debate concerning the need for restructuring the Swedish welfare system as well as the labour market and wage policies.[51] Virtually all parts of the social programmes are being scrutinised and reconsidered. The EES-agreement and the possibility of Sweden shortly joining the EU are additional new forces, which will have important implications for the functioning of the Swedish labour market and the design of social policies.[52] At the present moment it is still difficult to discern what will be the outcome of the economic and political processes that have been started.

As emphasised earlier in the paper, the division of labour between men and women and between work in the home and work in the market depends upon what value the family sets on home production compared with the monetary and non-monetary returns on market work and on how the returns from the different sectors are divided between men and women. This, in turn, is affected by all the factors discussed above - demographic changes, the development of demand, wages and wage structure, tax policy, family policy etc. What changes in these factors could the future bring about?

Swedish macroeconomic policy has switched its emphasis from the full employment goal to the goal of low inflation so as to maintain competitiveness in world markets and stimulate economic growth. The size of the public sector, with public expenditure corresponding to 75 per cent of GNP and a ballooning budget deficit, has provoked calls for policies to reduce public transfers along with public sector employment. This means that the sector which has been a steady source of demand for female labour in the past cannot be counted on for the future. At the same time, the next decade will see a growing demand for services which have traditionally been provided by the public sector, such as child care (as a result of high fertility and an increased population of fertile age) and care of the elderly (as a consequence of a rise in the number of very old persons). What can be expected to happen is privatisation of some of the services in these areas.

Up to now, however, men have been harder hit by the recession than women, since the effects have been concentrated on industry and building construction, while cut-backs in public employment have so far been less severe. On the other hand, this means that in the future women will probably meet increased competition from men in their traditional areas.

Whether privatisation will take the form of an expanding private labour market for care or more work at home will depend upon the incentives provided by the tax system and family policy. As mentioned above, the new tax system no longer holds

---

51 See SOU 1993:16. An English version is available as Lindbeck et. al. (1994).

52 An analysis of possible consequences for the economic situation of women in Sweden of membership of the EU is provided in Persson (1993).

the same strong incentives for equal market work by the spouses. In addition, high taxes make the tax wedge between (untaxed) work carried out at home and work available in the market at market prices so large that in most cases it will not be profitable for the households to buy social services at unsubsidised prices. The debate about this deterrent to the establishment of a private market for social services has recently led to a much-questioned proposal for tax deductions for home services.[53]

The two main criticisms of family policy have been that it is too expensive and that it provides a restricted choice for parents concerning the form of child care. The proposals for reform have been many. One set of reforms, already implemented, has focused on the production of child care and has opened the way for public subsidies of private child care centres, voucher systems etc.. The aim has not been to reduce the subsidy or provision of child care, but to increase efficiency and reduce costs by means of competition. Other proposals have focused on the money transfers to families. As an example, the replacement rate in parental insurance will most likely be reduced to 80 per cent (in line with reductions within other parts of the social insurance system). Another much debated proposal, which will attract women to work at home rather than market work, is a child allowance during a child's second and third year. It is proposed that the allowance may be used to finance either self-produced care or purchased care, but in the latter case at higher charges than before.

The profitability of work in the market will be determined not only by the design of taxes and child care subsidies but also by the development of wages and the wage structure. A most likely future scenario is a continuing wage differentiation accentuated by a growing demand for highly skilled labour, increased competition from neighbouring low-wage countries in the east, and the rapprochement towards the EU labour markets with their larger wage differentials. Such increased wage differentials are highly likely to increase sex differentials as well, especially since according to Blau Swedish women rank fairly low in the wage hierarchy.[54] But they will also mean greater economic incentives for Swedish women to pursue careers and move upwards in the wage hierarchy. What is likely to emerge from all this eventually is a future picture of Swedish women's work patterns and economic status that is much more differentiated than in the past.

---

53 Pålsson and Norrman (1994).
54 Blau (1993).

REFERENCES

Blau F (1993) Gender and Economic Outcomes: The Role of Wage Structure. Labour, no. 1.

Blomquist NS, Hansson-Brusewitz U (1990) The Effect of Taxes on Male and Female Labour Supply in Sweden. Journal of Human Resources, 25.

Burtless G (1987) Taxes, Transfers and Swedish Labour Supply, in BP Bosworth, AM Rivlin (eds) The Swedish Economy. Brookings Institution, Washington DC.

le Grand C (1994) Löneskillnaderna i Sverige: Förändring och nuvarande struktur, in Fritzell J, Lundberg O (eds.) Vardagens villkor. Brombergs, Stockholm.

Gustafsson S (1992) Separate Taxation and Married Women's Labour Supply: A Comparison of West Germany and Sweden. Journal of Population Economics, 5.

Gustafsson S (1993) Female Labour Supply and Pronatalism. An Economic History of Swedish Family Policies. Tinbergen Institute, Discussion Paper TI 93-19.

Gustafsson S (1994) Single Mothers in Sweden: Why is Poverty Less Severe? (forthcoming).

Gustafsson S, Bruyn-Hundt M (1991) Incentives for Women to Work. A Comparison between the Netherlands, Sweden and West Germany. Journal of Economic Studies, vol. 18, no. 5/6.

Gustafsson S, Jacobsson R (1984) Trends in Female Labor Force Participation in Sweden. Journal of Labor Economics, vol. 2, no.4, part 2.

Gustafsson S, Stafford FP (1992) Childcare Subsidies and Labor Supply in Sweden. Journal of Human Resources, 27.

Gähler M (1994) Svensk familjeupplösning och några av dess konsekvenser, in Fritzell J, Lundberg O (eds) Vardagens villkor. Brombergs, Stockholm.

Hakim C (1993) The Myth of Rising Female Employment. Work, Employment and Society, March.

Hoem JM (1993) Public Policy as the Fuel of Fertility: Effects of a Policy Reform on the Pace of Childbearing in Sweden in the 1980s. Acta Sociologica, 36.

Jonung C (1982) Kvinnorna i svensk ekonomi, in Södersten B (ed) Svensk ekonomi. Rabén & Sjögren, Stockholm.

Jonung C (1984) Patterns of Occupational Segregation by Sex in the Labor Market, in Schmid G, Weizel R (eds) Sex Discrimination and Equal Opportunity. Gower.

Jonung C (1993) Yrkessegregeringen på arbetsmarknaden, in Kvinnors arbetsmarknad. Arbetsmarknadsdepartementet, Ds 1993:8.

Jonung C, Persson I (1990) (eds.) Kvinnors roll i ekonomin. Bilaga 23 till LU90, Stockholm, Allmänna förlaget.

Jonung C, Persson I (1993) Women and Market Work: The Misleading Tale of Participation Rates in International Comparisons. Work, Employment and Society, Vol. 7, No 2.

Lindbeck A et al (1994) Turning Sweden Around. MIT Press, Cambridge, Mass.

Löfström Å (1989) Diskriminering på svensk arbetsmarknad. Umeå Economic Studies, no. 196, Umeå.

Meisaari-Polsa T, Söderström L (1993a) Recent Swedish Fertility Changes in Perspective, in Lundh C (ed.) (1994) Population, Economy and Welfare. Scandinavian Population Studies, Lund University Press.

Meisaari-Polsa T, Söderström L (1993b) Swedish Family Policy: Economic Aspects, in Lundh C (ed.) (1994) Population, Economy and Welfare. Scandinavian Population Studies, Lund University Press.

Myrdal A, Myrdal G (1934) Kris i befolkningsfrågan. Stockholm.

Nermo M (1994) Den ofullbordade jämställdheten, in Fritzell J, Lundberg O (eds) Vardagens villkor. Brombergs, Stockholm.

Nyberg A (1989) Tekniken -kvinnornas befriare. Linköping Studies in Arts and Sciences.

OECD (1988) Employment Outlook, Paris.

OECD (1990) Employment Outlook, Paris.

OECD (1991) Employment Outlook, Paris.

Persson I (1993) Svenska kvinnor möter Europa. Bilaga 16 till Långtidsutredningen 1992 (SOU 1992:19). Allmänna Förlaget, Stockholm.

Pott-Buter HA (1993) Facts and Fairy Tales about Female Labor, Family and Fertility. Amsterdam University Press, Amsterdam.

Pålsson A-M, Norrman E (1994) Finns det en marknad för hemarbete? SNS Förlag, Stockholm.

SACO (1992) Kvinnligt och manligt, (studier av löner och löneskillnader bland akademiker i statlig, enskild respektive kommunal tjänst 1991).

SCB (1963-1993) Arbetskraftsundersökningen, årsmedeltal, råtabeller.

SCB (Statistics Sweden) (1974) Arbetskraftsundersökningen, årsmedeltal 1963, redovisning enligt 1970 års tabellplan.

SCB (Statistics Sweden) (1992) Tidsanvändningsundersökningen 1990/91, Tabeller, Levnadsförhållanden, Rapport 80.

Silenstam P (1970) Arbetskraftsutbudets utveckling i Sverige 1870-1965.Industriens utredningsinstitut. Almqvist & Wiksell, Stockholm.

SOU 1993:16 Nya villkor för ekonomi och politik. Allmänna Förlaget, Stockholm.

Sundström M (1987) A Study in the Growth of Part-time Work in Sweden. Stockholm, Arbetslivscentrum.

Sundström M (1991) Sweden: Supporting Work, Family, and Gender Equality, in Kamerman SB, Kahn AJ (eds) Child Care, Parental Leave and the Under 3s: Policy Innovation in Europe. Westport, CT: Auburn House.

Sundström M (1992) The Growth in Full-Time Work among Swedish Women in the 1980's. Mimeo, Demography Unit, Stockholm University.

Sundström M, Stafford FP (1992) Female Labour Force Participation, Fertility and Public Policy in Sweden. European Journal of Population, 8.

Ståhlberg A-C (1994 forthcoming) Swedish Women's Pensions. Scandinavian Journal of Social Welfare.

Tegle S (1985) Part-Time Employment. An Economic Analysis of Weekly Working Hours in Sweden 1963-1982. Lund Economic Studies.

The Status of Women in Sweden (1968) Report to the United Nations. The Department of Foreign Affairs, Stockholm.

Chapter 4

Internal Migration
Tommy Bengtsson and Mats Johansson

It is generally considered that mobility is increasing in our society. Internationalisation is growing; travel is increasing; impulses, trends and new ideas from outside gain a more rapid foothold; distances diminish. At the same time, however, local ties are strengthening their hold in the sense that long-distance migratory movements are diminishing. High individual mobility - to places of work, education, recreation and service - is often possible without permanent migration. This, in broad terms, is the import of the "post-industrial paradox", as it is termed - a paradox which is not as paradoxical as it sounds.[1]

Transformation processes and diminished internal migration - an international survey

In Sweden, long-distance migration - i e movement across county boundaries - has been diminishing since the early 1960s. However, the high migration figures of the 1960s formed a parenthesis in what was a long-term trend. During the interwar period, the war years and the 1950s, long-distance migration had been exhibiting a declining tendency. The importance of migration in the Swedish urbanisation process was at its peak, for example, during the 1930s.[2]

Patterns of rapid economic growth have been associated as a rule with the movement of resources between different firms, trades and industries, which has also resulted in extensive geographical mobility. The latter was especially pronounced during the 1960s, which were characterised in Sweden by high growth, rapid structural transformation and shortage of labour - the industrial society stood at its zenith. Resources had to be shifted from low-productivity to high-productivity enterprises in order not to inhibit growth. This also formed the foundation of the so-called Rehn/Meidner model, in which a "wage-solidarity" (i e wage-equalisation) policy was combined with an active labour-market policy. Upward pressure on wage-levels in the least productive firms would cause them to go to the wall while at the same time wage increases in the productive firms would be restrained. For this policy to succeed it had to be possible for labour to be shifted swiftly and simply out

---

1 This essay is part of a larger study supported by Expert Group on Regional and Urban Studies (ERU) as a part of their research programme on migration.
2 Johansson and Persson (1991).

of low-productivity and into high-productivity firms.[3] Because these firms were not evenly distributed geographically the consequence was great geographical mobility during the 1960s. That decade can also be said to be the last - in Sweden at any rate - to be marked by the migration patterns of the industrial society.

However, there is nothing to suggest that the tendency towards diminished migration which has been observable in Sweden during recent decades is a phenomenon unique to Swedish conditions; there are indicators suggestive of the same trend in other countries as well. Migration between different regions within the European Union seems to have diminished since the early 1970s - at least if it is the mobility of European Union citizens that is being considered - and the southern regions seem to have largely ceased to function as reservoirs of labour for the north.[4] As far as Italy and Spain at least are concerned, there are studies which reveal a decline in internal migration as well.[5] There are indicators for Great Britain and France which point in the same direction, and the same applies to the traditionally highly-mobile United States. Moreover, migratory movements today do not seem to be characterised by "rural push" and "urban pull" - it is suburbanising and counter-urbanising tendencies that have made themselves increasingly felt instead.

What is it, then, that lies behind this development in the industrial or post-industrial countries of the western world? Is there any common explanation or is it a case of a multi-factor pattern of events in which the causes vary over time and between countries? This section singles out some factors and transformation processes which may well have had an inhibiting effect on long-distance migration in Europe and the United States - transformation processes whose effects are expected to continue into the future as well. Examples of such transformation processes - between which there are no watertight bulkheads - are decentralisation with changed preferences in regard to housing, growth of small and medium-sized towns (reconcentration), deindustrialisation, and reindustrialisation. Other processes which influence and will go on influencing long-distance migration are the new activity-patterns of trade and industry in combination with the labour market's increasing segmentation and a demographic trend towards a rising proportion of old people in the population. This also means that population and labour have become increasingly important factors in choice of location by firms - which are often know-ledge-based. These transformation processes are certainly influenced in part by trade-cycle movements but they are primarily structurally-conditioned.

What is meant by decentralisation in this case is that population and job opportu-nities move out from town centres to outlying places. These movements cannot be regarded as long-distance but more as short-distance, and they are dependent to a

---

3 The model took its name from two trade union economists, Gösta Rehn and Rudolf Meidner, who launched these ideas in the 1950s. However, it was not until the 1960s that they were translated into practice to form guidelines for labour-market policy.

4 Commission of the European Communities (1991), OECD (1993).

5 See e g Attanasio and Padoa Schioppa (1991), Milana (1990), Bentolila and Dolado (1991).

large degree on a functioning infrastructure. One ingredient of this process is migration out to the surrounding "countryside" adjacent to the large towns.[6]

These tendencies towards "counter-urbanisation" have long been observable in the United States. In Europe, decentralising tendencies were making themselves felt in Great Britain and the Benelux countries as early as the 1950s and 1960s, in Germany during the 1960s, and in France and Italy during the 1970s.[7] The population increase which has taken place in the major West European cities since the 1960s has resulted largely from increased in-migration from abroad.[8] But in Eastern Europe - with the exception of Hungary and Budapest - counter-urbanising tendencies have still not emerged; migration there is thought to be still characterised by "urban pull" and "rural push".[9]

Reconcentration - i e population increase in small and medium-sized towns - means that this development goes further and a multi-centre urban structure emerges. There is a shift away from big towns to smaller towns nearby. The term applied to the latter in the United States is "New Downtowns" or "Edge Cities".[10] Contraction of the large towns is offset by the growth of the smaller or medium-sized towns - but not literally so because the growth of these towns is not a direct consequence of the out-migration from the large towns. Only in part, therefore, are decentralisation and reconcentration different sides of the same coin. For the reconcentration process is conditioned in large measure by inward migration from the surrounding countryside.

Another central element of both decentralisation and reconcentration is that work and settlement are becoming increasingly separated - settlement gets higher and higher priority - which means that new settlement and migration patterns are emerging. Labour is becoming more and more mobile with respect to work tasks performed but more and more immobile in relation to settlement. The post-industrial society's priorities are different from those of the industrial society.[11] Thus, in many cases a good residential environment, proximity to nature, cultural and leisure facilities, plus - not least - access to good communications, become more important than being near to the place of work.[12] Commuting has become a real alternative to moving house. Developments in eastern and southern England illustrate this with particular clarity, even though the London region did show substantial net out-migration during the second half of the 1980s.[13]

The composition of the population in terms of age has also been a significant factor in the decline of propensity to migrate, firstly because older people move less than younger people, and secondly because a labour market is being created which has a diminishing effect even on age-specific migration intensities. For a high

---

6 Burns (1987), Cross (1990), Hall (1993).

7 See e g Cheshire and Hay (1989), Cross (1990), Hall (1993).

8 Commission of the European Communities (1992).

9 van den Berg et al (1987), Masser et al (1992).

10 Garreau (1991).

11 Inglehart (1977), Inglehart (1989), Johansson and Persson (1991).

12 Quigley (1989).

13 Cross (1990), Fielding (1993).

proportion of older people means that a labour market is created which is dependent on old people (care and treatment). The incomes of older people also have less tendency to "leak" than those of young people in the sense that a larger proportion of income is spent locally because services are most frequently produced where they are consumed. This means that the population itself has increasingly become a job-creating factor which partially inhibits out-migration from some of the traditional regions of out-migration - regions which have been transformed into "pensioner paradises".[14]

Deindustrialisation is intimately bound up with structural transformation of the economy.[15] However, friction-free economic transformation does not happen as a rule -disharmonies arise by virtue of the fact that resources are not shifted out of stagnating activities into expanding ones. The result instead is a stagnant economy with continually increasing unemployment, which has hit particularly hard in traditional industrial regions with a one-sided labour market.[16] This ought to give rise to increased out-migration from these decaying industrial regions - a migration analogous to the decline of the agrarian society and the rise of the industrial society. A neutralising factor which causes this to happen to only a limited extent, however, is the emergence of the post-industrial society, with its increasing segmentation of the labour market. The consequence is that there is no alternative target-destination for the labour force thrown out of work by deindustrialisation to migrate to, such as there once was for the farmer who had been rationalised out of existence. Instead, the districts hit by deindustrialisation become characterised by stagnation, depression and apathy, which have an inhibiting effect on the in-migration of both people and enterprise.

Simultaneously with deindustrialisation, however, reindustrialisation is going on. What this means is that new industries are replacing old ones and are a natural element of the transformation process. The problem is, though, that these processes do not coincide spatially; what frequently happens instead is that reindustrialisation occurs in districts quite different from the traditional industrial regions.[17] This also ties in with the changed alignment of investment. In the traditional industrial regions, productivity, profitability and expansion were associated in high degree with material investments in buildings and machinery - i.e. the investment pattern of the old industrial society. Today and tomorrow it is the non-material investments instead - R & D, product development, training and marketing - that form the foundation of profitability, productivity and expansion.

One element of this transformation process is increasing segmentation of the labour market. Labour and real capital used to be interchangeable to a large extent. Today the picture is different. The introduction of new technology requires labour with certain qualifications and thus also a certain degree of training - labour as a factor of production has become increasingly heterogeneous. Applying a production-

14 Cross (1990).
15 For a discussion of the deindustrialisation debate, see e g Rowthorn and Wells (1987).
16 Cheshire and Hay (1989), Fothergill and Guy (1990).
17 Cheshireand Hay (1989), Commission of the European Communities (1991) and (1993).

theory conceptual apparatus, we can say that there are "vintages" of both capital and labour.

One effect of increasing segmentation is the ever-growing incidence of both shortage and surplus of labour in the same firm, locality or region, or between regions. The segmentation of the labour market has become more and more of a regional segmentation as well. The result has been increased structural unemployment in which the long-term unemployed form a prominent element. In particular, poorly-educated young people, older people and immigrants have found difficulty in establishing a proper foothold in the labour market. Various studies have also shown that these are the very categories which have a low propensity to migrate.[18]

Thus it was characteristic of yesterday's industrial society that labour migrated to the firm. Dependence on raw materials and large-scale heavy investment in infrastructure, buildings and machinery made capital somewhat immobile. Today's picture is different - and so will tomorrow's be. When growing numbers of people are employed in the service sector and new - often knowledge-based - industries are being established and developed, it will become more and more common for firms to locate themselves in places and regions where skilled labour is to be found or is in process of being educated. Highly-trained labour and good communications are today considered to be the most highly valued location factors for this type of enterprise. The result has also been a number of location shifts from old densely-populated districts or traditional industrial regions to new and dynamic growth regions. One of the more striking examples of this phenomenon is the growth crescent around the Mediterranean from northeastern Italy via Provence and down to Barcelona on the Spanish east coast.[19]

The above-cited transformation processes have thus tended to work in the same direction, reinforcing one another. This has resulted in the emergence of a post-industrial migration and settlement pattern - the "post-industrial paradox". Thus, at the same time as mobility in society has increased generally, there are indicators suggesting that long-distance internal migration has diminished. But the statistics are defective in many cases, and it is difficult to form an overall picture of age-specific migration. As far as Sweden is concerned, however, these reservations do not apply, for the unique body of statistical material available here permits of a more detailed analysis of the "post-industrial paradox". This analysis will be made in the sections below.

From goods production to service economy - the case of Sweden

One of the most striking features of the transformation of the Swedish economy during the postwar period, just as in most western countries, is the deindustrialisation process. Six out of every ten employees in 1950 were involved in goods production, but that figure had dropped to one third by 1990. The change from an

---

18 See e g Greenwood and McDowell (1986).
19 Commission of the European Communities (1991) and (1993).

industrial to a service economy has resulted in a redistribution with respect to both production and consumption. The early 1950s saw barely half of the labour force involved in the production of goods and services for the local or regional market - today that figure is over seventy per cent.

The increasing importance of the service sector has had a stabilising effect on regional development, since the majority of services are produced where they are consumed. As a result of this enhancement of the local market's importance, the regions have become much less vulnerable to external factors of either national or international character. This structural change means that Sweden is approaching a stage where population settlement patterns determine the trend of employment at the regional level. This change from a goods-producing to a service-producing society - or from global to local production - has had a major impact upon regional development during the post-war period.

The most notable change during the period 1950-1985, however, must be the expansion of the public sector. This growth has been characteristic of three areas: care, education and local government administration. The rate of increase was especially notable in the 60s and 70s.

The public sector's expansion during the postwar period has had regional consequences. The 60s and 70s were a period of rapid expansion of government at the county and local level which led to large numbers of new jobs - primarily for women - throughout the country. As a result of this, most households in Sweden now have two incomes, the typical picture being one where the wife works in the public sector and the husband in the private sector. This development has reduced the sensitivity of regions to crisis and recession.

The rise of the service sector has also fuelled a reconcentration process in Sweden. Smaller and medium-sized towns have grown while big cities have stagnated or regressed in terms of number of inhabitants, while at the same time the sparsely-populated rural areas have been experiencing a population decrease too.

Structural transformation in different regions

In order to arrive at a better understanding of the possible effects of structural economic changes on migration, which is the purpose of this chapter, we have analysed out-migration from four regions with very different economic structures. The regions are: a metropolitan area (the Stockholm/Uppsala region), an old industrial district (Bergslagen), a sparsely-populated rural area (interior Norrland) and one "area" - twelve towns in northern Sweden - which can be characterised as regional service centres (Norrland towns).

By analysing the different regions' development patterns, we find that the metropolitan area (Stockholm/Uppsala) experienced rapid growth of employment during the period after 1960. This region's labour market is characterised by only a small percentage employed in the production of goods, and by deindustrialisation having already begun by the mid-60s.

We can see here that much of the change which would shape the national economy during the 70s and 80s had already begun in the metropolitan region by the mid-60s, so that this region was at an advantage when the boom came. The opposite also holds true - much of that which was to be phased out on a national level in the 70s and 80s had already been phased out in Stockholm/Uppsala in the 60s. As a result of this "head start", the region expanded vigorously during this period, and its dominance over the Swedish economy was reinforced.[20] The economy became characterised more and more by concentrations of knowledge-intensive activities, which influenced the labour market through increased demand for highly-educated labour.[21] As a result, the educational level of employees in the Stockholm area is notably higher than in the rest of the country. At the same time there are many employees of lower education working in the private service sector. The Stockholm/Uppsala region, like other metropolitan areas, becomes increasingly a dual and segmented labour market.[22]

The traditional style of industrial region is represented by Bergslagen, a region characterised by goods production and large-scale industry dominated by iron and steel and a small service sector.[23] The structural changes of the past decades have thus affected employment in Bergslagen severely. Its regional problems are directly linked to its industrial problems, with deindustrialisation and the decline of manufacturing accounting for much of the region's poor employment record. The structural crises of the past decades have hit the labour force hard, with long-term unemployment and early retirement as results.

The pattern of development of a sparsely-populated region with an economy closely tied to industries based on natural resources and raw materials (i.e. forestry, ore, and hydroelectric power) is here represented by interior Norrland. Decline in these activities has led to a decline in employment since the early 60s, mainly concentrated into the period 1965-1975, since when employment has risen somewhat primarily because of a rise in female labour force participation.[24] The region's development has been influenced by the structural rationalisation of, in particular, agriculture and forestry occurring mainly during the 60s and 70s. It was at this time that out-migration began to gather momentum. The fragile and unbalanced local industries were unable to absorb the labour freed by the rationalisation of the logging industry.

New jobs have been created in recent years, mainly through the growth of the public sector (which nevertheless was weaker than in other regions) from the mid-70s onwards. The public sector, including "transfer" payments, is more important for employment in interior Norrland than in any of the regions studied above.[25] Both the absolute and the relative expansion of the public sector, however, is a consequence of the lack of alternative employment opportunities. The lopsided age structure with its elderly population has led to increased employment in the fields of

20 SOU 1989:69.
21 See Johansson and Strömquist (1986), SOU 1989:69 and SOU 1990:36.
22 SOU 1989:67, SOU 1989:70, SOU 1990:20, SOU 1990:36, Bengtsson and Johansson (1992), Johansson (1993a).
23 Vinell and Ohlsson (1987), ERU and SCB (1991).
24 Johansson (1993b).
25 SOU 1989:67, Beckman and Lenntorp (1989), Holm and Tapper (1990).

health and social care of the elderly, the numbers employed here being greater than those employed in industries based on raw materials. The skewed age structure of interior Norrland has also resulted in a larger share of the labour force being employed in caring occupations than either in Norrland's towns or in the country as a whole.

The towns of Norrland can be described as regional service centres. The expansion of the public sector is one of the main explanations of the fact that the unemployment figures for these towns has been below the national average.

Despite these similarities, there are also differences in economic features. Some of the Norrland towns have a large share of the total labour force employed in manufacturing. These towns can be regarded as Norrland's industrial base, where industries based on raw materials have had a considerable impact on employment, Unfortunately, these industries have exhibited little capacity for growth since the mid-70s. The way these towns have developed can be compared to that in Bergslagen, with crises caused by international over-capacity dictating events on the labour market. The decline of the industrial sector has been offset by the rise of the service sector, especially the public sector. The regional service centres have taken advantage of the reconcentration process, which has been a central ingredient of the spatial development of employment and population in Sweden since the beginning of the 70s.

The slow-down of long-distance migration

Since the beginning of the 1960s the long-distance migration intensities - migration over county borders - of different age groups have exhibited a declining trend. It is often assumed that large birth cohorts have different migration propensities from small ones - larger cohorts are assumed to have relatively greater geographic mobility than smaller. This argument is based on the presumption that the possibility of finding work nearer home increases when the number of young people seeking jobs declines, and vice versa.[26]

However, we know that variations in the period migration intensities for different age-groups are not a function of the cohort sizes.[27] Regardless of cohort size, different age groups display very much the same development over time. Furthermore, there appears to be a cyclical pattern to the migration variations that is common to almost all age-groups. Those years which have been marked by high or rising migration intensity have also experienced economic peaks or upswings. In this light it would seem that migration could, at least in the short term, be explained by business cycles: cyclical upturns bring with them heightened migration intensity, while downturns have the opposite effect. This linkage holds true for both large and small cohorts.[28]

---

26 This phenomenon is often called the "Easterlin effect". See Easterlin (1968, 1980).
27 See Bengtsson (1989).
28 See Holmlund (1984), Bengtsson (1989).

The effects of cyclical variations are clear in the short run for all regions and most age-groups. As at the national level, the older age-groups show a weaker linkage to cyclical changes, as do children. This shows that families with small children are less sensitive to cyclical changes in their relocation patterns than singles or families without children. The same phenomenon can be found with regard to migration of different sexes. Female migration has a weak correlation with the over-representation of women in the noncompetitive public sector.

One method of eliminating the effects of cyclical variations in order to approach this question is to calculate the total migration intensity for each birth cohort over a ten-year period.[29] This method follows a cohort consisting of an entire age-group throughout the period, counting the number of movements across county boundaries. In this manner one follows a group of twenty year-olds until they turn thirty, thirty year-olds until they turn forty, etc. These groups will be referred to for the sake of simplicity by their age at entry into the cohort. The total migration intensity may be greater than 100%, since an individual can move across county boundaries more than once in the ten year period.

The result for the most mobile age-group, the twenty year-olds, is presented in Diagram 1. The total time periodcovered is 1961 to 1988, which means that total migration intensities for a ten-year period are calculated for those who were 20 years of age between 1961 and 1979. Examination of the graph discloses that longdistance

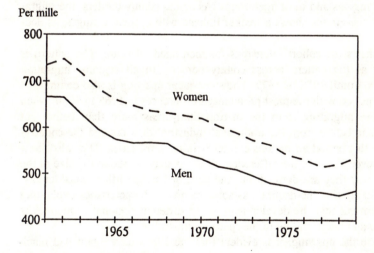

Diagram 1. Cohort migration intensities in ages 20-29 years for 20-year olds 1961-1979. Source: Bengtsson T (1989).

---

29 See also Bengtsson (1989).

migration declines over time for both men and women. The result is similar for other age-groups but at different levels.[30] There seems to be an increase in migration intensities at the end of the period. The question arises whether this is a sign of structural shift towards higher migration or whether it is an effect of the extremely lengthy boom of the 1980s. We will argue that the latter is likely to be the case. The fact that no correlation at all exists between cohort size and migration and that all age-groups show a similar development are clear evidences that the decline is not a result of changing cohort sizes. As business-cycle effects can also be ruled out, it is evident that the decline is a result of structural changes in the economy. In order to ascertain whether they are dependent on economic structure and change or are common to areas with different production structures, the out-migration intensities are calculated for different areas of Sweden.

The development of regional migration

The calculations of out-migration intensities are based on these cases of movements across regional boundaries, rather than county lines. Change in the yearly out-migration intensities from different regions tends to follow the same pattern as migration across county borders. The effects of cyclical variations are clear in the short run for all regions and most age-groups. As across county borders, the migration of the older age-groups shows a weaker linkage with cyclical changes, as does that of children.

Diagram 2 shows the cohort intensities for men aged 20 years. The pattern is much the same as the pattern across county borders. In all regions, migration declines from 1961 until 1978 or 1979. The subsequent upswing is also common to all regions. The period with the most pronounced differences is 1965 to 1970, when 20 year-olds were migrating from the metropolitan areas more than before but migrating less than before from the traditional industrial districts and the countryside. Apart from this period all regions exhibit striking similarities. They also show differences, however. Some of the differences in levels may be due to the size of the regions and the way they are defined, but the pace of change differs considerably. Thus it is most likely that the decline has some common characteristics explaining the overall pattern but that the development of the different regional economies is also important to an understanding of the speed of the decline.

With regard to the upswing, it is evident that the 1980s have again had much stronger migration; nevertheless we argue that this is not likely to be a result of a new structural change in the economy but rather of an exceptional boom. Normally, the impact of booms tends to be eliminated in these types of calculations, but because of the length and strength of the boom during the later part of the 80s, it did have a certain impact, especially on the traditional out-migration regions.

---

30 Bengtsson (1989).

   The Stockholm/Uppsala-region had a net in-migration of 20 year-olds throughout the period, even in the 70s.[31] This indicates that the net out-migration experienced by Stockholm county during the 70s results from out-migration among other
age-groups such as children and the middle-aged.[32] Out-migration from the region
was, and still is, primarily a family affair, consisting in large part of return migrants.[33] The metropolitan area was thus in some measure an ingredient of the
reconcentration process of the 70s and 80s, which resulted in a growth of smaller
and medium-sized towns.

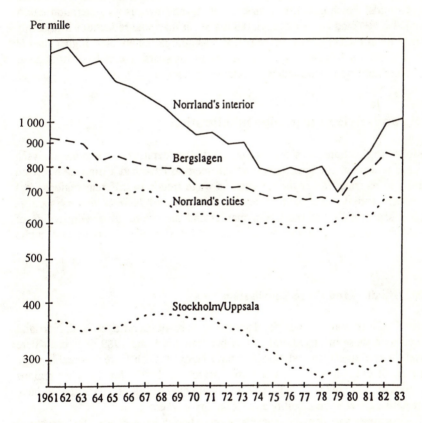

Diagram 2. Cohort migration intensities in ages 20-29 years for 20-year old men in 1961-
1983 in different regions.

Diagram 2 also shows that the aggregate out-migration intensity has fallen radically
in the traditional out-migration regions. The Norrland towns and interior, along

---

31 This region is clearly over-represented in 20 year-olds. See Johansson and Persson (1991).
32 See also Schéele (1991).
33 Regarding this situation during the late 80s, see Gustavsson and Johansson (1989).

with Bergslagen, all show this phenomenon. The same holds true for other age-groups, but at a lower level. Interior Norrland has felt the decrease most severely, with its out-migration intensity dropping to near the levels of its towns and Bergslagen. These reductions have not been matched by increased in-migration, however, with the result that these regions are still regions of out-migration.[34]

In conclusion, it can be said that the reduction in long-distance migration, both inter-regional and inter-county, is not a cyclical phenomenon. Generation effect, i.e. the influence of cohort size on mobility, has also been ruled out as an explanation. Migration intensity declined for 20 year-old cohorts of both large and small sizes. Migratory movements in other age-groups have followed the same general pattern as for 20 year-olds, which underlines our contention that there is no generation effect. It should also be noted that we are not talking about marginal reductions in mobility - the mobility at the beginning of the period was approximately 50% higher than at its end. The decline has been especially strong in the sparsely-populated rural areas interior Norrland and the old industrial area (Bergslagen).

Factors underlying the decline in migration

In the following sections we shall not attempt a more detailed or complete analysis, but instead will point out some factors which seem to have had a limiting effect on propensity to migrate: *direct factors* such as wage trends in different regions, real estate prices, and the rise of dual-income families; and *indirect factors* such as increasing segmentation of the labour market and the structural transformation of the Swedish economy with special reference to the rise of the service and public sectors.

Job Opportunities and Wage Equalisation

Diagram 3 shows wage trends for factory workers in Bergslagen and Norrland compared with those in Stockholm county between 1965 and 1989. It is clear here that workers in Bergslagen and Norrland have enjoyed much more favourable wage trends than Stockholm workers, a condition which holds true for the other regions compared with Stockholm as well. This regional equalisation of wages should have had a negative effect upon mobility among factory workers.

Simple supply and demand considerations should have caused the structural change which occurred in the "traditional" industrial regions during the 70s and 80s to have resulted in an increased, rather than a decreased, wage differential. The decreased differential, however, can be partially explained by the fact that it was industry with low productivity, and thus low wages, which went to the wall during the change. This process was reinforced by the "wage solidarity" policy which forced out the least productive companies. After unproductive enterprises were eliminated,

---

34 Statistics Sweden.

the wage level was raised as a result of the new composition of the market. The result was that wages rose despite increased unemployment.

Industrial (blue-collar) workers form only 13 per cent of the total labour force nationwide, and in the Stockholm/Uppsala region the figure is as low as 7 per cent. This means that wage trends among industrial workers reflect only a small part of the total labour market. Statistics on the trend of per capita incomes, however, show the same equalisation tendencies.[35]

For white-collar workers too there has been equalisation of wages, although the statistics at regional level are less reliable. From the beginning of the 60s to the end of the 70s an equalisation occurred between different white-collar occupations in Sweden. Between the end of the 70s and the middle of the 80s, the wage ratio between different white-collar categories was relatively constant. Since the middle of the 80s, however, the wage distribution in white-collar occupations has again become more unequal. This pattern also holds good for the wage ratio between male and females in both white- and blue-collar occupations. The differences between different categories, however, are not as large as they were in the 60s and early 70s.[36] These patterns seems to apply in different parts of the country as well.

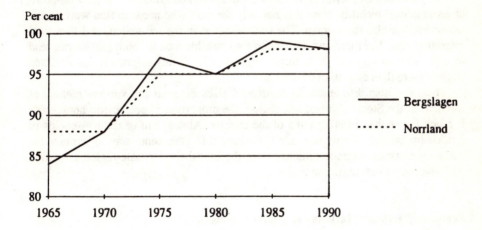

Diagram 3. Average wages for male industrial workers in Bergslagen and Norrland as a percentage to Stockholm county.

The expansion of the public sector seems also to exercise an income-equalising effect because of the more equal wage distribution in this sector compared with the distribution in the private sector.

---

35 Johansson (1993b).
36 Svensson (1992).

The conclusion is that wage and income equalisation between different regions, as well as different occupations and sexes, has reduced incentives to migrate, and that this in turn is one of the causes underlying the slow-down of internal migration during the past decades.

Dual-Income Families

Today, women have an employment frequency almost equal to that of men, about 85 per cent in the 20-64 years age-group. This figure is roughly the same regardless of civil status. The situation has changed drastically over the past thirty years, rising from a 25 per cent employment rate for married women in 1960.[37] However, these figures are overestimated in the sense that about half of Swedish women are only working part-time.

In earlier times, woman's occupation was not a factor for consideration in matters of geographic mobility. Women generally did not work, and a change in the husband's employment situation or prospects requiring relocation was not hindered by the wife. Often the wife began working only after the move, as moves were generally in the direction of larger towns with a more diversified, "female-friendly" labour market.

The increased employment of married women has contributed to a slowing-down of geographical mobility. Now it is not only the man who needs to find work in the new town, but also the woman. The time involved in the job-search, and thus total migration cost, has increased. Failure to find suitable jobs for both parties can lead to a decision to stay put. This factor explains why family migration has declined slightly more than migration of singles.

There are also differences in household sizes between the various regions of Sweden. In the Stockholm/Uppsala region, the proportion of one-person households is much larger than in other parts of the country. Almost half of the households in Stockholm consist of only one adult. Perhaps this goes some way to explain the relatively constant migration intensities in the Stockholm/Uppsala region compared with traditional out-migration regions.

Segmented Labour Markets - Regional Polarisation

In the Western world, the labour force skill level has become an important factor determining companies' choice of location, a consideration which holds especially true for easily-mobile companies in the so called "knowledge-intensive" sectors. This post-industrial trend diverges sharply from that of the industrial phase, when labour relocated to where employment existed. Localisation factors in that period were decided by considerations such as raw material supply, market conditions, and transport facilities.

---

37 Silenstam, (1970).

The sparsely-populated rural areas of interior Norrland can be said never to have entered the industrial phase in the sense that manufacturing never accounted for a large proportion of employment there. However, they did enter the industrial phase to the extent that they were affected by its development. One way in which the industrial phase affected these areas was in migration: the underemployed work force migrated - "rural push" - to metropolitan areas and industrial towns -"urban pull" - as long as there existed a lot of industrial and construction job opportunities.

Until the early 1970s the type of labour which moved away from the rural areas generally had no problem finding work once having arrived at the destination. Manufacturing required labour of low educational level with "standardised competence", that is, labour which could be directly placed in simple, repetitive tasks.

Today's picture is different. The labour required by the post-industrial urban labour market is different from that of the industrial phase. "Rural push" has declined as an activating force, and it seems that "urban pull" has come to dominate migration from depopulating areas to metropolitan areas and regional service centres.[38] However, the switch in demand signifies that a gap has developed between the type of labour in rural - and even industrial - areas and the type needed in cities and regional service hubs. It has been shown that young people of low education who have migrated to Stockholm have had difficulties establishing themselves in the more education-dependent labour market and quickly returned home, a process which was noticeable even during the economic upswing in the last half of the 1980s.

The result of these processes has been a further regional segmentation and polarisation of the labour force, a development which has hampered migration from the rural and old industrial areas. Consequently, there has been no benefit to these areas in terms of the location decisions of knowledge-based companies either.

Moving Costs and Real Estate Prices

Migration is not only associated with higher incomes or better working conditions but also with such expenditures as moving costs and cost of living in the new location. One factor that weighs heavily in the final decision to migrate is prices on the real estate market - whether rentals or purchase prices. Supply and demand theory suggests that the bigger the flow of migrants into a region, the higher the costs involved in migrating to this region. Moreover, to move from a stagnant or declining region also involves selling the former home at a low price. This has a limiting effect on both out-migration from a crisis area and in-migration to an expanding one.

The trend of prices of small houses during the period 1977-1989 in regions outside the metropolitan areas as a ratio of prices in the Stockholm area is un-

---

38 This is clearly seen in the studies which have been made of immigration to Stockholm during the economic upswing 1986-87. See Johansson (1989), Gustavsson and Johansson (1989). The same conclusion can be drawn from an analysis of migration to and from Västernorrland county. See Bylund (1992).

ambiguous. A small house outside the metropolitan regions sold for 62 per cent of the price of a similar house in the Stockholm area in 1977. Twelve years later - 1989 - the ratio had fallen to only 40 per cent. In only twelve years, prices in Stockholm had increased by 55 per cent compared with the rest of the country excluding metropolitan areas. This has naturally put a brake on movement from these regions to Stockholm and also the other metropolitan areas where the price ratio for real property has worsened, although not to the same degree as in Stockholm.

The Rise of the Public Sector

Simultaneously with the increased employment of married women, the structural transformation of the Swedish economy has resulted in a sharp increase in the proportion of employees working in the service sector in Sweden.

In the mid-60s, the service industry dominated employment only in the metro-politan areas, industrial production preponderating elsewhere. The highest propor-tion of industrial employees was to be found in the mills of Bergslagen. Twenty years later the picture was somewhat different, with service occupations predomi-nant in the country as a whole. The proportion has remained about the same throughout the expansion. This expansion suggests that availability of services has improved throughout the country.[39]

A good deal of the credit for the rapid expansion of the service sector should go to the public sector's expansion. Its proportion of the work force grew dramatically during the period 1965-1985, as can be seen in Table 1.

The "normal" public administration can be said to have experienced two distinct phases during the postwar period. The national administration was developed first, then the local administration. This has led to a situation in which public activities are the biggest "business" in many towns today - the largest employer is often the town hall or the hospital. This process has also resulted in a convergence between the different regions with regard to the proportion of employment accounted for by the public sector.

Thus the public sector's expansion in the postwar era has had strong regional consequences. During the 60s and 70s, the entire country was involved in the process through the proliferation of municipal and county administrative machinery.[40] This created vacancies which could be filled by women throughout the nation, and was a factor contributing to the rise of the dual-income family. Deindustrialisation ought to lead to increased mobility, but in this case it was counteracted by the rapid growth of the public sector. A common situation in Sweden today is that of the wife employed by the public sector and the husband by the private sector. This new situation has made the different regions more insulated from crisis effects than before, and it has also reduced geographic mobility, because work in the home region generally exists for at least one member of the household.

---

39 See Johannisson, Persson and Wiberg (1989).
40 See e.g. Bengtsson and Johansson (1992), (1993).

Table 1. The proportion employed in the public sector in different regions 1960-1990. (In per cent).

	1965	1975	1985	1990
Stockholm/Uppsala	22	34	34	33
Bergslagen	12	21	31	32
Norrland's cities	19	31	37	38
Norrland's interior	23	30	38	39
Total Sweden	16	26	34	34

Source: ERU.

Transfer Payments and Regional Policy

Concomitantly with the rise of the public sector, there has been a rise in public transfer payments. This has occurred partially through sector-directed policy, and partially through regional and social policy. Examples of the former are the siting of publicly-owned companies and plants, and the expansion of higher education at the regional level. Examples of the latter are different types of location assistance for companies, better unemployment relief, and early retirement plans to relieve the labour markets. These measures have also resulted in reduced migration intensity because the prospects for supporting or educating oneself in one's home region have improved, either directly by increasing the possibility of remaining there, or in-directly through increased services and job vacancies.

The rural areas and the traditional industrial districts have a skewed age structure in that they have a high proportion of old people. This results in a high dependence upon the social welfare system in the form of various types of govern-mental transfer payments. Some of these, such as pensions, are index-regulated, while others are associated with the the goal of ensuring an acceptable standard of living throughout the country. This has resulted in a high rate of subsidy-dependence, especially in depopulating rural areas - these areas are generally more dependent upon various governmental transfers to survive.[41]

Governmental transfers - especially pensions, services, and regional policy - have influenced the migration pattern in three ways. The first is that the possibility of staying on in the home region has increased. This is a direct result of the increased scope for sustaining an acceptable standard of living created by direct transfers for the purpose of reinforcing incomes. The second is that there are spin-off effects in rural and stagnating industrial areas in that a large proportion of old people generates employment for younger and middle-aged workers - primarily female - in the health care sector. Thus a new labour market has developed because of these

---

41 Beckman and Lenntorp (1989), Johansson (1993b).

areas' demographic structure. The third way in which migration has been affected is through the increased possibility of survival for other activities, based on increased purchasing power generated by governmental transfers and the existence of new employment opportunities.[42] Examples of this can be found in shops, post offices, and transport firms which would otherwise have been forced to close.

Both governmental, index-regulated transfer payments and regional policy have had the effect, *ceteris paribus*, that out-migration propensity in depopulating rural and traditional areas has declined.[43] These instruments have not been able to stop net out-migration from these areas, but we can safely assume that it would have been much higher in their absence.

A Post-Industrial Paradox?

Rapid economic growth is usually associated with transfers of resources between different companies, branches, or sectors. By transfers from low-productivity sectors to high-productivity sectors, transfer gains are experienced. These gains have been especially noticeable during the transition from agrarian to industrial society, where one prerequisite was for labour and capital to be transferred from the farming sector to the industrial sector, resulting in extensive geographic mobility. This was also a conspicuous feature of migration patterns in the industrial society.

The situation is different today. The service sector has supplanted industry, which means that transfer gains are more difficult to achieve because of the service sector's lower productivity. In addition, migration intensity has declined since the beginning of the 60s as one of the consequences of the post-industrial era. The slow-down of the propensity to migrate is an obvious fact in all age groups between 20 and 60 years.

Can it be that the post-industrial society does not require the same mobility of labour that the industrial one did? Is a new residence and migration pattern emerging on lines conforming to the economic development, and the values, of post-industrial society?[44]

The link between workplace and residence seems to be breaking down as the new age opens. The labour force is becoming more mobile in relation to the work performed, but less so in relation to place of residence. At the same time as society is becoming internationalised, it is also becoming more locally tied. This situation is not as paradoxical as it may seem, as the majority of Swedish workers today produce goods or services for the local or regional market.[44] Their proportion has increased during the postwar period, mainly as a function of the rise of the service sector. The

---

42 See Artle (1984), Cross (1990), Bengtsson and Johansson (1992).

43 This phenomenon is also noticeable in Italy. Different forms of assistance and income guarantees have served dramatically to reduce migration in general and especially migration from southern Italy. This decline occured despite the wide differences in productivity and labour market conditions between the north and the south. See Milana (1990), Attanasio and Padoa Schioppa (1990).

44 See Johansson and Persson (1991) for discussion of residence and mobility patterns in the post-industrial age.

increase in service production, often local in character, has led to a better and more evenly distributed access to services nationwide. At the same time, both spouses have begun working, at least one of them, usually the woman, being employed in the local or regional service sector. It has also become more common to work, for example, one day a week at home, some days at the workplace and possibly some days at another location. The development of patterns of this sort has caused many individuals to question the validity of the distinction between work and leisure.

The priorities of the post-industrial economy are also different from those of the industrial. Quality of life, environment, cultural activities, recreational areas, and good transport facilities become more valuable than proximity to the workplace for many.[45] The result is increased local ties, which are reinforced by the increasingly local or regional nature of service production and the loosening of the links between residence and work for a larger proportion of the labour force - a process which will be continued in the future.

However, this post-industrial paradox is not unique to Sweden. As was observed in the first part of the chapter, it seems to be an international phenomenon as well. Decentralisation and reconcentration of settlement patterns, the rise of female participation in the labour force and dual-income families, deindustrialisation, growth of service production and population ageing, are all development patterns indicative of a slow-down of internal migration, and they are common to most industrialised or post-industrialised Western societies. In some aspects Sweden is in front, in other cases lagging. What we have shown in this chapter, however, is that this post-industrial paradox with regard to mobility and migration is not unique to specific ages and regions - rather, it seems to be common to all ages and all parts of the country.

---

45 See e.g. Inglehart (1977), Inglehart (1989), Quigley (1989).

REFERENCES

Attanasio OP, Padoa Schioppa F (1991)Regional Inequalities and Mismatch in Italy, 1960-86, in Padoa Schioppa F (ed) Mismatch and Labour Mobility. Cambridge University Press.

Beckman B, Lenntorp B (1989) Staten i geografin. SOU 1989:65. Stockholm.

Bengtsson T (1989) Påverkar generationsstorleken migrationen, in Broomé P, Ohlsson R (eds) Generationseffekten. Kristianstad.

Bengtsson T, Johansson M (1992) Population Structure, Community Development and Employment in Post-Industrial Sweden. Paper presented at The First International Symposium on Population and the Comprehensive Development of Community. December 1992, Haikou, China.

Bengtsson T, Johansson M (1993) Economic and Social Factors behind the Slowdown of Migration in Norrland, in Jusila H, Persson L O, Wiberg U (eds) System Shifts at the Top of Europe. NordREFO.

Bentolila S, Dolado JJ (1991) Mismatch and Internal Migration in Spain, 1962-86, in Padoa Schioppa F (ed) Mismatch and Labour Mobility. Cambridge University Press.

Burns L S (1987) Urban Growth and Decline as a Force in Regional Development: Issues and a Research Agenda, in van den Berg L, Burns LS Klassen LHF (eds) Spatial Cycles. Aldershot UK.

Bylund M (1991) Borta bra men hemma bäst? Flyttare och återflyttare i Västernorrlands län. ERU-rapport 72. Stockholm.

Cheshire PC, Hay DG (1989) Urban Problems in Western Europe. London.

Commission of the European Communities (1991) Europe 2000. Luxembourg.

Commission of the European Communities (1993) Regional Studies. Luxembourg.

Cross DWF (1990) Counterurbanization in England and Wales. Aldershot, UK.

Easterlin RA (1968) Population, Labor Force and Long Swings in Economic Growth. New York.

Easterlin RA (1980) Birth and Fortune. New York.

Fielding AJ (1993) Migration and the Metropolis: South East England 1971-1991. Paper presented at the conference Migration and Mobility in Metropolitan Areas. Urbanization in a New Era. June 5th-9th 1993 in Umeå.

Fothergill S, Guy N Retreat from the Regions. Corporate Change and the Closure of Factories. London.

Garreau J (1991) Edge City: Life on the New Frontier. New York.

Greenwood MJ, McDowell JM (1986) The Factor Market Consequences of U. S. Immigration. Journal of Economic Literature. Vol XXIV.

Gustavsson K, Johansson M (1989) Stockholm. Tur och retur - vilka flyttar ut och varför? Statistik om Stockholm 1989:2.

Hall P (1993) Migration and the Future of the Cities. Paper presented at the conference Migration and Mobility in Metropolitan Areas. Urbanization in a New Era. June 5th-9th 1993 in Umeå.

Holm E, Tapper H (1990) Geografin i den ekonomiska politiken. Ds 1990:74. Stockholm.

Inglehart R (1977) The Silent Revolution. Changing Values and Political Styles Among Western Publics. Princeton.

Inglehart R (1989) The Rise of a New Political Style. In SOU 1989:33, Urban Challenges. Stockholm.

Johannisson B, Persson LO, Wiberg U (1989) Urbaniserad glesbygd - verklighet och vision. Ds 1989:22. Stockholm.

Johansson B, Strömquist U (1986) Teknikspridning och importsubstitution. Stockholmsregionens teknikförnyelse. Länsstyrelsen i Stockholms län 1986 nr 7:2.

Johansson M (1993a) The Polarization of a Metropolis in a Welfare State - The Example of Stockholm. Scandinavian Housing and Planning Research, May 1993.

Johansson M (1993b) Migration Patterns in Depopulating Areas,in Wiberg U (ed) Marginal Areas in Developed Countries. CERUM Report 1994. Umeå.

Johansson M, Persson LO (1991) Regioner för generationer. Gothenburg.

Masser I, Svidén O, Wegener M (1992) The Geography of Europe's Futures. London & New York.

Milana C (1990) Wage Differentials, Regional Productivity Gap and Output Growth in a Dualistic Economy: The Case of Italy. Paper presented at the conference Labour Markets and Labour Market Policy in Europe in the 1990's, 20-23 September 1990.

Nilsson J-E (1988) Industrisamhällets omvandling - från varor och tjänster. Länsstyrelsen i Skaraborgs län.

OECD (1993) The Changing Course of International Migration. Paris.

Ohlsson L, Vinell L (1987) Tillväxtens drivkrafter. Stockholm.

Quigley JM (1989)The Quality of Housing. In SOU 1989:33, Urban Challenges. Stockholm.

Rowthorn RE, Wells JR (1987) De-industrialization and Foreign Trade. Cambridge.

SCB (1986) Information i prognosfrågor.

Schéele S (1991) Stockholmare och andra. Demografiska fakta, utvecklingstendenser och framtidsfrågor. Stockholm.

Silenstam P (1970) Arbetskraftsutbudets utveckling i Sverige 1970-1965. Uppsala.

Svensson L (1992) Politik eller ekonomi? En diskussion om orsaker till variationerna i kvinnliga tjänstemäns och arbetares relativa löner i den privata sektorn 1955-1990. Lund. Duplicated.

SOU 1989:12 Den regionala problembilden. Stockholm.

SOU 1989:67 Levnadsvillkor i storstadsregioner. Stockholm.

SOU 1989:69 Storstadsregioner i förändring. Stockholm.

SOU 1990:20 Välfärd och segregation i storstadsregionerna. Stockholm.

SOU 1990:36 Storstadsliv. Rika möjligheter - hårda villkor. Stockholm.

Chapter 5

Immigration and Economic Change
Christer Lundh and Rolf Ohlsson

By the beginning of the 1930s the wave of emigration to America had abated, and Sweden turned from a country of emigration into one of immigration. Large-scale immigration has been taking place all through the postwar period. An average of 37 000 persons per year have immigrated, which has resulted in there being 1.4 million people of foreign origin in Sweden (see Diagram 1).[1] This means that Sweden is one of the most heavily immigrant-populated countries in Europe. Only Belgium, France, Germany and Switzerland have a higher proportion of foreign citizens than Sweden.[2]

However, the pattern of immigration, the economic role which immigrants have played, and immigration policy itself have undergone radical change during the postwar period. On the basis of these criteria immigration during the postwar period can be divided into two phases.

Labour immigration predominated from the end of the war until the early 1970s, after which the elements of refugee and associated immigration came to play an ever-increasing role. During the former period immigration was free in principle, but since then it has been controlled for non-Nordic immigrants. Labour immigration came principally from Nordic countries. In addition, labour was imported from Germany, Austria and Italy during the 1950s, and from Yugoslavia and Greece during the 1960s. Towards the end of the 1960s immigration policy was changed and immigration of non-Nordic labour ceased. From the middle 1970s onwards immigration of labour from the Nordic countries declined because of diminishing differences in the standard of living.

Immigration of refugees, chiefly from the Third World and Eastern Europe, has increased since the early 1970s instead. Another change has been that immigration of relatives has increased. Some of these have consisted of relatives of the earlier immigrant workers from Greece and Yugoslavia, but mainly they have been members of refugee families (see Diagram 2).

In this study we examine what causal links have existed between Swedish economic development and immigration, but we also discuss what effects immigration has had on economic development. In our opinion there is a great difference between the period before and after 1970 with regard to both the causes of

---

1 This is a slightly revised version in English of chapter 7 in our book Lundh and Ohlsson (1994). For a more detailed documentation of the statistics in this article and for further references, see this book.
2 Castles and Miller (1993), SOU 1993:113.

immigration and its socioeconomic effects. We conclude by outlining briefly some conceivable future scenarios.

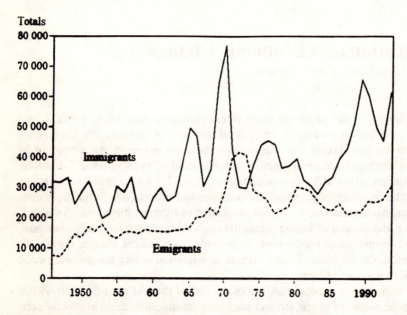

Diagram 1. Immigration to and emigration from Sweden 1946-1993.
Sources: SOS Befolkningsrörelsen, SOS Folkmängdens förändringar, SOS Befolkningsförändringar, SOS Befolkningsstatistik.

Causes of immigration

Our starting point is the "push-and-pull" theory so frequently cited in migration analyses, the basic idea being that migration flows can be explained in terms of conditions in both the home country and the target country and of sundry institutional obstacles to migration.[3] It is customarily the task of concrete analysis to determine which factors were most crucial in each individual case. However, our object is not to make a regular push-and-pull analysis, and especially not to establish the explanatory power of the various factors by means of econometric methods or formal models. Instead, our object is to discuss on a broader plane how economic conditions *in Sweden* have influenced immigration during the two phases. In conjunction with this we discuss changes in immigration policy, which in our opinion are determined primarily by economic conditions.

---

3 Lee (1969).

Economic and industrial growth

Swedish industry found itself in an exceedingly favourable position at the end of the war. In the war-torn countries of Europe whose production apparatus and infrastructure had been wholly or partly destroyed there was a great need for imports, while the production capacity of Swedish industry was greater than it had ever been. Moreover prices had risen less in Sweden than in other countries. There were therefore great prospects of a massive

expansion of exports. Even in Sweden itself there was a great latent need both to consume and to invest after the controls of wartime, and this manifested itself in a strongly rising home demand.

The great need to import means of production and transport in conjunction with reconstruction of industry in the war-ravaged lands had positive repercussions on developments in Sweden's engineering industry and shipyards. One of the results of this was that employment expanded substantially in these industries during the 1940s. But the limited import competition, too, in combination with a strongly rising home and international demand for consumer goods, furnished the scope for a significant expansion of the textile, ready-made clothing, shoe and leather industries.

It was during this period that the free labour immigration policy was established. The opportunities for economic expansion were judged to be good, but shortage of labour was felt to be a problem. The solution therefore seemed to be to import labour. The previous restrictive immigration policy was scrapped and immigration of labour into Sweden was free in practice from the beginning of the 1950s. This immigration policy was characterised by completely free access of Nordic citizens to the Swedish labour market, by cooperation between firms and the Labour Market Board (Arbetsmarknadsstyrelsen, or AMS) in endeavouring to establish organised forms for importing non-Nordic skilled workers for keyjobs in industry, and by the permitting of other non-Nordic workers as well to come to Sweden on their own initiative in order to seek work without being hampered by major administrative problems.

The period from the end of the war to the beginning of the 1970s was a period of industrial expansion characterised by high economic and industrial growth. Between 1947 and 1970 the average annual rise in GNP was 4.3 per cent (see Diagram 3). Industrial growth was even higher at times, notably during the first half of the 1960s. This economic and industrial expansion resulted in a permanent excess demand for labour. Part of this demand was met through an increase in the female labour supply. In 1945, 31 per cent of adult females (aged 15-64 years) were gainfully employed: by 1965 the proportion had risen to 44 per cent. But the demand for labour was greater than the increase in the female labour supply.

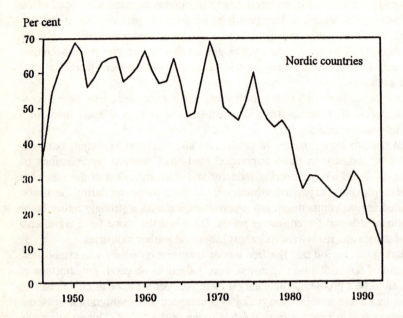

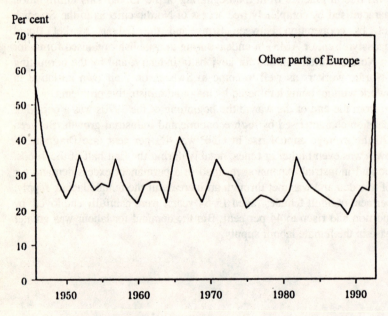

Diagram 2. Proportions of immigrants from different regions 1946-1993.
Sources: See diagram 1.

Per cent

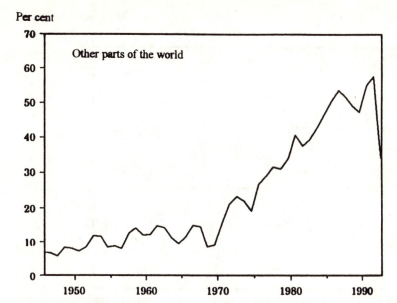

Diagram 2. Continued

The demand for foreign labour to which economic and industrial growth gave rise furnished the background to the great immigration of labour into Sweden up to the beginning of the 1970s. Between 1950 and 1967 a total of 531 000 persons migrated to Sweden. Of these, 24 000 were refugees, which means that more than 95 per cent of immigrants during these years came to Sweden either to work or to accompany an immigrant worker.[4] It may be added that even the refugees who fled to Sweden as a result of the Second World War or of the Hungarian uprising of 1956 established themselves quickly on the labour market and thus became part of the labour force.

By degrees certain negative consequences of this labour immigration became apparent.[5] Free labour immigration caused foreigners to dominate the workforce at certain factories and in minor industrial areas while at the same time the housing shortage was becoming serious. The immigration of new groups from Yugoslavia and Greece in the middle 1960s hampered communication at workplaces because of linguistic confusion and cultural differences. At the same time the trade union movement regarded free labour immigration, which gravitated particularly towards low-paid occupations, as a threat to successful implementation of the "wage solidarity" (i e wage equalisation) policy. The tendency towards a slight growth in unemployment towards the end of the 1960s also contributed to the decision of 1968 to establish barriers against free labour immigration from non-Nordic countries.

---

4 SOU 1982:49.
5 Lundh (1994).

Per cent

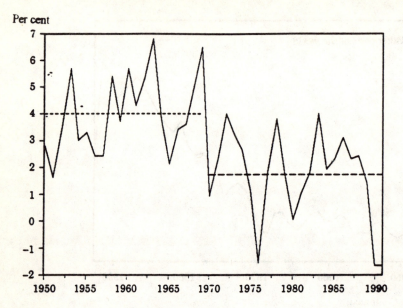

Diagram 3 Annual change in GNP 1947-1992.
Source: SOS Nationalräkenskaperna.

As Diagram 3 shows, the pace of economic growth has been considerably lower since the beginning of the 1970s. During the period 1970-1990, GNP increased by no more than 1.5 per cent per year, which was not even half the previous growth rate. Industrial growth too subsided to a considerably lower level than before.

The decreased demand for foreign labour meant that the control of non-Nordic immigration which was introduced in 1968 in practice brought non-Nordic labour immigration to a complete halt. Nordic immigration, especially of Finnish workers, gradually declined as well, partly because of a narrowing of differences in living standards between Finland and Sweden. Immigrant workers have been replaced by other kinds of immigrant instead (refugees of various kinds and associated cases), where the immigrants' primary motives have been other than that of seeking work. Another new feature has been that non-European immigration has come to form a rapidly-growing proportion of total immigration.

In 1991, a total of 50 000 people migrated to Sweden. Of these, fewer than one quarter were from Nordic countries. Of the 36 000 applications for residence permits by non-Nordic citizens approved by the Immigration Board between July 1990 and June 1991, 35 per cent consisted of refugees, 61 per cent of relatives, 3 per cent of adoptive children and 1 per cent of workers. Even though many non-Nordic citizens know that the chances of being granted entry for labour-market reasons are small and therefore cite family relationships in their applications for residence permits, the difference compared with the period prior to 1970 is obvious. If all the reasons cited in applications for residence permits are correct, no more than one immigrant in four came to Sweden in the late 1980s in order to work but for other reasons.

Business cycles

Numerous studies have shown that there has been a strong correlation between immigration into Sweden and business cycles in the various immigrant groups' home-lands and Sweden. This was particularly the case during the period up to the middle 1970s and with regard to typical labour immigration, e g from Finland. For the period 1946-1970 we can find a relatively strong link, for example, between trade cycle movements and the annual changes in external immigration, so that immigration was high in times of boom and vice versa (see Diagram 4). Detailed scrutiny shows that there was often a delay of a year between the peak (and trough) of the boom and the immigration maximum (and minimum). The delay between economic peak and immigration peak is explained by the fact that it takes time for information to spread.[6]

During the period after 1970, however, it would seem that labour market condi-tions played a minor role in immigration into Sweden. This is the result not only of the replacement of labour immigration by refugee immigration but also of other fac-tors. In spite of the fact that in the mid-1970s, unemployment in Finland was increas-ing while simultaneously it was constant in Sweden, immigration from Finland was in decline at that time. On the other hand, it has been discovered that there was a clear economic co-variance between Swedish cyclical fluctuations and the immigra-tion of Chileans who were formally granted residence permits on refugee or family grounds.[7] The probable explanation is that many of the family-associated cases arriv-ing from Chile during the 1980s considered the economic factors before deciding to migrate.

It seems as though Swedish labour market conditions have greater general effects on emigration from Sweden than on immigration into Sweden. The statistics show that a large proportion of immigrants re-emigrate after some years in Sweden, and it is evident that hard times in Sweden do hasten return migration. Statistics of the number of foreigners registered for work in Sweden for the period up to the middle of the 1970s exhibit a strong co-variance with the Swedish industrial cycle. The trend of net immigration also displays this link, more for the period prior to the mid-1970s. In both cases, it is return migration more than immigration which gives this immediate correlation.[8] One explanation of this is that return migration takes place in immediate conjunction with a worsening of economic conditions, e g through dismissals, while immigration into Sweden is delayed because of impediments to information.

---

6 Wadensjö (1973), Ohlsson (1975) and (1978).
7 Gustafsson, Zamanian-B and Aguilar (1990).
8 Geschwind (1958), Widstrand (1962).

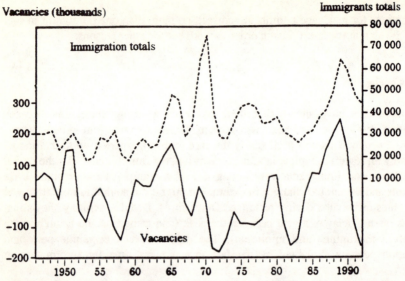

Diagram 4 Immigration to Sweden and vacancies in trade and industry (deviation from the trend).
Source: SOS Befolkningsrörelsen; SOS Befolkningsförändringar; Statistiska meddelande.

Structural transformation

The period up to the middle of the 1970s can be described as one of industrial expansion. As mentioned above, the industrial growth rate was high until the middle 1970s. The highest annual growth took place during the "record years" of the early 1960s. Between 1950 and 1965, industrial production measured at fixed prices doubled, and the numbers in industrial employment were rising until the middle of the 1960s, when about 1.6 million persons were working for industrial firms.

The background to this was among other things that blockade and protectionism during the 1930s and 1940s had caused home market-orientated branches such as the textile, clothing and foodstuffs industries to account for a large proportion, approximately one third, of total industrial production by the war's end. This was almost as much as the export-orientated branches such as engineering, pulp and paper industries produced all told. The bulk of exports at the war's end consisted of raw or almost raw materials.

The industrial expansion which took place after the war and was helped along in large measure by the demand generated by reconstruction work in Europe brought in its train large-scale structural changes in Swedish industry. The importance of branches orientated towards the home market diminished while that of the export-orientated sector was simultaneously expanding. The foodstuffs industry declined in relative terms because home market demand was limited, while the textile and clothing industry was soon faced with increasingly fierce international competition which squeezed profit margins and led to reductions in the volume of production and employment.

Instead it was the export branches such as the shipbuilding industry, the car industry, the engineering industry and the steel industry that became the "powerhouse" of industrial expansion during the 1950s and 1960s. The expansion was facilitated by the market integration which was taking place within the framework of GATT, the EEC and EFTA.

This industrial expansion was the background to the import of labour. Industry needed labour and it was considered that Swedish labour would not be sufficient. This was the context in which the import of foreign labour came about. According to the statistics, something like half of all immigrant workers were employed in industry during the 1950s and 1960s. Moreover, the tendency was for the proportion employed in industrial jobs to increase. However, these figures mean that the importance of industry to immigrant labour is underestimated. Firstly, there was a large group of foreign citizens employed on Swedish ships, a fact which was not new in the postwar period, and secondly, there was a special demand for foreign domestic servants during the 1950s. If these somewhat specialised categories of foreign labour employed outside the industrial sector are deducted, the importance of industry for employment emerges as even more vital. Furthermore, it has to be borne in mind that many immigrants who made their way to Sweden on their own initiative worked in the restaurant branch to begin with, going over to industrial jobs after a short time.

Since the middle of the 1960s, the industrial sector's relative significance in the total national economy has diminished. Towards the end of the 1960s, industry (including building construction) accounted for 46 per cent of GNP; by 1990 it had dwindled to 27 per cent. If we look at industry's importance for total employment in the nation the decline is even more striking. (See Diagram 5.) The proportion employed in industry increased up to the beginning of the 1960s, when it was 45 per cent. After that, the corresponding proportion fell and in 1990 amounted to 29 per cent. The impact on the demand for labour stands out even more starkly, perhaps, from the fact that the decline was not only relative but absolute. Thus in the early 1990s, 300 000 fewer people were working in the industrial sector despite the fact that the total labour force had increased by 800 000.

Alongside the fact that the relative decline of industry is an international phenomenon in highly-developed economies, the tendency towards increased international competition was strengthened in Sweden. By the middle 1960s the rebuilding of European industry had been more or less completed. The currency system had been restored, the national and international credit markets had been put in order and great free trade areas had been established, giving rise to increased investment all over Europe. By the middle of the 1960s, therefore, there were new factory installations, modern production equipment and well-adapted marketing organisations.

Per cent

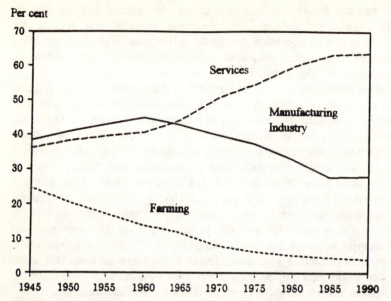

Diagram 5 Proportion employed in the agricultural, industrial and service sectors.
Source: Statistisk årsbok.

At this time Swedish industry, both exporting firms and those aligned towards the home market, was beginning to encounter considerably more severe international competition than before. However, the competition that confronted industry came not only from European countries but also from Japan. During the 1970s and 1980s, competition from newly-industrialised countries in the Third World, the so-called NIC countries, also affected Swedish industry. This international competition subjected large sectors of Swedish industry, including textiles and clothing, shipyards, the steel industry and parts of the engineering industry, to heavy pressure for change. The crisis which hit Sweden in 1973/74 resulted not only from increased oil prices, excessively high wage costs and ordinary cyclical marketing difficulties: it was a structural crisis as well.

At this time a structural transformation of industry commenced which involved a sharp decline in certain branches such as textiles and clothing while other branches were adapting more easily to the new conditions. For most industries the more intense competition meant that efforts were made to squeeze costs by reducing personnel and increasing efficiency. The structural problems also hastened the trend towards more highly-refined products. By the early 1980s, raw and near-raw materials formed less than one third of total export values, while the engineering industries alone accounted for 40 per cent. The branches which, during the entire postwar period, had increased the most are precisely those with highly-refined products, for example the car industry, the electrotechnical industry and the chemical industry. The structural transformation since the middle of the 1970s has brought increased investment in knowledge-intensive and high-technology production.

Because it was primarily industry that demanded foreign labour during the period of free labour immigration, the decline of that sector has meant a drastic reduction of the demand for foreign labour. The relatively increased importance of the service-producing sector has not brought any corresponding degree of augmentation of the demand for foreign labour, partly because of the lower growth rate compared with before.

The trend towards increasingly information- and communication-intensive processes, both through the growth of the service sector and in industry, has created a demand on the labour market to which the skills-structure offered by the new immigrant groups corresponds less and less. The transaction costs involved in exploiting the skills of immigrants satisfactorily have increased dramatically, and the adaptation costs have become higher than in the period 1946-1974 both for firms, administrative organs and the state. Culture-specific requirements have given Swedish women an advantage in the competition for many jobs, notably in public service production. Therefore the female employment intensity has continued to rise during the most recent decades, while at the same time immigrants have found it increasingly difficult to establish themselves on the Swedish labour market.

Renewal - efficiency drive - renewal

Economic advance in the postwar period can be described on the basis of different levels of growth rate for different periods or in terms of its business cycles. It can also be viewed as an irreversible structural trend, in which the industrial sector expands until the middle 1960s and diminishes in importance thereafter, while the service sector increases in socioeconomic importance throughout the period. But industrial advance can also be viewed in a cyclical structural perspective, in which phases of renewal and transformation are followed by phases of expansion and efficiency drives. In the Swedish case a full cycle may be said to have covered about 40 years.[9]

According to the cyclical structural perspective, increased investment leads to the diffusion of innovations, the establishment of new products and techniques, and the rise of new firms. During this phase of renewal, production is aligned chiefly towards the home market. Gradually, as the home market's expansive force ebbs away, expansive firms turn to the international market. Industrial expansion continues, activity quickens, but now investment is directed mainly into the same sort of technology, products and plant as have already been developed. In step with the sharpening of international competition, firms are compelled to resort more and more to investment which enhances efficiency and reduces costs. When international competition becomes too intense, a structural crisis supervenes which again enforces renewal and transformation.

In Sweden's postwar economic history the period up to 1958 can be termed a renewal phase, whereas the period 1958-1974 was a phase of expansion and efficiency drives. The crisis which occurred in conjunction with the oil-price rises of the mid-1970s has already been designated as not only a cyclical but a structural crisis. Thereafter the Swedish economy entered upon a new phase of renewal and transfor-

---

9 See Schön (1991) and (1993).

mation.

From the structural and cyclical perspective it may be presumed that different kinds of labour are in demand during the different phases of a structural cycle. During the renewal phase many technicians, specialised workers and skilled workers are required, whereas during the expansive efficiency-drive phase, unskilled but cheaper labour is more in demand. This tallies well with the demand for foreign labour prevailing on the Swedish labour market during the postwar period.

Apart from the refugees who came directly after the war, to a large extent it was skilled workers who migrated to Sweden during the period 1946-58. This resulted from the fact that there was a shortage of skilled workers in Swedish industry. It was primarily in the expansive branches of industry such as engineering and shipbuilding that the need for skilled workers was great, while the proportion of unskilled workers was higher in the stagnant branches such as the textiles and clothing, shoes and rubber industries.

It was chiefly well-educated skilled workers capable of going directly on to the production line who were recruited. The majority of these skilled workers came from West Germany as it then was, Italy, Austria, Finland and Denmark, where the scope for recruitment was enlarged by the readjustment problems facing those countries after the war. The immigration of this period can be characterised to a certain extent as an immigration of specialists in which, in addition to skilled workers, there were a relatively large number of technicians, engineers and civil engineers. Most of these specialists found jobs in either the engineering or the building industry. But the hotel and restaurant trade also recruited skilled cooks, head waiters and waiters from abroad during this period.

During the 1940s and 1950s, immigrants constituted a mainly *complementary* labour force. An increased demand for labour in a particular branch of industry meant that firms took on *both* more Swedish workers *and* more immigrants. The demand orientated towards foreign sources pertained to particular categories with specialised qualifications and usually constituted a demand which was impossible to satisfy on the home labour market. But the demand, whether for Swedish or foreign labour, was of the same character.[10]

Immigration played a very large role in the great industrial expansion and efficiency drive after 1958. During the first half of the 1960s labour immigration accelerated, but it also partially changed its character compared with what had gone before. The elements of unskilled labour now increased; many came from rural areas and lacked previous experience of industrial work. South and southeastern Europeans (as well as Nordics) were in a clear majority in this immigration flow. In contrast to the previous situation, in which they had formed a complementary labour force, immigrants functioned as a *supplementary* or replacement labour force during the 1960s. It can also be said that it was the branches of industry in which employment of Swedes fell most heavily that the bulk of foreign workers were employed.[11]

The background to the realignment of the demand for labour was chiefly the fact that industry was entering a more expansive phase in which investment was aimed at

10 Ohlsson (1978).
11 Op cit.

winning a share of the international market and squeezing costs down. In this way there was an increase in the demand for unskilled labour, both Swedish and foreign. A contributory factor may also have been that it was becoming increasingly difficult to recruit skilled foreign workers. From the early 1950s onwards, expansive firms, with the help of the Labour Market Board, had organised collective transfers of skilled foreign workers, but towards the end of the decade it became more and more difficult to recruit this type of labour. At the same time there was a continuous influx into Sweden of unskilled foreigners seeking work, and many firms found it easier to employ these than to get into the tedious "importing business" involving not only the Swedish Labour Market Board but also the labour-market authorities in the countries of emigration. In the early 1960s the Labour Market Board made renewed efforts to bring in skilled workers by organised routes, but these produced little practical result, and the great majority of Yugoslavs, Greeks and Finns who arrived during the 1960s were not skilled workers.

At this point we may cite parts of the engineering industry as examples to illustrate that the processes of change which were in train in industry were increasing the demand for unskilled foreign labour. As has already been remarked, the engineering industry had employed mainly highly-skilled workers from Northwestern Europe and Italy during the 1940s and 1950s. Gradually, as the economic difficulties of those countries were overcome, the scope for Swedish recruiting diminished. From the late 1950s onwards the shortage of skilled labour increased, while at the same time the traditional areas were considered to provide an insufficient basis for an intensified recruiting drive. Workers from other countries therefore began to be recruited. Yugoslavia, Greece and Turkey in particular were added to Finland as new catchment areas. At first recruitment was confined to fully-trained workers capable of going straight into production, but gradually the recruiting policy changed. To an increasing extent the immigrants employed lacked training and industrial experience. After recruitment they were put through crash courses of a few weeks to train them as welders or sheet-metal workers for example.

These variations of training and recruitment policy were intimately bound up with the technological and organisational changes which the engineering industry was undergoing. The changes meant that it was becoming possible to a greater extent than before to replace skilled labour with unskilled, which lowered the trade-skills requirement on recruitment. The new technology was also making it possible to make more efficient use than before of the firm's skilled workers.

Similar developments in technology and labour organisation were taking place in most industrial branches during this period, with intensified division of labour, specialisation, automation, rationalisation and large-scale production as the main characteristics. The changes in technology and labour organisation were also becoming diffused to the service and the public sector. All these changes meant that it was becoming increasingly possible to use unskilled labour, and therefore immigrants, in the production process.

Since the middle of the 1970s it has become more and more difficult for immigrants to establish themselves on the labour market. The renewal undergone by the economy may be one explanation of this. The elements of R & D-intensive activity have been augmented, and administrative decentralisation and team working have been introduced. It is mainly the newly-arrived immigrants to Sweden who have had difficulty in finding a place on the labour market, but many of the earlier arrivals already established on the labour market have also had problems in keeping themselves there. One explanation of this is the very fact of the sudden switch of demand for labour brought about by the economy's having moved into another renewal phase. What is in greater demand now is labour possessing specialised knowledge in the new fields which can be considered the forcing ground of a new economic expansion. The factor common to many of these is that the work involved contains large elements of culture-specific knowledge in which language, communication and familiarity with the way Swedish society functions play a large role.[12]

For the skilled workers who were taken on during the 1950s or those less skilled who came to Sweden in the 1960s, cultural and language differences did not constitute a barrier in the same way. For those originating from Denmark and Norway such differences are scarcely worth mentioning, while for Finns and West Europeans it was mainly language that was the problem. National culture, workplace culture and trade union traditions did not differ very much from those to which they were accustomed. In the case of skilled workers and specialists, the sort of technical training which they had had in their home countries could be transferred to Swedish conditions relatively easily. The problems were greater for the Yugoslavs, Greeks and Turks who came during the 1960s. For them both language and culture were obstacles to adaptation, and this caused difficulties at the workplace and generated trade union opposition to the free labour immigration policy. But the simple tasks to which these unskilled foreign workers were assigned in industry were nonetheless easy to learn, despite the fact that the cultural and linguistic gap was great.

There are many indications that the renewal undergone by the economy since the middle of the 1970s has made it more difficult for the new immigrant groups to establish themselves on the labour market. On this point, however, the fact cannot be ignored that these groups made their way to Sweden for reasons other than to work, and that therefore, for obvious reasons, their selection did not take place in response to the demand signals which the Swedish labour market was sending out. Even so the fact remains that the new immigrant groups have had very great difficulty in getting on to the labour market. Recruitment intensity has been very much lower, unemployment higher and dependence on social security greater than for Swedes. Even very well-educated immigrants find it difficult to establish themselves on the Swedish labour market. A study made among its members by SIPA (the Swedish International Professional Association) showed that only 20 per cent were in employment appropriate to their education in their home countries. A study made by the National Swedish Audit Bureau (*Riksrevisionsverket*) points in the same direction. Five years after residential registration with local authorities only one half had any sort of regular employment at all, 40 per cent were undergoing some form of training and 10 per cent were sick or unemployed. The immigrants who have succeeded in establishing themselves quickly in their occupations have often been those with internationally

---

12 This is the main hypothesis in the research project "The immigrants in the post-industrial society" in which we are taking part together with Tommy Bengtsson, Mauricio Rojas, Piet Bevelander and Kirk Scott, all at the Department of Economic History in Lund, Sweden.

transferable training, e g doctors.[13]

The problems of new immigrants in establishing themselves on the labour market do not arise solely as a result of language and communication difficulties in the purely technical sense, although language skills are certainly a basic condition. Much of the knowledge required at work in Sweden today is difficult to formalise and has very subtle dimensions. The "new growth theory", as it is called, has begun to pay attention to this type of experience-based expertise ("tacit knowledge"), which is acquired through personal participation in work processes, work teams or firms, and which people learn from one another within the firm. This means that formal general school knowledge plays less of a role in how people establish themselves on the labour market, while other personal qualities and attainments are of greater importance.[14] This is confirmed by the responses received by the Labour Market Board to its questions in a survey of the factors to which employers attached importance when employing people. Only 11 per cent of the respondent employers considered a good school record to be of any significance, while 55 per cent felt that vocational training was important. More than two thirds of the responses, however, considered other factors to be of greater significance, such as an applicant's creating a good impression at the job interview, fitting into the work environment, possession of job experience and good references.[15]

Structural and cyclical pull factors

If we are looking for a couple of factors capable of explaining postwar immigration into Sweden in a general way, these would probably be the high Swedish standard of living and the liberal immigration policy. As Diagram 6 shows, over the postwar period as a whole an average of more than two thirds of total immigration came from countries with a considerably lower standard of living than Sweden's. The imports of labour in the 1950s and 1960s came from countries which had been hard hit by the war such as Germany, Austria and Italy, and from countries with considerably lower levels of industrialisation such as Finland, Yugoslavia and Greece. As economic development has proceeded in many of these countries and their living standards have been raised, emigration from them to Sweden has dwindled. This happened with immigration from Germany and Austria during the 1960s and from Finland from the late 1970s onwards. With countries of about the same level of living standards as in Sweden, the exchange of migrants has been fairly even, i e about as many have migrated to them as from them.

The fundamental background to the great labour immigration up to the early 1970s was industrial expansion. High economic and industrial growth and a growing industrial sector resulted in a demand for foreign labour. The variations in demand which arose because of economic fluctuations had repercussions on the foreign labour force. Return migration increased during periods of recession, and after a certain

---

13 Riksrevisonsverket (1992).
14 See Romer (1986) and Lucas (1988).
15 Arbetsmarknadsstyrelsen (1992).

delay immigration declined.

Efforts were made from the Swedish side to overcome the barriers to migration existing during this period, because there was a positive attitude to the import of foreign labour. Swedish immigration policy was liberalised and labour immigration became free in practice. Swedish labour market authorities made contact with their counterpart authorities in foreign countries with a view to coordinating the migration of labour. Recruitment offices were established abroad in order to bridge the information gaps, and workers who were transferred to Sweden on the initiative of Swedish firms and authorities were spared having to pay the costs of the move themselves. Efforts were made to overcome the social obstacles as well by giving assistance in obtaining housing in Sweden and by facilitating the transfer of workers' families either at the same time or later.

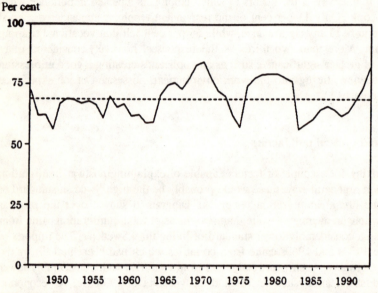

Per cent

Diagram 6 Proportion of total immigration to Sweden from countries where GNP per head was less than 80 per cent of Sweden's.
Source: SOS Befolkningsrörelsen, SOS befolkningsförändringar, Korpi, W, Halkar Sverige efter?

As far as concerns the second phase of the history of Sweden's postwar immigration, from the middle of the 1970s onwards, it is difficult to find obvious domestic economic causes for continued high immigration other than the high Swedish standard of living. The industrial sector has been declining in significance since the middle 1960s, and since the mid-1970s the rate of economic and industrial growth has been considerably lower than before. This has made the demand for foreign labour much smaller than before. Moreover, the growth of the service sector and the renewal and change undergone by the Swedish economy have produced a situation where what is demanded is a kind of culture-specific proficiency which foreign labour lacks for the very reason that it is foreign. Therefore the position of immigrants on the labour market has weakened drastically since the middle of the 1970s.

It is therefore clear that it has not been because there was a demand for foreign labour that immigration has continued at the same high level, and has even increased, during the most recent decades. However, it is easy to identify causes of this immigration in situations in other countries, for example where war and oppression have given rise to an overall increase in the migration of refugees. Because the migration flows have not been evenly distributed between countries having about the same standard of living as Sweden, it is clear that the barriers to such migration have been lower here.

After some years' delay, the reversal of immigration policy in 1968 brought non-Nordic labour immigration to an effective halt, as was the intention. On the other hand the exceptions to the rules allowed in the legislation, and especially in practice, made continued high immigration possible. At two points in particular, Sweden's approach is more liberal than that of most other countries. Firstly, the definition of a refugee has been stretched in Swedish practice so that it has also come to cover war refugees, *de facto* refugees and persons citing so-called humanitarian grounds. In this way regular refugees as defined by the Hague Convention have come to constitute only a small proportion of those granted residence permits on quasi-refugee grounds. Secondly, the rules on immigration of relatives are very generous in Sweden. The bulk of non-Nordic immigration into the country today consists of the immigration of relatives. On the other hand, Swedish law and practice do not differ greatly from other countries' rules with respect to "Convention refugees". But it is possible that what has motivated many refugees to choose Sweden when seeking asylum has been the high Swedish level of aspiration with regard to settlement in the host society along with social security and the favourable prospects of relatives' being able to follow the original migrant. Sweden accepts more refugees than any country in the world in proportion to its population.

The economic effects of immigration

The main economic argument for free immigration during the 1950s and 1960s was that immigration would relieve the shortage of labour in expansive branches of the economy and during boom periods. It would thereby have a stabilising effect on the trade cycle, counteract excessive wage claims and contribute to economic growth generally. In that spirit, Sweden supported the OEEC's labour statute in 1953, undertaking to facilitate European labour migration, and the 1954 agreement on a common Nordic labour market.

No exact estimates of what labour immigration has really signified in terms of industrial growth have been made, and such calculations by and large are impossible. However, it is a commonly-held opinion that the imports of foreign labour, especially during the renewal phase up to the late 1950s, prevented production bottlenecks from occurring as a result of labour shortages. This is especially the case with respect to the foreign technicians and skilled workers who came to occupy important key positions in the expansive firms when new methods, machinery and products were being introduced during the industrial transformation. In this way immigration contributed not only to the increase of production but also to higher productivity.[16]

During the 1960s, when the industrial expansion phase began, the function of immigration was somewhat different. The shortage of labour was now more general, and even though unskilled workers were mutually interchangeable, the expansion could not have been accomplished without imported labour. The advantages of large scale which were exploited during this phase in order to raise productivity were based among other things on the supply of labour.[17]

One argument put forward against imported labour during the 1960s, in the trade union movement and the Social Democratic party for example, was that the supply of cheap foreign labour was inimical to structural economic change.[18] Instead of committing investment to technological measures which would increase productivity (and therefore wages), stagnating firms and branches opted to take on foreign workers. If the supply of foreign labour had not existed, low-productivity firms and branches would have gone to the wall, their workforces being transferred to the expansive sectors of the economy.

It is conceivable that the increased supply of cheap labour, especially during the 1940s, delayed a necessary structural rationalisation, in the textile and clothing industries. In this way the textiles crisis of the 1950s became more serious than it otherwise need have been. However, it does seem as though the effects of external migration on structural changes in industry were relatively marginal during the 1950s, since immigration during that period was relatively low. During the 1960s, finally, immigrants were taken on in branches which the Swedish labour force was tending to leave. This can be interpreted to mean that the structural transformation was delayed because of immigration. Another perspective on this is that immigration made it easier for Swedes to switch over to work in the expanding service sector and that in this way it helped structural change along.

There are no Swedish studies of how immigration influenced wages and the work environment, but foreign studies suggest that such influence was small. However, two studies have been made of the distribution effects exercised by immigration via the public sector. Both studies focused on groups of labour immigrants. The study of 1969 showed that the immigrants paid a couple of thousand *kronor* (in the money values of 1969) more in taxes than they received in the form of transfer payments and public services.[19] The second study, made in 1976, indicated the same thing, although the amount was smaller. In both instances this is explained by the fact that the immigrants had a younger age-pyramid and higher employment intensity than the Swedish average.[20]

Discussions of the socioeconomic effects of immigrants during recent decades have tended to revolve mostly around the costs occasioned by immigration. In particular, the costs of "home-language instruction" and refugee reception have stood at the centre of debate. Figures for these costs have varied widely as a result of different periods having been utilised as the basis of calculation and the inclusion of

---

16 See Ohlsson (1978).
17 Op. cit.
18 See Lundh (1994).
19 Wadensjö (1973).
20 Ekberg (1983).

various kinds of overhead costs. A common feature of this debate is that these costs have not been viewed in relation to the incomes which the immigrant may be expected to generate later in life - the refugee when he has found a job, or the second generation immigrant who has a job which allows use to be made of bi-cultural and bi-linguistic skills. This may possibly result from the fact that the prospects for immigrants on the labour market today are so depressing and predictions so difficult to make. Without doubt, a study along the lines cited above of the claims made by immigrants on transfer payments and public services compared with their tax contributions would show very disheartening results, especially in respect of the recently-arrived immigrant groups.

As this chapter has shown, we know extremely little today about the economic effects of immigration. There is surer ground for expressing an opinion on short-term costs and revenues in limited fields than on long-term effects. Certain studies do exist, after all, and it is probably safe to assume that firms which have employed immigrants have made a correct judgment in the context of the conditions set by their own activities in the short-term perspective.

But in our opinion it is well nigh impossible to give an empirically-based answer to the question whether immigration is economically profitable in a longer-term perspective. We know that even in the future, labour will be needed in order to ensure economic growth. But we can no more determine what economic effects today's immigration will have than we can determine whether it is economically profitable in a dynamic long-term perspective for children to be born.

Future scenarios

What, then, can we say about immigration into Sweden in future? Very little, one reason being that it is the Swedish people and their political representatives themselves who will decide the matter. We can, however, express ourselves with greater assurance regarding the prerequisites of such a decision. Two things do seem virtually certain.

Firstly, it is improbable that the Swedish economy will experience such a shortage of labour as prevailed from the end of the war until the middle of the 1970s. Not even when the present recession ends and the Swedish economy enters upon a new expansionary phase is it likely that the demand for labour will become so strong that foreign labour has to be imported. Moreover, it is probable that the demands for culture-specific skills which make it difficult at present for immigrant groups to establish themselves on the labour market will continue to exist and perhaps even intensify in future.

Secondly, it is probable that international migration flows will continue with unabated vigour. War, dictatorship, ethnic conflicts, poverty and hunger in the Third World and in Eastern Europe will continue to form a basis for refugee migration and generate a permanent migration pressure towards Western Europe. On the other hand, if Sweden joins the European Union it is unlikely to be particularly heavily affected by labour migration within the Union, because the social obstacles to migration have shown themselves to be too strong.

Sweden's present policy with regard to immigration and immigrants was shaped between the mid-1960s and mid-1970s. In 1968 the government decided to control non-Nordic immigration, and after this a policy was developed for the adaptation and integration of foreign minorities into Swedish society. A strong contributory factor in the new policy was that immigration of new, culturally and linguistically divergent groups had increased enormously since the beginning of the 1960s - Yugoslavs, Greeks, Turks. The object of the decision of 1968 was to limit non-Nordic immigration, and success in this was achieved. The exceptions to this halt on immigration which were inserted into the regulations to cover contingencies such as refugees and their families were conceived merely as exceptions to be applied on a limited scale, approximately as before. But by degrees practices changed, so that during the 1980s a very large proportion of immigration into Sweden was taking place by reference to these exceptions. Just as in the early 1960s, but now on a very much larger scale, the massive immigration from countries with different cultural, religious and linguistic backgrounds - this time from the Middle East - has caused Swedish policy towards immigration and immigrants to be called into question.

REFERENCES

Arbetsmarknadsstyrelsen (1992) Kompetensbehov, kvalifikationskrav och rekrytering till lediga platser. Rapport från Utredningsenheten 1992:4.

Ekberg J (1983) Inkomsteffekter av invandring. Växjö.

Geschwind H (1958) Invandrares vistelsetid i Sverige. Statistisk tidskrift, nr 3.

Gustafsson, Zamanian-B, Aguilar (1990) Invandring och försörjning. Uddevalla.

Lee E S (1969) A theory of migration, in Jackson, J A (ed.) Migration. Cambridge.

Lucas R (1988) On the mechanism of economic growth. Journal of Monetary Economics, Vol. 22.

Lundh C (1994) Invandrarna i den svenska modellen - hot eller reserv? Fackligt program på 1960-talet, in Arbetarhistoria. Vol. 18, No. 70.

Lundh C, Ohlsson R (1994) Från arbetskraftsimport till flyktinginvandring. Kristianstad.

Castles S, Miller M J (1993) The Age of Migration. International Population Movements in the Modern World. London.

Ohlsson R (1975) Invandrarna på arbetsmarknaden. Lund.

Ohlsson R (1978) Ekonomisk strukturförändring och invandring. Kristianstad.

Riksrevisionsverket (1992) Utländsk kompetens - ett resurstillskott på arbetsmarknaden. Förvaltningsrevisionen granskar. F 1992:11. Stockholm.

Romer P M (1986) Increasing returns and long-run growth. Journal of Political Economy, Vol. 94.

Schön L (1991) Development blocks and transformation pressure in a macro-economic perspective - a model of long-term cyclical change. Skandinaviska Enskilda Banken Quaterly Review, No. 3-4.

Schön L (1993) 40-årskriser, 20-årskriser och dagens ekonomiska politik. Ekonomisk Debatt, No. 1.

SOU 1982:49. Invandringspolitiken. Bakgrund.

SOU 1993:113 Invandring och asyl i teori och praktik. En jämförelse mellan tolv ländrs politik.

Wadensjö E (1973) Immigration och samhällsekonomi. Lund.

Widstam T (1962) Invandringen till Sverige och återutvandringen under 1950-talet. Statistisk tidskrift, nr 5.

Chapter 6

The Pension System
Agneta Kruse

Public expenditure on consumption and transfers to households has increased dramatically in Sweden; from 33 per cent of GDP in 1970 to 52 per cent in 1992. The national pension system more than doubled in relation to GDP during the period, from 5 per cent to 12, thus being one of the most important factors underlying this expansion. Pensioners' standards have been significantly improved, and pensioners collectively are today one of the groups with the lowest proportion of poor. The national pension system is the most important means of support for pensioners. This chapter gives a description of this system, its history and its design.

As well as distributing incomes over an individual's life-cycle, the pension system also distributes available consumption between the current working generation and pensioners. This distribution is determined by the pension system's rules and by economic and demographic developments. A condition of a stable pension system, i e one in which the implicit social contract between generations embodied in the pension system will not be broken, is that this distribution should be regarded as fair. A second condition is that the rules are formulated so as not to jeopardise the functioning of the economy, for example through distortions of saving and labour supply. In the second part of this chapter it is shown that the Swedish pension system is untenable in the long run and that this is the consequence partly of expected demographic developments, with an aging population, but also of its design. Alternative designs for establishing a long-term stable system are discussed.

Means of support in old age and the rise of the pension system

By far the major part of support in old age is provided by the national pension system, which consists of the national basic pension (*allmänna folkpension*) giving the same amount to everybody, and a supplementary pension based on previous income. These publicly-provided pensions constitute about 70 per cent of pensioners' incomes. The rest consists of contractual pensions, i. e. pensions negotiated between the parties on the labour market, private pension insurances and incomes from private savings.

The first component, or its predecessor, national pension insurance, was introduced in 1913.[1] Sweden was thus the first country in the world to introduce national pension insurance, i e an insurance which included all men and women irrespective

---

1 Elmér (1960) p. 16, Edebalk (1991).

of occupation or income.[2] Hitherto the the most important alternative means of support had been the family, which firstly consisted of several generations and secondly, from a dependency perspective, also included servants in accordance with the Servants Act (*legohjonsstadgan*). Anyone not supported within the family had to rely on his own savings and/or poor relief. Certain occupations did have their benefit societies, but these were of extremely marginal significance. The only occupational group which enjoyed any degree of support out of pension prior to the national basic pension was the civil service.

Poor relief was a matter for local authorities and became increasingly onerous, partly as a result of a shrinking agrarian sector and a growing industrial sector - with increasing difficulties for old people trying to carry on working. One important reason for the introduction of the national basic pension was to relieve the pressure on local authorities and to transfer responsibility to the central government. Prior to 1913 there was no definite retirement age: work was phased out gradually as capability dwindled. With the introduction of national pension insurance a legal retirement age of 67 came into force and was the same for both men and women.

National pension insurance consisted at its inception of two components, a contributory pension and a means-tested element. Contributory pensions were financed by means of fixed contributions which were the same for everybody and a supplementary contribution which depended on income. The benefits deriving from this component of the pension insurance were strictly linked to the contributions paid, and it would be impossible to receive a full pension before 1965. The part of the retirement pension which became of any significance worth mentioning was thus the means-tested component. The original system in this way combined a premium reserve system and a pay-as-you-go (PAYG) system. Table 1 shows that for a long time after its introduction the national pension insurance scheme provided very meagre support. The family can therefore be said to have been of continued importance as a support institution even after the introduction of the national basic pension, and it was not until 1956 that the law imposing on children the duty of supporting their parents was repealed.

The national basic pension has been reformed a number of times since its inception and in 1946 (with effect from 1948) it assumed the shape it still has today. The link between contributions and benefits was cut, while benefit levels were raised substantially and made uniform except for the introduction of a housing supplementary allowance, which was differentiated in five housing-cost categories. From that year on, the pension system's degree of coverage in Sweden was 100 per cent. This differs markedly from the situation in other countries. Thus, for example, the degree of coverage at the end of the 1940s was less than 70 per cent in Britain, just under 60 per cent in Germany, about 50 per cent in Denmark and about 40 per

---

2 Several other countries had already introduced pension insurance schemes, including Germany (1889), Denmark (1891), Austria (1906) and the UK (1908). However, these were either means-tested or based on previous work. Sweden was first with national insurance for the entire population.

cent in Austria, rising to between 80 and 100 per cent in these countries only during the 1980s.[3]

Table 1. National pension insurance and national basic pension as a percentage of an average industrial worker's wage.

	Contributory pension	Means-tested pension	National basic pension
1914		11.3	
1921	0.003	8.8	
1926	0.006	16.4	
1936	0.009	16.2	
1948	16.6		35
1956	16.4		35

Source: Elmér (1960) page 195, 256

Nevertheless the standard enjoyed by Swedish pensioners was still low compared with that of the working generation (see Table 1), and there was intensive debate during the 1950s over the need for supplementary pensions. These existed for salaried staffs via agreements negotiated between the parties on the labour market, but the groups represented by the Swedish Confederation of Trade Unions (*Landsorganisationen*) did not have such agreements. The introduction and shaping of the national basic pension in 1946 had not occasioned any major political conflicts. The Conservative and Farmers' parties pursued the question: the Social Democrats recommended means-tested pensions but the decision was finally taken in relative unity. This is in sharp contrast to the political drama which preceded the introduction of the national supplementary pension scheme (*allmänna tilläggspensionen)*, referred to hereafter by its Swedish initials, ATP.[4] The dispute revolved around strengthened basic security unrelated to previous income *versus* a compensation principle based on (loss of) previous income, a funded system *versus* a PAYG system, and compulsion *versus* the voluntary principle. The supplementary pension is one of the few issues on which Sweden has had a referendum. The referendum was followed by new elections to the Riksdag, elections which produced an exactly equal division of seats between non-socialists and Social Democrats + Communists. The 1958 Riksdag adopted the ATP system by a one-vote majority through the abstention of one non-socialist member.

The ATP scheme came into force in 1960. It is compulsory and based on the PAYG principle, which also applies to the basic pension. A PAYG system functions by using today's contributions received to fund the benefits disbursed to today's pensioners, without there existing any intermediate fund.[5] Moreover, ATP is based on

---

3 See Palme (1990) p. 47.
4 See Edebalk (1991) p. 14 ff.
5 Initially, higher contributions were levied than were disbursed on pension payments and the

the loss of income principle inasmuch as it makes good 60 per cent of the average during the fifteen years of maximum income. The loss of income principle is not fully applied because the pensionable income is limited by a floor and a ceiling. Thirty years of pensionable income suffice for a full pension; years in excess of thirty do not affect benefits, while the pension is reduced by 1/30 for each year below 30. Both pensionable incomes and pension awards are indexed ("inflation-proofed") by being linked to a so-called "base amount" which is determined by the consumer price index. Table 2 give some data on the scope of the Swedish pension system and its most important characteristics.

Both the national basic pension and ATP consist not only of old-age pension but also of disability pension and a survivor's benefit. There was formerly a widow's pension. This was abolished in 1990, but with a long period of transitional rules, and has been replaced by a one-year "adjustment allowance". Perhaps this can be regarded as an adaptation to the fact that Sweden has a high female participation rate and that households which consist of two adults are dual-breadwinner households. Moreover, there are children's pensions both from the national basic pension and from the ATP for children under 18 years: these are paid to children whose parent dies.

The pension age was lowered from 67 to 65 years in 1976. At the same time the partial-pension system was introduced for occupationally-active people in the 60-64 years age group. In addition it is possible, within the national system, for the individual himself to decide the timing of retirement by taking an early or deferred pension between the ages of 60 and 70 years. The pension is reduced or increased in this event by an actuarially-calculated amount. Disability pensions can of course be paid at all ages up to the legally-fixed retirement age. However, the 55-64 years age group accounts for more than 80 per cent of the newly granted disability pensions each year, which means that such pensions function as an aid to early retirement from work. Even though the legally-fixed retirement age today is 65 years, the disability pension and partial pension are used to such an extent that the pension age is *de facto* about 62 years. An extremely small proportion of people avail themselves of the opportunities of early or deferred withdrawal but make use instead of the considerably more advantageous opportunities for early retirement through disability pension or partial pensions.[6]

Thus Sweden, like most other industrialised countries, opted to organise its national pension system in accordance with the PAYG principle. There are advantages and disadvantages in such a design compared with a funded system, and we shall revert to these in the next section. With funded systems it takes a long time before benefits can be paid out. With a PAYG system benefits can start being paid out immediately. This avoids the problems which had caused the pension insurance scheme of 1913 to fail to survive, being reformed in the 1940s instead: the system would not have reached its fully-functioning stage until 1965 and provided such low benefits during the building-up phase that they were felt to be inadequate.

difference was consolidated. The declared purpose was to offset a feared reduction of savings by means of public savings. Today the funds amount to about 450 thousand million SEK, or about 5 times the amount disbursed in one year.

6 See Kruse and Söderström (1989).

Table 2 Characteristics of the Swedish pension schemes, 1991.

	Basic Pension	Supplementary Pension
Number of pensions paid (1 000s)		
old age	1 562	1 193
disability	367	323
survivors	58	370
adjustment pension	2	2
Total benefits paid (thousand million SEK)		
old age	43.7 (56.3*)	63.9
disability	9.8 (14.4*)	17.1
survivors	1.5 (1.6*)	8.4
adjustment pension	0.1	-
Average old-age pension benefit (SEK)		
	28 000 (36 000*)	54 000
Contribution rate, per cent of the wage sum	7.45**	13.0***
Income bases for calculating benefits	-	Average of 15 best years
Number of years required to qualify for		
any pension	-	3
full pension	-	30
Floor (ceiling) for calculating		
benefits	-	yes (yes)
contributions	no (no)	no (no)

* incl. pension supplement, municipal housing allowance, children and handicap supplement.
** Contribution covered 72 per cent of costs. The remainder was defrayed from the national budget.
*** Contribution covered 95 per cent of costs. The remainder was defrayed from interest accrued on ATP funds.
Source: RFV. Socialförsäkringsstatistik, Fakta 1992.

The ATP system was not introduced as a pure PAYG system with immediate effect but with certain transitional rules, with lower benefits initially than a pure system would have yielded. In spite of this the introduction of ATP was exceedingly advantageous to the initial generation. Thus an average old-age pension rose from about 30 per cent of the wage sum per person of occupationally-active age[7] in the

---

7 The wage sum is computed "net", which in this context means exclusive of pension contributions and inclusive of the benefits from sickness, parental and unemployment insurance.

early 1970s to about 65 per cent in the middle 1980s, a level at which it was then stabilised with minor fluctuations.[8] Now this is not wholly explained by basic pension and ATP - the basic pension alone without any other benefits gives a low standard and there were relatively large numbers of pensioners who had not qualified for ATP; indeed, there still is such a group even though its numbers are diminishing. For those with low ATP or none, an additional pension benefit, called a pension supplement (*pensionstillskott*) was introduced in 1969. This is linked to the base amount and can today amount to a maximum of 54 per cent of a base amount for an old-age pensioner and to 104 per cent for an early retirement pensioner entirely without ATP. According as more people have succeeded in qualifying for ATP and at higher and higher levels of income-replacement, the numbers of people in receipt of pension supplement is falling: in 1980 there were 778 000 old-age pensioners in receipt of additional pension benefit (56 per cent of all old-age pensioners); by 1991 this had fallen to 497 000 (32 per cent).[9] In addition there is a means-tested housing supplementary allowance, which goes to pensioners with low ATP or none.

The substantial improvement in pensioners' standards is also shown by Diagram 1, showing the trend of pensioners' income standard compared with other age groups. In 1975, 35 per cent of old-age pensioners had an income standard below the margin forming the social security norm, so that they had a much higher proportion of poor people than did the 18-64 age group, of whom just over 10 per cent were at a similar low income standard (Annex 19 to LU 90). As Diagram 1 shows, this situation has changed appreciably; in the 1980s 10-12 per cent of old-age pensioners had a low income standard, a figure which fell to about 5 per cent towards the end of the 1980s. One explanation of this improvement of standards is the fact that the ATP system covers more and more people with higher and higher pensions. In this way younger pensioners have a higher standard than older pensioners, a circumstance which will persist until the system reaches the fully-functioning stage. The system's maturation process is shown by Tables 3 and 4; there are considerably more older people than younger people who have only the national basic pension, and the ATP pension is significantly lower for the older pensioners than for the younger ones.

In addition to the public pension system there are contractual pensions, which are pension systems negotiated between the two sides of the labour market. The great contractual areas are private-sector salaried employees (ITP), private-sector workers (STP), and central and local government employees. These four agreements cover almost the entire labour market. They are based on the loss of income principle and all four systems make up 10 per cent of income reductions for incomes up to 7.5 times the base amount. ITP and contractual pensions in the public sector also make up for income reduction above 7.5 times the base amount (= the ceiling in the ATP system), in broad terms about 65 per cent for incomes between 7.5 and 20 times the base amount and 32.5 per cent on incomes between 20 and 30 times the base amount.[10]

---

8 See Kruse (1988) p. 31.
9 RFV. Socialförsäkringsstatistik
10 See Ståhlberg (1993) chap 3 and Edebalk and Wadensjö (1989) for precise expositions.

Per cent

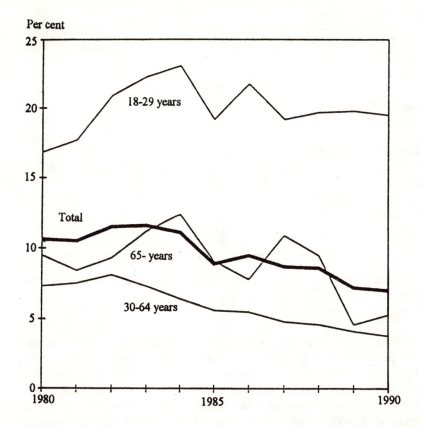

Diagram 1. Proportion of persons with income standard below 1.0.
Note: "Income standard 1.0 is equivalent to an income just on the margin of the social security norm." (cited Annex 19 to LU 92, page 13)
Source: Annex 19 to LU 92, page 21.

Table 3 suggests that contractual pensions may become more important as time goes on by virtue of the fact that more young pensioners than old have contractual pensions, even though contractual pensions form a somewhat higher proportion of the incomes of older pensions than of younger, (see Table 4). But it is still the case that the national system accounts for the vast bulk of pensioners' incomes.

Table 3. Proportion of old-age pensioners with different pension benefits 1990, distributed by age and sex.

	65-69	80-89	All
Basic pension only			
Men	2.2	7.4	4.2
Women	15.3	27.9	22.8
Basic pension + ATP only			
Men	23.1	44.0	29.2
Women	26.5	41.5	33.0
Basic pension + ATP + ITP/STP*			
Men	51.1	29.5	45.1
Women	23.2	9.3	17.0
Basic pension + ATP + govt or local govt contractual pension			
Men	23.6	19.1	21.4
Women	34.9	21.3	27.2

Note: ITP = contractual pensions for private-sector salaried employees, STP = ditto for private-sector workers
Source: Ståhlberg (1993), p 40.

Thus, the national pension system has led to material improvements in the standards of pensioners as a group, both in absolute figures and relatively to the working generation. Within the group, however, there is a broad spread, with the younger pensioners having higher incomes than the older and men higher than women. For example, older men have only about 67 per cent of the incomes of younger men, while older women have about 85 per cent of younger women's incomes. This is a phenomenon which will disappear in part with the maturation of the ATP system, when increasing numbers will have qualified for ATP. However, with economic growth the younger pensioners will always have higher pensions that the older, since the benefits are calculated on previous income. Furthermore, women always have lower pensions than men, e g younger female pensioners have about 67 per cent of the incomes of younger males. This results from the fact that pensions are based on the loss of income principle and reflect the differing labour-market behaviour of men and women and the differing conditions prevailing on the labour market. It does not mean that women can be said to be disadvantaged by the system itself - a point to which we shall revert.

Table 4. Pensioners' income structure 1989. 1000s of *kronor*

	Income after tax	ATP	PT*	Widow's pension
Men				
66-69	81.2	68.8	0.4	
80-84	54.4	29.1	1.6	
Women				
66-69	54.2	25.4	3.5	5.2
80-84	46.1	5.9	6.6	4.6

Proportion of aggregate income					
	Basic pension	ATP	Income from capital	Income from employment	Contractual pension
Men					
66-69	18.7	53.0	6.2	6.8	14.9
80-84	30.3	37.3	10.9	1.3	16.5
Women					
66-69	31.2	33.2	9.5	3.7	10.4
80-84	44.8	10.3	12.6	-	11.2

* PT is the pension supplement to those with low ATP or none.
Source: RFV (1992)

Today's pension system. Problems and possible solutions

There are a number of problems inherent in the present design which make the pension system untenable in the long run. This section deals with some of the causes of this and discusses solutions to the problems.

In the first place, the system is extremely growth-sensitive; at an annual growth rate of 2 per cent, contributions would only need to be raised marginally during the next 25-year period, whereas they would need to be raised by over 50 per cent at 1 per cent growth and to be doubled at zero economic growth (see Table 5).[11] The economics of the system are therefore completely unpredictable. There is in addition the fact that the distribution between the working generation and pensioners is determined by the rate of growth and not by what is regarded as reasonable or fair.

Moreover, the PAYG system is sensitive to demographic changes; the aging population which can be predicted in Sweden will exercise pressure on the pension

---

11 These figures are presented in the main report by the government committee which was working between 1984 and 1990. The committee pointed out a number of problems of the Swedish pension system but abstained from making recommendations for change. The only point on which unity was achieved was the abolition of widows' pensions and their replacement by survivor's benefit. See Kruse and Ståhlberg (1992) for comments.

system. The increased contributions shown in Table 5 are in part a reflection of the aging population. The rates of contribution which are shown in the table are nevertheless calculated for only one demographic alternative. The figures for alternative population scenarios can show us how contributions and benefits will vary within a range of conceivable population changes.

As well as sensitivity to growth and demographic changes, the design of the system has given rise to a number of other problems, primarily caused by the fact that the linkage between benefits and contributions is weak. This in turn gives rise to redistributions of income, both between generations and within a generation, which are not always consistent with traditional distribution policy. Furthermore, it causes an increasing proportion of the contribution to cease being a contribution and become a pure tax, with the distorting effects and excess burden which follow from this.

Growth sensitivity, the index method and the ceiling

In principle, the pension system can be organised as either a funded system or a PAYG system. In both systems, the individual sets aside a certain proportion of his income during the working period of life. In the one case, the setting aside takes place in the form of a premium which is consolidated, in the other case in the form of a payment into a PAYG system where the contribution is utilised to pay the pensions of current pensioners. In the funded system, the pensions are "guaranteed" by the fund and the return earned by it. The yield on the premiums paid in are thus determined by interest rates on the capital market. In the PAYG system, pensions are "guaranteed" through the "promise" by future generations to pay pension benefits, a "promise" which subsists by virtue of the PAYG system's implicit social contract between the generations. The yield of the PAYG system is determined by the economy's rate of growth, which in turn is determined partly by the trend of productivity and partly by the trend of population.

The PAYG system's budget restriction, $q \cdot w \cdot L = p \cdot R$, where q = rate of contribution, w = average wage, L = number of persons in the labour force, p = average pension benefits and R = number of pensioners, gives a simple and intuitive understanding of how a PAYG system functions.[12] The left-hand term gives the sum of payments-in and the right-hand term the sum of pensions paid out. In a pure PAYG system the contribution payments of a given year are used to pay the pension benefits of the same year. The system then shows neither surplus nor deficit. It appears from the budget restriction, for example, that with positive economic growth ($w \cdot L$ rising) it will be possible for pension benefits to be raised. At a fixed contribution rate, the consumption potential of the working generation rises at the same rate as that for pensioners.

Now the Swedish system is not organised as a pure PAYG system. Inflation-proofing is not effected by means of the growth rate. Instead, an unchanged purchasing power in real terms is guaranteed through linkage of the benefits to the base

---

12 See e g Marchand and Pestieau's formulation in a two-period overlapping generation model.

amount. This design means that with high economic growth, the consumption potential available to the working generation increases relatively to that of pensioners, while with low growth the situation of pensioners improves relatively to that of the working generation. Therefore the distribution between the working generation and pensioners is determined by the growth rate. Furthermore, pension payments depend on pensioners' incomes during the 15 highest-income years while occupationally active; in this way the system acquires a "memory" of earlier economic growth. All in all this gives an exceedingly growth-sensitive system, as is revealed by Table 5, which shows the contributions which will require to be levied in order to cover the pension benefits which are promised under today's rules.

Table 5. Expenditures on pension benefits as a percentage of the wage sum at different growth rates of GDP.

Year	Yearly GDP growth rate		
	0%	1%	2%
1995	26.5	24.7	23.3
2015	43.7	32.7	25.1
2025	48.1	33.1	23.3

Source: SOU 1990:76, p. 30.

It is also possible to read off from the table the distribution of consumption possibilities between the working generation and pensioners; the higher the contribution the less the consumption possibilities of the working generation, *ceteris paribus*. Because the benefits are established via the system of rules, the entire adaptation to changed economic and demographic circumstances is expected to be borne by the occupationally-active part of the population. We can say that at 2 per cent annual growth the contribution barely needs to be raised at all. The reason for this is that when there is growth, an increasing number of people will have incomes that exceed the ceiling, which limits benefits but not contributions.[13] The ATP system then ceases to function according to the loss of income principle and becomes a reinforced basic pension - in other words, growth causes the system to change its guise for the majority of pensioners. However, it is in such a situation that contractual pensions become really significant. In all contractual areas except that applying to private-sector workers, the contractual pension replaces income losses above the ceiling. These pensions are financed by means of contributions charged on the pay roll of the occupationally-active.[14] Thus, when growth is high the contributions to the national system are low, as is shown by Table 5, but on the other hand contributions to contractual systems

---

13 In 1992, 15 per cent of men and 2 per cent of women had earned the maximum pension points. With 2 per cent annual growth this will apply to 60 per cent of men and 25 per cent of women by the year 2015, and to 75 per cent of men and 50 per cent of women by 2025. (SOU 1990:76).

14 In the ITP scheme the premiums are consolidated, while contractual pensions in the public sector are organised on the PAYG principle.

become higher at the same time. All in all this can be said to signify that the distribution which will apply if we include contractual pensions is the one between the working generation and pensioners that can be read off indirectly from Table 5 at low or zero growth. With this system, pensioners will enjoy a higher standard than the working generation, a factor which can hardly be said to promote the system's stability.[15]

Defective linkage between benefits and contributions. Effects of distribution between generations, between social groups and between men and women.

In a distributionally neutral system the relation between expected payments-in and expected benefits is the same for all.[16] Such is not the case under the Swedish pension system, which thus gives rise to redistributions between generations, between different social groups and between men and women.

In PAYG systems the initial generation is usually over-compensated, which follows from the fact that the benefits can be paid with immediate effect, without being preceded by long contribution periods; this is a point frequently cited as one of the advantages of such systems. As was noted earlier, Sweden had transitional rules limiting the initial generation's benefits. The ATP system was naturally very profitable for these age groups in spite of this, as can be seen from Table 6, which shows the ratio between benefits and contributions and the net transfers as a proportion of life-incomes for different age groups. A ratio of 1 means that the system always works out evenly for the group, which is another way of saying that the system is distributionally neutral.

For the oldest cohorts, the system means that they received a return of between four and six times the cash contributed and that the life-income is enhanced by a maximum of four per cent. When the ATP system was introduced, persons born in 1944 were 16 years of age, which is the lowest age at which pension rights can start being earned. This cohort, which is thus the first to have entered the fully-functioning system, will pay more into the system than it is expected to receive in benefits, as will all subsequent cohorts, so that the system has the effect of reducing life-incomes. This may be taken as further confirmation that the system is untenable in the long run. A further redistribution between generations arises as a result of the system's growth-sensitivity, which has already been described; the birth cohorts which happen to be pensioners during a period of economic growth lose relatively to the currently working generation, and the converse applies to those who are pensioners during a period of economic stagnation.

---

15 See Kruse (1988).

16 There is a problem here with how narrowly or widely different risk groups are defined, i e within what limits expected results are the same. For example, in Sweden the premiums/contributions or benefits are not differentiated according to sex in spite of the fact that expected lifespan is longer for women than for men. In the 1913 pension insurance scheme women had lower pension benefits, which was justified on the ground of their longer expected lifespan.

Table 6. Benefit/contribution ratio and net transfers as proportion of life-income under ATP. (Calculations made with a discounting factor of 2 per cent)

Cohort	Benefit/contribution ratio	Net transfers as proportion of life-income
1905-14	5.9	0.02
1915-23	3.7	0.04
1924-33	2.0	0.04
1934-43	1.2	0.01
1944-40	0.8	-0.02
1964-70	0.8	-0.02

Source: Ståhlberg (1993), page 68.

A picture of the differences between men and women was given in Table 4, differences in pensions which preserve, through the operation of the loss of income principle, the differences which existed during the working period of life. How time is spent by men and women respectively is reported in Rydenstam.[17] Men and women seems to spend about the same amount of time working, viz about 60 hours per week. However, the distribution between work on market terms and non-market work differs widely. Men work an average of 41 hours per week on the market and 20 hours on domestic tasks, while the corresponding time-distribution for women is 27 and 33 hours respectively per week. Because the ATP system is based on the previous income, this division of labour will result in different levels of pension benefits for men and women.

Men and women differ in many other respects as well as in the time spent working on market terms. For example, we have an extremely sex-segregated labour market. Jonung shows that in 1980, 68 per cent of women would have needed to change their occupation to make their occupational distribution conform to men's.[18] In 1990 this had decreased to 65 per cent; changes do occur after all and they do move in the right direction as well - but at the present rate, according to Jonung's figures, it would take between 100 and 150 years before we arrive at a sex distribution of at least 40-60 in each occupation. Women, to a larger extent than men, are employed in areas with low wages and almost without exception in lower positions. Table 7 shows that today's female pensioners have very low ATP compared with males, at lowest 15 per cent among the older pensioners and at most just under 40 per cent for younger pensioners. This reflects, *inter alia*, an economy with a low female participation rate, a phenomenon which applied to those who are pensioners today but does not apply to tomorrow's female pensioners. The table also reveals that it has proved impossible to fulfil the ambition to introduce a system based on loss of income principles. "We", or "the political system", cannot stand by and watch the unequal income distribution among pensioners which would come about; various types of extra allowances have been introduced for those who have low income-related

17 SCB (1992).
18 Jonung (1993).

pensions or none.[19]

The national pension system evens out many of these differences so that women's pensions (including Kbt and PT) come up to about 95% of men's despite the fact that their ATP is only about one third of men's.[20]

Table 7. Women's pensions as percentages of men's, 1989.

	FP, ATP, Kbt, PT*	Own ATP
66-69	91	37
70-74	87	29
75-79	95	22
80-84	100	20
85-89	95	15
90-	94	20

Note: Kbt = municipal housing allowance, PT = pension supplement.
Source: RFV 1992:6

Thus, women's benefits are frequently lower than men's. In saying this we are not saying that men are favoured more by the system in a general sense. To enable us to say anything about the distribution effects, expected payments-in must be compared with expected payments-out - and on average women pay in less than men. Table 8 shows a comparison between expected payments-in and expected payments-out under the ATP system - at a benefit/cost ratio equal to 1, these are thus equal. It breaks down the result from Table 6 by social group and sex for the two youngest age groups. We can see a clear pattern, even though it is broken in some cases, a pattern which shows that the ATP system redistributes incomes from low income-earners (Social group III) to high income-earners (social group I) and from men to women. The reason is that the 15- and 30-year rules work to the disadvantage of persons with many years on the labour market and with evenly-distributed life-incomes, while favouring persons with few years on the labour market (more than 30 years bring only contributions with no increase in benefits) and with unevenly-distributed incomes. The latter description fits a pattern on the labour market characteristic of highly-educated persons with career occupations, but it is also consistent with the pattern for women on the labour market. It is worth pointing out that this does not apply to women in social group III. Women in this group born between 1944 and 1950 are the

---

19 An alternative interpretation is cast more in terms of public choice: it is easy to win votes by introducing benefits into a PAYG system. The resultant profits go to a well-defined group while the costs are spread over a large group that includes forthcoming generations. See e g Browning (1975) or Verbon (1993) for a public choice analysis of social insurance.
20 Both Kbt and PT are means-tested allowances and are granted only to persons with low ATP or none. PT is reduced *krona* for *krona* against ATP, thus having a 100 per cent marginal effect in low-income brackets.

ones who come out worst of all. This is one of the results which demonstrate the system's "perverse" redistribution effects, i e from low-income earners to high-income earners. The higher life expectancy of women constitutes a further explanation of the fact that on average women are favoured by the system.

Table 8. Benefit-cost ratio under ATP for the generation born 1944-1950 and 1964-1970.

Social group and sex	Benefit-cost ratio	
	1944-1950	1964-1970
Men		
I	0.88	0.71
II	0.80	0.74
III	0.78	0.77
I+II+III	0.80	0.75
Women		
I	0.94	0.83
II	0.82	0.91
III	0.65	0.77
I+II+III	0.77	0.85
Men and women	0.79	0.79

Note: Social group I consists mainly of higher salaried employees and larger businessmen, social group II of lower salaried employees and small businessmen, social group III of workers. On average, income-earners in social group I have the highest life-income and income-earners in social group III the lowest.
Source: Ståhlberg (1993)

Internationally speaking, Sweden today has very high female participation rate. More and more women have been coming on to the labour market from the 1960s onwards. Women born in the middle of the 1940s are the first generation of women who do not leave the labour market during their childbearing years but instead stay at home for a brief period during their children's infancy.[21] Future female pensioners can therefore count on higher pensions than today's female pensioners. But although women on average receive a higher dividend on their contributions (a higher benefit/contribution ratio), even future female pensioners will receive lower pensions than men because they have lower wages. Women still take a greater responsibility for looking after the home and children, with shorter working time on the labour market as a consequence. There is no possibility today of a division of pension rights between spouses, which would dispose of part of these problems.

---

21 Parents' insurance, which covers 90 per cent of income reduction for 12 months, is pension-qualifying income.

An aging population, labour market participation, pension age and old people on the labour market

The fact that the pension system is organised as a pay-as-you-go system means that the sum of the contributions paid in by the occupationally-active over one year is utilised to pay out the pension benefits of the same year. As was remarked above, this can be summed up in a budget restriction which shows clearly the significance of population changes. A rewriting of the budget restriction as $q = p/w \cdot R/L$, where p/w is the replacement ratio and R/L is the pensioner ratio, shows that at the given replacement ratio the contribution must rise with an aging population. If the rate of contribution is fixed, an aging population will lead to reduced benefits if the system is not to run at a deficit.

Sweden has a rapidly-aging population and therefore an increasing dependency burden. The main cause is declining fertility, but increasing lifespan has been a contributory factor.[22] Table 9 shows the age structure since 1960 along with a forecast of continued aging in accordance with Statistics Sweden's (SCB) main alternative for population projections.

Table 9. Age structure of the Swedish population.

	0-15	16-64	65+	Old age dep ratio 65+/(16-64)	Total dep ratio [(0-15)+65-]/ (16-64)
1960	0.24	0.64	0.12	0.18	0.56
1970	0.22	0.64	0.14	0.22	0.56
1980	0.21	0.63	0.16	0.25	0.59
1985	0.19	0.63	0.17	0.28	0.58
1990	0.19	0.63	0.18	0.29	0.59
2000	0.20	0.63	0.17	0.27	0.59
2010	0.19	0.62	0.18	0.29	0.60
2015	0.19	0.61	0.20	0.33	0.64
2020	0.18	0.61	0.21	0.34	0.64
2025	0.19	0.60	0.21	0.35	0.67

Source: SCB. Demografiska rapporter 1989:1.

The proportion of children has fallen markedly, by 5 percentage points, between 1960 and the present, but it is expected to remain relatively constant from now on. The proportion of old people has risen very considerably, by 10 percentage points during the period from 1960 to 1990, a rise which is expected to persist throughout the period of the forecast. At the same time there will be a steady decline in the proportion of population of occupationally-active age.

---

22 See Bengtsson and Ohlsson in this volume.

If we base ourselves on the budget restriction for a pure PAYG system and assume that a replacement ratio of 60 per cent is reasonable or desirable, a contribution rate of 10.8 per cent would have sufficed at the pensioner ratio of 0.18 which applied when the ATP system was introduced in 1960. The pensioner ratio of 1990 requires a contribution of 17.4 per cent and in the year 2015 a contribution of 19.8 per cent. (Note that the discussion of contribution rates here refers only to the old-age pension: early retirement pension and survivor's benefit are additional.) Every increase of the pensioner ratio by 1 percentage point requires a rise in the contribution rate of 0.7 percentage points.

The pensioner ratio shown in Table 9 is calculated as the ratio between the number of persons aged 65 and older and the number of persons aged 16-64, a ratio which is determined by fertility, mortality and migration. The number of persons of occupationally-active age, however, is merely one of the factors influencing the development of the PAYG system. The development of the contribution base (w·L in the budget restriction's left-hand term), which determines pension benefits, is determined by the wage trend (productivity trend) and by the supply of labour.[23] Of course "the number of persons of occupationally-active age" is a fundamental determinant of the labour supply, but the latter is also determined to a high degree by participation rate, by the number of years of which a working life consists, by the number of weeks of which a working year consists, and by the number of hours of which a working week consists - these in turn being determined by individual choices and institutional conditions.

Since the ATP system was introduced, great changes have taken place on the labour market. Entry of young people on to the labour market has been shifted to a later point as a result of expansion of education after compulsory basic schooling; age 20 rather than age 16 can be said to be the lower age limit of the workforce. The pension age has been lowered from 67 to 65 years. The relative figures for men aged 60-64 in the workforce has fallen by almost 20 percentage points between 1970 and 1992, from 79.5 to 60.8 per cent. The retirement age is therefore *de facto* nearer to 62 than 65 years.

The biggest change on the labour market consists of the increased female participation rate. Between 1970 and 1985 the workforce increased by almost 600 000 persons, an increase which is wholly explained by the entry of women into the labour market. In every age group the participation rate rises over time. Thus for example the participation rate for women aged 20-29 years was 55 per cent in 1968, 77 per cent in 1978 and about 90 per cent in 1988.[24] This increased labour supply has naturally had a positive effect on the contribution base; the system's finances have been regarded as healthy, which may have been a contributory cause of the "generous" changes which have been implemented, e g reduced retirement age and the introduction of partial pensions.

Despite this increase in the number of persons in the workforce, the number of hours worked fell, both in absolute figures and per person aged 16-64 years. The

---

23 In other words, the yield of a PAYG system is determined by the economy's growth-rate - productivity growth and population growth. See Samuelson (1958).
24 See Jonung and Persson (1990).

number of hours worked per person fell by almost 6 per cent during the 1970s, rose again in the 1980s and then fell once more in the early 1990s. A reduced labour supply is always costly under the PAYG system.[25] The design of the ATP system makes it extra costly because a diminished labour supply reduces the contribution base but has almost no effect at all on pension benefits because of the 15- and 30-year rules; if there is any effect it is exceedingly marginal.

All in all these changes on the labour market mean that the pensioner ratio which is shown in Table 9 considerably underestimates the reality. The reduction of actual retirement age from 65 to 62 alone increases the pensioner ratio by between 7 and 10 percentage points.[26] A pensioner ratio defined as number of old-age pensioners in relation to number of persons in the workforce would have given a ratio of 0.37 in 1985 instead of the 0.28 shown in Table 9, with higher rates of contribution ensuing in order to cover pension expenditures.

Increased lifespan in Sweden along with lowered retirement age may serve as yet another illustration of how important demographic changes are in a PAYG system. Since 1950, the expected remaining lifespan at age 60 has risen by 5.1 years for women and 2.0 years for men.[27] Taken together with the lowering of the retirement age to 65 in 1976, the expected number of years as pensioners has thereby increased by 63% for women and by 39% for men. For women, the pensioner ratio has then risen so that the balanced contribution rate in an actuarial system would require to be raised by 8 percentage points. For men the corresponding rise is 3 percentage points.

An aging population is a well-known problem of PAYG systems and easily leads to tensions between generations.[28] If the cause of the aging population is falling fertility, perhaps the working generation's dependency burden may increase less dramatically than if the cause is declining mortality. In the first case, part of the resources which are now not needed for children may possibly be transferred to the elderly.[29] When mortality is declining, dependency has to be borne for more years than before. In principle this can be accomplished by reducing pension benefits per year or by raising contributions. In Sweden at present it is the latter which applies, since the system is benefit-determined. The burden is thereby laid on the working part of the population.

In this way the expected demographic changes constitute a form of pressure on the pension system in themselves. The rules of the ATP system are so worded that this pressure is reinforced by the fact that they give an incentive to reduced working time. It is the lack of linkage between contributions from and benefits to the individual that gives rise to such incentives. The existence of the 15- and 30-year rules and the

---

25 In Samuelsonian terms this can be interpreted as a negative population trend, with negative interest (= yield) ensuing in consequence.

26 See Kruse (1989) p. 123.

27 See Table 4 in Bengtsson and Kruse (1992).

28 This does not mean that demographic changes would be problem-free in funded systems. See Bengtsson and Kruse (1994) for an analysis.

29 Marchand and Pestieau (1991) discuss the point along these lines. However, experience up to now suggests a low substitution-elasticity between expenditure on children and old people respectively. See also Cutler, et al (1990).

ceiling frequently causes increased working time to lead only to increased contributions while benefits are not affected.

Different demographic scenarios and effects on contribution rates and/or pension benefits.

The National Social Insurance Board makes projections of necessary rates of contribution for a number of growth rates. Some of these calculations have been shown in Table 5. However, only one demographic scenario is utilised throughout, viz the one which is the SCB's main alternative in population projections. By making alternative assumptions concerning future population developments the pension system's sensitivity to demographic changes can be elucidated. In Bengtsson & Kruse calculations are made for a number of demographic scenarios.[30] These include a model for projections of pension payments-out and contribution payments-in with the specifically Swedish characteristics. The model consists of two parts, one for population projections and one pension model.

Because the main object in Bengtsson & Kruse was to study effects of different population developments, growth was assumed to be 0, despite the fact that the Swedish system is sensitive to growth rate.[31] In the next study, therefore, the model has been enlarged to include this feature as well.[32] One reason why economic growth makes such a strong impact on the pension system's finances is the so-called ceiling. Contributions are paid even on income above the ceiling, but they generate no pension benefits. If there is growth, an ever-increasing proportion of income-receivers break through the ceiling. Calculations are therefore made with and without the ceiling.

The data of 1985 are the base-data used for the projections. These base-data have been retained here too, except for participation rates, where 1989 and forecasts from that year have been utilised. Both participation rates and pension points are calculated as averages in 5-year age groups for men and women. The same applies to the "labour market factor", i e the 30-year rule.

Data for 1985 are also used in the population model as starting values with the number of men and women in 5-year age groups and actual transition propensities during the period 1980-84. Three scenarios are used: one which is virtually identical to SCB's main alternative (Nat 1), one where high fertility is assumed (HF) and one with low mortality (LM).

In Nat 1 it is assumed that fertility first falls somewhat, then rises to 1.9 years in the year 2010 for all women. Thereafter the total fertility rate (TFR) is assumed to be constant. Mortality is assumed to fall until 2010 and then to remain constant. Expected lifespan rises by 1.4 years for men and 2.0 years for women compared with 1989. In HF, fertility is assumed to rise to reproduction level until the year 2005 and then to remain constant. In LM, the death risk is assumed to fall by 30 per cent for

---

30 Bengtsson and Kruse (1992).
31 Bengtsson and Kruse (1992).
32 Bengtsson and Kruse (1994).

women and 45 per cent for men until the year 2005, remaining constant thereafter. This signifies an increase of 8-10 years for men and of 4-5 years for women.[33]

A mere glance at the budget restriction for a PAYG system gives an intuitive understanding that HF must be the most favourable scenario for the pension system. Higher fertility signifies an increase of the labour force, though with a time-delay of about 20 years. LM is the least favourable because the number of years as pensioners rises. HF and LM can be said to form a sensitivity band around the main prediction. It is worth noticing, however, that no scenario is based on extreme assumptions but that all are fully conceivable. The population developments to which these demographic scenarios give rise are illustrated by the ratio between old-age pensioners and labour force in Table 10.

Table 10. Ratio between pensioners and labour force.

	1985	2000	2015	2030	2050
Nat 1	0.37	0.34	0.42	0.46	0.45
High fertility	0.37	0.34	0.43	0.46	0.41
Low mortality	0.37	0.36	0.51	0.62	0.66

Source: Bengtsson and Kruse (1992)

Until the turn of the century, the pensioner ratio falls in all scenarios. The small birth cohorts from the 1930s reach retirement age during the 1990s and the large cohorts from the baby boom of the mid-1940s are still on the labour market. During the early decades after the turn of the century the ratio rises dramatically, by between 8 and 15 percentage points up to 2015, by a further 3 and 11 percentage points up to 2030. In 2015 there are 2.4 occupationally-active per pensioner in the Nat 1 case and only 2 per pensioner in the low-mortality case.

Pension expenditures are going to rise regardless of demographic scenario. From Diagram 2 it can be seen that the rise is most vigorous up to 2015, that it continues until 2030 (though to a negligible degree in the HF alternative) and then levels off. The rise up to a point immediately after the turn of the century results partly from demographic developments, partly from the fact that only then does the system reach its fully-functioning stage. The sharp increase during the first 15 years of the next century can be ascribed in high degree to the large cohorts of the 1940s, who by then have retired on pension and for the most part are still alive.

Different population developments do not have any effect on pension benefits until the turn of the century - in all three cases, expenditure rises by 40 per cent. After that the differences in population developments make a substantial difference to pension expenditure: in 2015 the differences in expenditure between the high- and low-fertility cases is 35 per cent, a difference which has risen to 50 per cent by 2030.

---

33 See Bengtsson and Kruse (1992) page 11ff for a more precise description.

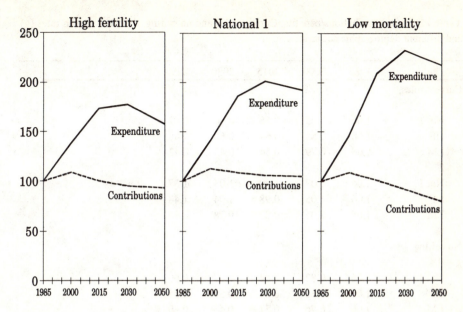

Diagram 2 a-c. Expenditure and contributions according to three different scenarios. Index 1985=100.
Source: Bengtsson and Kruse (1994).

Of course pension expenditures say nothing about the future finances of the pension system because contributions paid-in will also be affected in high degree by the population trend. Diagram 2 shows how these develop as well.

In all cases, contributions rise until the turn of the century, then fall off in varying degrees. At the end of the period, contributions in the low-mortality case run at about 25 per cent below the level of contributions in the middle of the 1980s. The explanation lies in the changed population structure expected, with repercussions on the labour supply, with a heavy decrease of the labour supply in all scenarios, and a very sharp rise in the number of pensioners in the low-mortality case.

The calculations recorded in Diagram 2 apply to present system with 0-growth. Not in any demographic scenario will contributions in this case cover the benefits. A deficit of at least 15 per cent appears as early as the turn of the century, and by 2015 contributions suffice only for between 54 and 65 per cent of the benefits. Effects of different population scenarios are shown clearly by these calculations. A difference of 6 percentage points between "best" and "worst" population alternatives has already emerged by the turn of the century, a gap which widens to 10 percentage points by 2015, to 15 by the year 2030, and to 20 by 2050.

In systems which are designed so that benefits are fixed, this development means increased contributions, especially in the low-mortality case. Table 11 shows the proportion of benefits which are covered by contributions, given the rate of contribution applicable in 1985.

Table 11. Ratio contributions/benefits. Current rules and no ceiling, different growth rates (g) and different demographic scenarios.

	1985	2000	2015	2030	2050
Current rules,					
g = 0					
Nat 1	1.06	0.85	0.65	0.60	0.62
HF	1.06	0.85	0.64	0.60	0.68
LM	1.06	0.79	0.54	0.45	0.42
g = 2					
Nat 1	1.06	1.07	1.00	1.03	1.37
HF	1.06	1.05	0.98	1.04	1.48
LM	1.06	1.01	0.83	0.78	0.94
No ceiling					
g = 0					
Nat 1	1.06	0.82	0.62	0.57	0.60
HF	1.06	0.80	0.61	0.58	0.65
LM	1.06	0.76	0.51	0.43	0.40
g = 2					
Nat 1	1.06	1.03	0.93	0.89	1.00
HF	1.06	1.02	0.92	0.90	1.08
LM	1.06	0.97	0.77	0.68	0.69

As already observed, the system is growth-sensitive, and Table 11 shows that at 2 per cent annual growth the system would run at a surplus both if Nat 1 and if HF were to apply. But not even 2 per cent annual growth suffices to offset such an aging population as will be the case in the scenario with low mortality.

One of the main explanations of the fact that the system functions so much better at 2 per cent growth is the so-called ceiling. With growth, as was remarked earlier, an increasing number of people come to enjoy incomes above the ceiling, incomes which do not qualify for pension but which affect contributions alone. Therefore Table 11 also shows calculations in which the ceiling has been removed. The deficit is smaller with growth than without it even when the ceiling is removed (and in th in the HF-case it is actually non-existent over the entire period). The reason is the lag which arises because the benefits are calculated on earlier incomes. It is obvious that growth reduces the problems in the pension system, but that an annual growth of 2 per cent is insufficient to cope with a population development in which a certain degree of continued increase of lifespan is assumed.

In a somewhat special sense, therefore, we can speak of a trade-off between growth and population developments: high growth permits a "more difficult" population trend than low growth. Thus, for example, contributions cover only just over half of the benefits of 2015 in the low mortality case if we do not have growth, whereas they cover 83 per cent if we have annual growth of 2 per cent.

However, to present it as a trade-off conceals some important aspects. In the first place, it tends to suggest that growth and population developments are politically controllable magnitudes - a notion which may at best be characterised as wishful thinking. In the second place, it obscures the fact that the system is not designed to be capable of coping either with fluctuations in the economic growth rate or the demographic development to be expected with an aging population.[34] As has been shown above, the optical illusion results from the fact that the ceiling limits the commitments in the public system. Nevertheless the commitments remain but are transferred to the contractual insurance system. In order to cope with the fluctuations in the economic growth rate, the method of indexing must be changed from inflation-linking to growth-indexing. The problems of coping with fluctuations in the age structure and an aging population are alleviated if the pure PAYG system is combined with buffer-funding.[35]

Concluding comments

We have called attention to a number of problems in the Swedish pension system. Some of these are the result of "design faults" and some of the fact that an aging populations puts pressure on a PAYG system. Compared with other countries, the Swedish system is of extreme design inasmuch as the combination of replacement ratio, number of years on the labour market required for full pension and price-indexing exposes the system to greater strains than the combinations selected in other countries.[36]

It is obvious, and today generally accepted, that the present pension system has to be reformed. In the spring of 1994 a parliamentary commission put forward proposals for reform which, if implemented, will resolve a good many of the problems in the present system. The proposal involves going over to a pension based on the life-income, i e abolition of the 15- and 30-year rules. Apart from a few exceptions (e g care of children) this leads to a complete linkage between benefits and contributions, which in turn means a reduced tax ratio and an end to the subsidising of leisure time by the pension system. Wage-indexing is also proposed instead of the price-indexing of today, so that the system will be obedient to economic trends instead of sensitive to changes in growth as at present.

To base pensions on the entire life-income and utilise a wage index is not enough, however. The experiences of the German and Finnish pension systems, for example, both of which are based on life-income and wage-indexed, show that despite this design there can be problems in meeting pension commitments, and these have forced changes to be made in the pension rules in those countries. In order to avoid this type of problem, therefore, the parliamentary commission proposes that the system should be contribution-determined instead of benefit-determined. In this way the system

---

34 With a Samuelsonian (1958) design of the pension system there occurs a genuine trade-off between economic growth and an aging population.
35 See also Kruse (1989).
36 See Gonnot (1994) for comparisons of pension systems in various countries.

becomes financially closed.

The majority of industrial countries introduced similar systems to Sweden's at about the same time. It is easy to understand that Sweden, like other countries, opted for a PAYG system at that point. In a PAYG system the pensions are "guaranteed" by the growth rate, i e the return on contributions is determined by the growth of production, unlike what happens in funded systems, where the "guarantee" comes from interest, i e the return is determined on the capital market. If the growth rate is higher than interest rates, which was the case during the 1950s and 1960s when the systems were introduced, the PAYG system is manifestly more advantageous than funded systems. But PAYG systems are more sensitive to certain types of demographic changes than funded systems and therefore give rise to conflicts over distribution. In all countries the present systems are untenable in face of expected population changes involving aging populations. These demographic strains are less noticed than "design faults". The aging of the population is a lengthy process. Many of the demographic changes can be foreseen, which gives time e g for buffer funding so as to cope with the demographic fluctuations. From Table 10 we know for example that in Sweden the pensioner ratio will fall until the turn of the century and that it will not be back at the 1990 level until 2010. To make use of this time for buffer funding would seem an obvious thing to do.[37]

---

37 The results of simulations of buffer funding are given in Hagemann and Nicoletti (1989) page 73.

REFERENCES

Bengtsson T, Kruse A (1992) Demographic Effects on the Swedish Pension System. IIASA WP-92-35.

Bengtsson T, Kruse A (1994)Demographic Changes and Economic Growth in Pension Systems, with Sweden as an example. Included in Gonnot, Keilman, Prinz Social Security, Household and Family Dynamics in Aging Societies. In course of publication, Swets & Zeitlinger Förlag, Amsterdam and Lisse.

Browning EK (1975) Why the Social Insurance Budget is too Large in a Democracy. Economic Inquiry, vol XIII.

Cutler DM et al (1990) An Aging Society: Opportunity or Challenge? Brookings Papers on Economic Activity, 1:1990.

Edebalk P-G (1991) Drömmen om ålderdomshemmet. Åldringsvård och socialpolitik 1900-1952. Meddelanden från Socialhögskolan, 1991:5.

Edebalk P-G, Wadensjö E (1989) Arbetsmarknadsförsäkringar. Rapport till Expertgruppen för studier i offentlig ekonomi. Ds 1989:68.

Elmér Å (1960) Folkpensioneringen i Sverige. Gleerup, Lund.

Gonnot J-P (1994) Demographic Changes and the Pension Problem: Evidence from Twelve Countries. Included in Gonnot, Keilman, Prinz Social Security, Household and Family Dynamics in Aging Societies. In course of publication, Swets & Zeitlinger Förlag, Amsterdam and Lisse.

Hagemann RP, Nicoletti G (1989) Population Ageing: Economic Effects and Some Policy Implications for Financing Public Pensions. OECD Economic Studies 12.

Jonung C (1993) Yrkessegregeringen på arbetsmarknaden. Included in Kvinnors arbetsmarknad. 1990-talet - återtågets årtionde? Arbetsmarknadsdepartementet, Ds 1993:8.

Jonung C, Persson I (1990) Kvinnans roll i ekonomin. Bilaga 23 till LU 90.

Kruse A (1988) Pensionssystemets stabilitet. En samhällsekonomisk analys av värdesäkring och långsiktig stabilitet i det svenska pensionssystemet. SOU 1988:57

Kruse A (1989) Demografi och pensioner. Included in Ohlsson R, Broomé P Generationseffekten. Befolkningsekonomiska problem. SNS Förlag

Kruse A, Ståhlberg A-C (1992) Pensionerna i framtiden. Ekonomisk Debatt nr 4.

Kruse A, Söderström L (1989) Early Retirement in Sweden. Included in Schmähl W (ed) Redefining the Process of Retirement. Springer Verlag, Berlin Heidelberg.

Marchand M Pestieau P (1991) Public pensions: Choices for the future. European Economic Review 35.

Palme J (1990) Pension Rights in Welfare Capitalism. Stockholm.

RFV (1992) Socialförsäkringsstatistik. Fakta 1992.

RFV Hur långt räcker pensionen? En analys av ålderspensionärers inkomstförhållanden år 1989. RFV redovisar 1992:6.

Samuelson P (1958) An exact Consumption-Loan Model of Interest with or without the Social Contrivance of Money. Journal of Political Economy.

SCB (1989) Sveriges framtida befolkning. Prognos för åren 1989 - 2025. Demografiska rapporter 1989:1.

SCB (1991) Sveriges framtida befolkning. Prognos för åren 1991 - 2025. Demografiska rapporter 1991:1

SCB (1992) Nationalräkenskaper 1980-1991. N 10 SM 9201.

SOU 1990:76 Allmän pension. Huvudbetänkande från Pensionsberedningen.

Ståhlberg A-C (1993) Våra pensionssystem. SNS förlag.

Verbon H (1993) Public pensions. The role of public choice and expectations. Journal of Population Economics, vol 6, no 2.

Chapter 7

Social Care and the Elderly
Per Gunnar Edebalk and Björn Lindgren

Modern forms of care for the elderly began to emerge in Sweden immediately after the turn of the century. At that time Sweden was a mainly agrarian society which found itself in a phase of rapid economic and social transformation.

In this chapter we shall describe the development of public-sector care of old people since the turn of the century. There has been a pattern whereby ideological shifts have taken place whenever crisis situations have been experienced. These have been characterised by tensions between need and demand on the one hand and available resources on the other. Special emphasis is laid on current developmental trends and reforms, and the current situation will be analysed from the economic perspective.

Care for the elderly is an integral feature of the Swedish welfare state. Although relatives may make an important contribution, nevertheless in the last resort the care of old people is a government - i e local government - concern. It is also mainly tax-financed. The current situation is characterised *inter alia* by strong demographic pressure and ever-deteriorating local government finances. It provides a distinct illustration of the present crisis of the Swedish welfare state and of strategies for finding new paths out of the crisis.

Old people's homes

Around the turn of the century it was customary for old people to be looked after by their children. Such arrangements were based on law and tradition. Faithful retainers might find a last refuge with their employers. Those who were poor and lacked private alternatives had to trust to local authority poor relief. This applied to actual subsistence of course, but it also meant housing and care if occasion arose. A serious problem was generally the multitude of small local authorities on which poor relief constituted a heavy burden.[1] This, in combination with wide freedom in the design of poor relief, resulted in "stingy" schemes of poor relief. The situation was especially bad in rural areas, where the majority of old people lived. Four forms of assistance which were particularly prevalent in rural areas will be cited here:

1. Boarding out. This meant that the local authority provided reimbursement to a family looking after a person in need of care. This form of assistance was applied to

---

1 Edebalk (1991).

children and to old people as well. The boarding-out system showed its worst aspects when an old person became decrepit and unable to make any contribution by his own labour.

2. Auctioning off. This was an open auction procedure for getting recipients of relief boarded out. The principal rule was that the lowest bidder, i e the bidder willing to accept the lowest level of reimbursement from the local authority, became the "care provider". The saying current at the time was that "a pauper buys a pauper", meaning that the purchasers were frequently crofters and others hoping to improve their own situation by means of the boarding allowance. That abuses occurred is self-evident, and the auction procedure itself was of course extremely offensive to the poor.

3. "Group rotation" *(rotegång)*. Persons in need of care were rotated between different farms, staying at each one for a brief period. This form was resorted to mainly in the poorest rural districts in order to avoid paying boarding allowances, or else because physical feebleness and other such factors made the recipients of relief in question difficult to board out. Thus, those who were most in need of care were continually being shunted about between the various members forming the group.

4. Institutions. Institutional care of the elderly was provided by "pauper shelters" *(fattigstugor)*, "poorhouses" *(fattighus)* and "workhouses" *(fattiggårdar)*. The most common of these were the small "pauper shelters", the main function of which was to provide a roof over the heads of those in distress. The poorhouses were of varying character. As a rule there was neither superintendent nor communal food preparation. In these poorhouses, according to a contemporary observer, there prevailed "great disorder and untidiness, and many of them are real moral plague-spots, in which all kinds of itinerant riff-raff gather".[2] "Workhouses" were linked to farming operations in which the inmates helped with the work according to capability. A common feature of the poor relief institutions, with certain exceptions among the larger institutions in big cities, was the undifferentiated mixing of those receiving assistance: the old and decrepit, the chronically sick, the mentally deranged, orphans, alcoholics etc.

One tendency was manifest with regard to the various forms of relief: institutions were assuming a growing importance in relief of the poor. In 1874, 14.5 per cent of all those relieved were living in institutions, compared with 19.1 per cent in 1907.[3] In the major towns, huge institutions had started being built with room for over a thousand inmates (thus making differentiation possible).

Shortly after the turn of the century a socio-political "breakthrough" occurred in Sweden. Rapid economic development along with the impending franchise reform (decisions bringing in universal male suffrage were taken in 1907 and 1909) were among the contributory causes. In particular, note was taken of the harsh situation of the poor and aged, a factor which should also be viewed in the context of a rapid increase in the numbers of old people. The population over 65 years of age had reached nearly 170 000 by 1850; in 1900 the figure was 430 000.

The view taken at the time was that a dignified old age required differentiated and purpose-equipped institutions, and by about the year 1910 the term "old people's

---

2 Social handbok (1908) p. 123.
3 Edebalk (1991).

home" was becoming more common. The old people's home can be regarded as a logical consequence of differentiation. It was to be reserved for the aged poor and to have the character of a home. The function of old people's homes was to provide subsistence, lodging, and care. All the functions were important: there was no public pension scheme; the plight of the aged poor with regard to housing (if they had anywhere to live at all) was often wretched; and trained superintendents and decent accommodation would be the guarantee of good care. The latter especially should be viewed in the context of the forms of help prevailing at the time.

A public pension scheme was introduced in the year 1913.[4] One main reason was to relieve the strain on local authority poor relief and to provide more dignified forms of help. Even though the amounts paid out were small, a reduction in the subsistence function of old people's homes ensued. A reform of poor relief was effected in 1918.[5] This reform enlarged the area of obligatory poor relief; the right of appeal was introduced and "auctioning off" and "group rotation" were prohibited. One of the most important objects of the reform was to improve the standard of institutional care. Every local authority was instructed to have an old people's home.

Within ten years, the local authorities would have resolved the question of old people's homes. An enquiry at the end of the 1930s reported that all local authorities had old people's home facilities, that the majority of them were very small, and that a large proportion of the inmates were mentally disordered or chronically sick. There were links here firstly with the inadequacy of government provision for care of the mentally ill and secondly with the fact that responsibility for nursing homes was unresolved. Difficulties in the recruitment of competent staff formed part of the picture as well. The care of old people in Sweden, meaning old people's homes, was nothing to boast about at the end of the interwar period.

Special housing for the aged, known as "pensioners' housing" (*pensionärshem*), had begun being constructed as a policy measure complementary to the public pension scheme. This constituted a category of accommodation devoid of institutional character and representing a move away from poor relief. This type of housing formed one of the elements of a local authority policy of providing old people with good living accommodation at a low, i e subsidised, rental. The target group consisted of pensioners who either had hopelessly old-fashioned dwellings or were forced to rely on poor relief to pay their rents. In 1939, the Riksdag resolved in favour of government subsidies for "pensioners' housing".

Two decisions of fundamental importance were taken with respect to the care of old people at the end of the Second World War.[6] Firstly, the Riksdag resolved in 1946 in favour of a reform of local government boundaries to establish larger local authority areas, one of the objects being to create bigger and better old people's homes. This reform came into effect in 1952. Secondly, an improved old age pension based on the minimum standard principle was decided on in that same year. In this way the inmates of old people's homes would become paying guests instead of poor relief claimants. These decisions were accompanied by new and more up-to-date

---

4 Elmér (1960).
5 Edebalk (1991).
6 Edebalk (1991).

guidelines for old people's homes. One of the effects of these guidelines, which were adopted by the Riksdag in 1947, was that old people's homes were no longer to be poor law institutions and that the "mixing of clients", as it was termed, was to cease. County councils were to be assigned responsibility for nursing homes so that these could be enlarged with a view to relieving the strain on old people's homes. A definitive decision was taken in 1951. Care of the mentally ill was also to be developed, and special government provision was made for this in the early 1950s.

The proposed old people's homes were to be open to all old people in need of care, irrespective of status with regard to income or capital assets. Old people's homes were to offer at least the same material standards as pensioners' housing. Single rooms were to be in the majority and the number of places was to be not less than 25 in each home. Modern old people's homes were to be attractive places in which to work so that skilled staff could be recruited. There was a real and expected shortage of care assistants in consequence of the full employment prevailing after the war (hence, there were many other attractive job opportunities), and also of the fact that new entrants to the labour market were relatively few because of the low birth rates of the early 1930s. A high demand for old people's homes was expected to materialise as soon as the creation of modern old people's homes got under way. Consequently, with the growing numbers of old people particularly in mind, a large-scale building programme was launched. The rule of thumb at the time was to the effect that about one pensioner in ten would be living in old people's homes by the time the expansion was completed. This expansion was to be stimulated with the assistance of central government subsidies.

Development of the "live-at-home" ideology

To carry the guidelines of 1947 into effect involved a gigantic building programme. There was one obvious obstacle, however, viz the state of the Swedish economy, which bore the marks of overheating. This led to a halt on reform by the end of the 1940s, and the outlook for the 1950s held out no hope of relief. The situation for the reform of old people's homes was one of grave crisis.[7] On the one hand a tight rein had been kept on building during the 1940s (which had included the war), and no change for the better was in sight. On the other hand, the number of old people was increasing relatively sharply. This tendency had existed for a long time, but the repercussions on old people's care were not perceived until the latter part of the 1940s. In 1940 there had been 503 000 persons over 67 years of age. By 1950 the figure was 560 000, and a forecast made in 1949 gave a figure of 920 000 for 1980.

Up to about 1950, the care of old people was synonymous with old people's homes. During the economic crisis a new ideologue, the author Ivar Lo-Johansson, appeared on the scene. He wrote a series of newspaper articles describing conditions in Swedish old people's homes. He spoke of Big Brother attitudes, melancholia, passivity, the loss of human dignity and zest for life. In Lo-Johansson's view it was not a matter of reforming old people's homes. Placement in an old people's home

---

7 Edebalk (1990).

meant tearing the aged away from the familiar framework of their lives. It was one's own home that gave life its meaning, and it was there that the old ought to be provided with help and supervision. Lo-Johansson's slogan was "*hemvård i stället för vårdhem*", a play on words roughly translatable as "care at home, not a nursing home". As a result of Lo-Johansson's efforts, the care of old people received much attention from the mass media, and his commitment brought influence to bear on public opinion.

The critical situation with regard to old people's care around 1950 provided the stimulus for a reorientation. An important initiative was launched by the Red Cross in Uppsala in 1950, when it started the first organised home-help service for old people. The object was to delay the moment of transfer to old people's homes, and the services provided were to include cleaning, feeding, home visits and nursing assistance. Favourable reports of the new home-help service were received and disseminated from a very early stage. Three main positive results were observed:

1. Old people liked this form of help.
2. The demand for places in old people's homes diminished.
3. Recruitment (particularly of middle-aged housewives, who normally were not available to the labour market) was a relatively simple matter. Moreover, an important factor for the future was that women in the 40-60 year age group showed a clearly predicted increase right up to the 1960s.

Hourly-paid housewives and low wages kept the costs of the home-help service down. An abundant supply of "cheap" labour furnished the conditions for expansion, and the new ideas quickly gained currency among local authorities and in the Riksdag. Reasonable living conditions are one of the prerequisites for providing help to claimants in their homes. This is the point at which help with home improvements for old people is specially noticeable. A resolution of the 1952 Riksdag brought intensified action on home improvement. It was primarily a matter of providing dwellings with such facilities as water and drainage, and suitable forms of heating. Government assistance took the character of interest-free permanent loans which became in reality a straight grant.

According to the new ideology, the home-help service was to be the primary form of old people's care. The home-help service was not encumbered with the character of poor relief in any way and was general in principle. Old people's homes were to remain as a necessary alternative, but their role was greatly played down.

The home-help service continued its expansion all through the 1950s, and by degrees it became more and more common for local authorities to take over the entire task. Home improvement activity accelerated, and towards the end of the 1950s government grants were introduced for the fitting of specialised equipment in the homes of handicapped persons. However, the urbanisation then in progress, along with a diminuition of family cohabitation and a growth in numbers of old age pensioners, brought a situation of constant shortfall. In the middle of the 1960s the government made a vigorous effort, using three main weapons to tackle the problem:[8]

---

8 Edebalk (1990).

1. Temporary central government subsidies for building nursing homes.
2. Intensified home improvement activity.
3. Central government subsidies for local authority home-help services.

Concurrently with these measures, central government grants towards the building of old people's homes were abolished, and housing policy decisions were made whereby central government loans on favourable terms could also be extended to the provision of common facilities in pensioners' housing (service housing). The political decisions of the middle 1960s gave local authorities strong incentives to allocate resources to home-help services, and to county councils to build nursing homes. The "live-at-home" ideology received another and more powerful boost. Old people in need of care were to live at home for as long as possible with the aid of the home-help service, and for those impossible to care for at home there were the county council nursing homes.

It could be questioned whether the viewpoint of the most influential politicians allowed old people's homes any (long-term) right to exist at all. The decision to introduce a specially-designated central government subsidy for home-help services while abolishing subsidies for old people's homes tends to suggest this. Moreover, the climate of opinion was influenced during the 1960s by international currents that recommended "de-institutionalisation" for the care sector generally. A book which attracted attention in its day, published in 1962 by the English sociologist Peter Townsend, contained a blistering attack on old people's homes. Its chief line of argument was the same in principle as that propounded by Lo-Johansson 13 years earlier.

The situation after the Riksdag decisions around the middle 1960s can be formulated as follows. Both local authorities and pensioners had incentives to opt for living-at-home with home-help service. Local authorities received central government subsidies towards home-help service but not for building or running old people's homes. Pensioners residing in old people's homes had to pay relatively high board-and-lodging charges whereas those living in their own homes had the benefit of government property loans on favourable terms, of housing allowances towards rent, and of low, subsidised home-help service charges. Old people's homes also became expensive for the individual pensioner compared with county council nursing homes, where, as with in-patient treatment generally, there was a very low flat rate charge.

Thus it came about that the home-help service expanded considerably: the main lines of development are shown in Table 1.

Table 1. Number of individuals per 1000 pensioners aged 65 + receiving home help and residing in old people's homes respectively

	1973	1980	1987
Home help	253.4	255.5	202.9
Old people's homes	48.3	41.3	27.9

Source: Statistisk årsbok, various years

The 1970s were characterised by favourable financial conditions, and the care of old people as a whole underwent rapid expansion. In addition to the more conventional home-help services, hair care, bath services, security alarms, mobility services etc became included. Home-help services expanded sharply during the 1970s. At the same time the cost per care-hour was rising. Structural changes formed one of the reasons for the increase in costs.[9] Four points merit special notice here:

1) Because a larger number of very old people were being afforded the opportunity of remaining in their own homes, the work tasks falling to the lot of care assistants and others came to include some elements which were new. Attendance on personal needs (toilet assistance etc) thus became an important feature. This imposed demands in terms of staff training for instance. At the same time, this "new" group of care receivers were often consumers of home nursing as well, so that coordination with the county council nursing service made heavier demands on resources than in the case of institutional residence.

2) From 1976 inclusive, the majority of care assistants went over to monthly-paid employment instead of hourly-paid as previously. As a result, journeys to and from the care receivers became a cost defrayed by local authorities whereas previously it had fallen in part on the home helps themselves. Likewise - and probably more importantly - labour became more expensive inasmuch as the risk of wasted time became magnified in consequence of the coordination and planning problems involved in its use. Finally, of course, this entailed an increased administrative strain in itself.

3) Full employment, along with the increased frequency of gainful employment of women in Sweden, meant that the reserve of labour in the form of "cheap" housewives began to run dry. Recruitment of new groups of caring staff tended in this way to raise wage levels.

4) Towards the end of the period new models of work organisation were being developed, based on group organisation and work teams to which responsibility was allotted for a certain number of care receivers. One of the objects was to achieve greater flexibility of organisation. The establishment of work teams required leadership, time, information, coordination of holidays and timetables, which increased the consumption of resources without any quantitative changes in performance.

The local authority expansion of the 1970s was not matched by any corresponding cost-consciousness. Only towards the end of the period did such questions begin to be looked at seriously in the field of old people's care. The system of central government subsidies was deficient in direct built-in incentives for local authorities to keep costs down by trying to find cheaper solutions. The expansion of the public sector began to slow down during the 1980s. The prevailing economic climate was such that increases in the cost of the home-help service led to relatively fewer old people receiving home help, while help became increasingly concentrated on the more onerous care cases. At the same time a drastic reduction of the relative numbers residing in old people's homes was taking place (see Table 1). Difficulties in recruiting new staff for work in the home-help service made themselves felt, as also did a relatively high turnover of staff, with concomitant quality problems. By now, the mid-1980s, the almost fanatical faith in the "live-at-home" ideology was beginning to give way to a certain element of doubt.

---

9 DsFi 1987:6.

The organisation of old people's care began to be questioned, and enquiries were set up. The reports of these enquiries clearly showed an increased awareness of the need for complementary forms of housing.[10] It was observed that the costs of different forms of old people's care varied widely, and that it was probably only in the less serious cases that the cost was lower for persons living at home and in receipt of home help. This was confirmed later by various studies. Svensson, Edebalk and Persson found that the annual cost of service and care for a home-help receiver with a small help requirement was only 5 000 *kronor*, whereas a home-help receiver with a large help requirement could cost up to 435 000 *kronor*; these figures refer to the 1990 level of cost.[11] The corresponding costs in the more onerous cases were considerably lower in old people's homes, varying between 161 000 and 289 000 *kronor*.[12] Moreover, studies revealed that home-help receivers whose help requirements called for large-scale efforts were less satisfied with the home-help service received than those with more modest help requirements.[13] The de-institutionalisation objective became less absolute, although the official political aim in Sweden still emphasises that living at home, possibly supplemented by home-help service, home nursing and other assistance from the public sector, is to be the primary solution to old people's needs for housing, care and service.

In government bill 1990/91:14, the then Social Democratic government submitted to the Riksdag a proposal for reforming care of the aged and handicapped. The bill declared the necessity of improving efficiency in the use of resources allotted to the social services and to health care so as to enable the growing need for care and treatment to be met by an economy in balance. Sector boundaries liable to have a negative effect on the utilisation of resources must be removed. Activities ought to be decentralised and responsibility delegated to a greater extent than today, while at the same time the need to follow up results and reappraise the utilisation of resources must be given high priority. The judgment of the cabinet minister presenting the bill was that there was good reason to suppose that the existing resources employed in current activities could be used to better effect.

The bill did not merely emphasise the requirement of greater efficiency. It also stressed the need to change the organisation because aged and handicapped people would eventually come to demand more influence over the services provided than previously. It was therefore considered that the supply of services must become more varied so as to afford opportunities for the individual to make his own choices, and more flexible so as to facilitate easy adaptation in accordance with the needs and wishes of the individual.

In December 1990, the Swedish Riksdag voted to reform the care of the aged and handicapped; the reform came into effect on 1 January 1992. We shall shortly give an account of its contents, but first it may be as well to describe how matters stood at its inception.

---

10 SOU 1987:21 and Ds 1989:27.
11 Svensson, Edebalk and Persson (1991).
12 Edebalk, Lindgren, Persson and Svensson (1992).
13 Lundh (1992).

Structure, costs and financing of old people's care at the beginning of the 1990s.

During the 1980s there were considerable changes in the type of housing on which local authorities concentrated their efforts (Table 2). The number of places available in old people's homes decreased while those in pensioners' housing with social service ("service housing") increased.

Table 2. Number of places/flats for aged and handicapped persons, 1985 and 1991.

	1985	1991	% change
Old people's homes with or without full board and lodging	51 733	36 099	- 30 %
Service flats in service housing or in ordinary residential blocks	33 292	49 278	+ 48 %
Long-stay wards	48 600*	41 915*	- 13 %
Group dwellings	0	5 105	-
Total	**133 625**	**132 397**	**- 1 %**

Source: Lindgren and Prütz (1993)
* Number of persons in long-stay wards

Day centres have been built since the 1960s, and by 1991 there were 1570 in total. The transportation service has been expanded considerably as well. The number of persons with entitlement to transportation service increased between 1973 and 1990; in 1991, however, a degree of decline could be observed in the numbers entitled. Approximately 440 000 persons had access to the transportation service in 1991. The number of single journeys made per year was rising up to 1980, in which year each entitled person made an average of 44 journeys. By 1991 the number had fallen to 35 single journeys per person.

Since 1980 there have been no major changes in the number of persons receiving home-help service, despite the fact that the number of old people rose substantially. Between 1990 and 1992, however, the number of entitled persons diminished by 10 per cent, from just over 302 000 to a little more than 271 000. On the other hand the number of service hours per person increased during these years, from 360 to 371 per year.

Table 3 reveals that it is mainly persons over 75 years of age, especially those over 85, who avail themselves of old people's care (and handicapped care). Table 4 likewise shows that persons over 85 years of age have a help requirement which is considerably greater than in the case of the younger age groups; it also shows what proportion of persons in different age groups have access to local authority services.

Table 3. Proportions of different age groups making use of social services. 1991. Per cent.

	64 years and younger	65-74 years	75-84 years	85 years and older
Old people's homes with or without full board and lodging	1	6	37	56
Service flats in service housing or in ordinary residential blocks	7	14	55	34
Group dwellings	7	11	48	34
Home-help service	15	17	41	27
Transportation service	12	16	44	28

Source: Lindgren and Prütz (1993).

Table 4. Use made by old people of social services related to different age groups, 1991. Per cent.

	65-74 years	75-84 years	85 years and over
Old people's homes with or without full board and lodging	4	6	12
Service flats in service housing or in ordinary residential blocks	6	8	11
Group dwelling	1	1	1
Home-help service	17	38	51
Transportation service	30	53	69

Source: Lindgren and Prütz (1993).

Because the care of old people is a local government matter, there are also wide differences between municipalities with regard to both special housing, social home-help service and transportation service.[14] In 1991 the total costs for primary local authority care of old people averaged 20 580 *kronor* per inhabitant over the age of 65. The local authority housing supplementary allowance (*bostadstillägg*), as it is termed, is not included in this. About 75 per cent of the cost consists of staff costs. The cost varies considerably between local authorities, from 13 219 *kronor* per inhabitant over the age of 65 in the municipality with the lowest costs to 29 194 *kronor* per inhabitant over the age of 65 in the municipality with the highest costs.

Care of the aged and handicapped is financed chiefly via local income tax. In 1991 local income tax met 64 per cent of the cost. For the rest, central government subsidies covered 14 per cent and user charges about 10 per cent; "other sources of income", including loans, defrayed the remaining 12 per cent. It may be added that

14 Lindgren and Prütz (1993).

during the 1980s, primary local authority expenditure as a whole increased by 9.7 per cent in real terms while income increased by only 6.1 per cent; the widening gap between income and expenditure was offset by increasing borrowing and running down reserves. Here too we are dealing in national averages; there are very great differences between local authorities as regards the breakdown between different sources of finance. There are some municipalities whose charges to users amount to only 3 per cent, while other municipalities may take up to 22 per cent. At least one municipality did not claim any central government subsidies at all; in another municipality, central government subsidies accounted for 32 per cent of its finance.

Regeneration of old people's care

The rise in local authority borrowings reflects a general financial crisis in the public sector in Sweden. Total public expenditure at present, including transfer payments, amounts to about 75 per cent of the national income, whereas revenue forms only 65 per cent. A rapidly-increasing national debt, in combination with low or negative Swedish economic growth rates and a fairly widespread belief among leading politicians that Swedish taxes ought not to be severely increased, manifestly limits the scope for financing any continued expansion of expenditure on traditional lines. The entire Swedish welfare system is under strain. Demographic pressures make the situation seem even more difficult for local government care of old people.

A reorientation is needed. In Sweden today there is a general aspiration to improve public sector efficiency and to give the Swedish people greater direct influence over services which have traditionally been supplied by the public sector. For example, a current government report suggests that the pricing of public services must be compatible with efforts to achieve economic efficiency in the utilisation of resources.[15] The government considers that increased competition will promote efficiency and strengthen consumer influence (prop 1992/93:43). One of the proposals of a commission headed by Professor Assar Lindbeck is to the effect that all public business other than exercise of the state power should be subject to competition, and that uniform and appropriate accounting must be required of all local authorities along with effective follow-up and inspection of local government activities. The aim is for more quasi-market organisational forms, in which decentralisation, buying/selling and profit-centres are some of the watchwords, in the conduct of public business.[16] These are some of the manifestations of a general tendency which can be summed up in the concepts of efficiency, freedom of consumer choice, competition between producers, and (cautious) privatisation. This is not unique to Sweden. The pattern can be recognised in many other European countries; perhaps it has been most conspicuous in Great Britain.

In the field of Swedish old people's care, these aspirations have produced such results as a changed distribution of responsibility between primary local authorities and county councils, changes in the systems of consumer's changes and central

---

15 SOU 1991:110-111.
16 Ds 1992:7, Ds 1992:108, SOU 1993:48, SOU 1993:73.

government subsidies, and changes in the conditions and terms for the conduct of private providers.

Changes of relative responsibility between primary local authorities and county councils.

The shared responsibility of primary local authorities and county councils for health and social care, and the blurred boundaries between areas of responsibility, have long been known to be a problem, but the seriousness of the problem has gradually been aggravated as expenditure has risen and the scope for financing it has narrowed. Blurred responsibilities and cost containment measures encourage people to act in such a way as to avoid, as far as possible, accepting costs for which someone else can take responsibility equally well. This often works to the detriment of the private individual, who may find himself being "shunted about" between different institutions and different authorities. The situation can also have adverse effects on the economy as a whole, since the individual's need for care and treatment may then be met at the "wrong" level. One example is the incidence of discharge-ready patients in somatic hospitals, one cause of which is the inadequacy of the incentives for county councils to move patients into cheaper forms of care and for local authorities to accept persons who while no longer emergency cases still require substantial provision of care and treatment.

In the reform of old people's health and social care which came into effect on 1 January 1992, local authorities were assigned overall responsibility for long-term service and care of the aged and handicapped. One example of the obligatory duties allotted to local authorities as part of the reform is the responsibility (formerly belonging to county councils) for operating local nursing homes and other institutions of long-stay medical care. Local authorities also had a legally-regulated responsibility imposed on them to defray the cost of any somatic long-term medical treatment for which they did not have operational responsibility; similar cost-responsibility was also introduced for discharge-ready patients in somatic emergency and geriatric care. The reform also contains several voluntary elements. One example is that a local authority may assume responsibility for home nursing by agreement with its county council. A second example is that a local authority may be allowed the opportunity of offering primary health care (otherwise a matter for the county council) over a five-year trial period, subject to agreement between the county council and local authority concerned and the sanction of the National Board of Health and Welfare (*Social-styrelsen*). According to Ministry of Health and Social Affairs (*Socialdepartementet*) figures, the total scale of this reform amounts to 20.3 thousand million *kronor* at 1991 prices, which is approximately equivalent to 21 per cent of county council expenditure on health care as it was prior to the reform.

The reform in question is thus a very comprehensive one in financial terms. It is far and away the most radical of several shifts of responsibility in the field of health care since the war, and by virtue of its scale alone it probably has the potential for considerable direct effects on the activities in question as well as on the Swedish economy as a whole. Important objects of the reform are to improve the conditions for increasing the efficiency of county councils and local authorities in utilising resources, and to stimulate them to seek organisational and production solutions which raise productivity in the utilisation of resources in the slightly longer term. It is expected that the changes in the distribution of responsibilities should afford scope for reaping the benefits of coordination. The local authorities' responsibility for costs in respect of medically discharge-ready patients is expected to give strong incentives to local authorities to send such patients home and provide them with assistance either in their own homes or in one of the specialised types of housing (nursing homes now also being in this category).

From the outset 110 local authorities availed themselves of the opportunity of taking over home nursing, while seven local authorities assumed responsibility for primary health care. No evaluation is yet available. But responsibility for funding seems to have fulfilled expectations, according to the early studies which have been made of the effects of responsibility for funding.[17] The level of remuneration for the care of discharge-ready patients, which is exactly the same throughout the country, is set by the government once a year. In 1992, somatic emergency treatment was re-munerated at the rate of 1800 *kronor* and geriatric care at 1 300 *kronor* per day or part thereof. This rate of remuneration is clearly higher than the cost of special forms of housing, so that the incentive to bring the patient home is probably quite strong. It may be mentioned that it is estimated that about 15 per cent of all patients staying in somatic hospitals in 1989 and 1990 were discharge-ready. In 1993 the number of discharge-ready patients had diminished by 50 per cent in somatic hospitals and by just over 60 per cent in geriatric care as a result of local authorities' new funding responsibilities.

Thus the demand for in-patient treatment has declined, and this is expected to cause the number of hospital beds for somatic care to be reduced by 1 165 (or 3 per cent of a total of about 37 000 beds) and those for geriatric cases by 884 (or just under 13 per cent of a total of about 7 000 places). It is estimated that this will reduce the running costs of county council health services by 435 million *kronor* in 1992 and 1993. At the same time the number of places in special housing has risen, a development which has been encouraged, *inter alia*, by the designated government grants introduced for the building of group dwellings and flats in special housing and for the establishment of more single rooms in nursing homes. If existing plans come to fruition, the number of places in special forms of housing will increase by 5 184; primary local authorities' running costs are expected to rise by 969 million *kronor* as a result of the expansion and the improvements to the special forms of housing.[18]

Neutral central government subsidies and new charging structures for consumers

Until the end of 1992, Sweden had a system of central government subsidies based for the most part on the principle of making designated grants to local authorities (and county councils). There are a number of problems in such a system. It can produce

---

17 SOU 1993:49.
18 SOU 1993:49.

uncertainty and irregularity in local authority planning because of changed ideologies and vagaries occurring at central political level. It can give incentives to local authorities to involve itself in activities which are not efficient in a wider economic perspective instead of being developed and adapted to suit the local authority's own conditions and the wishes of its inhabitants. Also, the local authority's responsibility for its activities is limited, since it is unable to influence the orientation of its activities to the extent desirable - not, at any rate, if it does not want to lose all its subsidies from central government. In the sphere of local authority old people's care (and the county council health service for the aged), government grants have led to the provision of unjustifiably elaborate home-help services to facilitate living at home, and of too many county council nursing homes (most of which have now been taken over by local authorities). Old people's homes have been neglected, only a few new ones having been built during the 1980s.

A new system of central government subsidies to local authorities came into force from 1 January 1993 onwards. As part of the government's move towards a more general subsidy system, 12 of the former designated subsidies to local authorities have been abolished. The new tax-equalisation subsidy system consists of three parts: (a) a subsidy to equalise local authorities' tax incomes up to a general basic level, (b) an addition to, or deduction from, the subsidy based on differences of climate, age structure and other structural conditions not easily susceptible to influence, and (c) a supplement for declining population. The new tax-equalisation subsidy is calculated only on the local authorities' tax base and ignores completely what activities the local authority engages in. Overall, the central government expects that government subsidies to local authorities will diminish. At the same time the government is encouraging local authorities to adapt themselves to the development of the Swedish economy as a whole, to take more responsibility for their activities in future, and to find alternative ways of financing them.

The present rules for consumer charges in respect of old people's care and treatment have also created distorted incentives, to the detriment, *inter alia*, of old people's homes. At the beginning of 1992 the maximum daily charge for treatment in local nursing homes, formerly county council-owned but now taken over by the local authorities, was 65 *kronor* according to government regulation. The rates for old people's care were governed by similar regulations. At old people's homes run by the municipalities, the level of charges at most could be such as would leave the individual sufficient funds for personal expenditure; as in all local government business, however, the charge was not allowed to exceed the local authority's prime costs. This rule generally meant a considerably higher charge than in the nursing homes. In addition, the cost of any medicines and of dental or medical treatment was included in the nursing home charge, whereas those living in old people's homes could be charged normally for these services over and above the fees payable to the home.

New legislation, cancelling the distorted detailed regulations previously applicable, has been in place since 1 March 1993. Local authorities now have the option of developing uniform principles of their own for charging in respect of all forms of special housing and other services offered to old people in the local authority district. Many local authorities have also opted to include a cost ceiling of their own limiting the total of all charges which can be levied on any inhabitant of the local government district for care and treatment during any one year.

The evidence so far of the effects of the new charging rules is that there are great differences in charging between one local authority and another. Most local authorities have increased their nursing home charges. However, many authorities do not avail themselves of their scope for differentiating charges according to the content of the service, but a surprising number of authorities continue to apply the full board and lodging principle in old people's homes, and have also introduced that same principle into nursing homes. Viewed overall, local authorities' total charges seem to have increased.[19] In years to come, local authorities with poor finances may be expected to increase their charges to the individual. But there are limits to the increases that can be brought in. If local authorities do not introduce cost ceilings at reasonable levels, there will firstly be a risk that individuals will begin to reduce their saving so as not to have any substantial assets or income from capital in old age, and secondly there will be the possibility of intervention by the state to regulate the expenditure of local authorities in detail again.

Competition among providers, freedom of choice for consumers, and privatisation

The present Swedish government considers it important to increase competition in activities which have traditionally been both financed from public funds and supplied by public producers. There is a wish to raise efficiency in the utilisation of resources by increasing competition. Competition between private and public alternatives is also seen as a means of realising the government's ambition to increase freedom of choice for the individual. Existing Swedish legislation contains a number of formal obstacles to the development of private forms of management. There have also been some more informal obstacles. Work is going on to identify these obstacles and to remove or limit the ones considered unnecessary.[20] Since 1 January 1993, therefore, changes in the laws relating to social services and to health care have made it possible for local authorities and county councils to contract with other parties to carry out the duties assigned to them in such fields as the care and treatment of old people.

However, the running of a private nursing home is an old tradition in Sweden; such business is governed by special regulations.[21] There are just about 270 private nursing homes in Sweden, or almost exactly one third of the country's 810 or so nursing homes. Apart from this, interest in running private businesses devoted to the care and treatment of old people seems moderate so far. A study carried out during the spring of 1992 reported that 71 local authorities and 6 county councils had put parts of their child care and old people's care businesses out to contract. Such contracts were most commonly with private firms, but there were trusts and

---

19 Socialstyrelsen (1993).
20 Ds 1992:108.
21 SOSFS 1985:16.

cooperatives as well.[22] There may be a number of reasons for interest being lukewarm. One reason is the various kinds of formal obstacles which required legislative changes to clear away, so that the texts of the amended statutes are so new as not to have succeeded in making any major impact as yet. Another reason, obviously, could be that private entrepreneurs simply do not see any prospects of profit in the care of old people. A third reason is that private entrepreneurs consider the terms and conditions of the business not to be sufficiently stable, partly because of the politically-loaded character of the services, the prevailing political and parliamentary system with three-year parliaments, county councils and primary local authorities, rapidly-shifting political power-relationships, and minority governments. There is great uncertainty as to the future configuration of care and treatment and their funding; not unexpectedly, therefore, one finds private firms establishing themselves chiefly in fields of enterprise aligned towards target groups wider than the old and handicapped and in which capital investment is low, such as chiropody and food services.

A fourth reason why private enterprise has not yet become noticeably more active in the areas which have traditionally formed part of the government's domain in Sweden has to do with the more informal obstacles. As representatives of the public choice school and several other researchers all declare, it is not certain that it is in the interests of all local government politicians and senior officials to run local authority enterprises as efficiently as possible.[23] To maximise the size of his own administrative machine may be quite an important private goal of the politician or senior official, a circumstance which naturally may make him less inclined to subject his own activities to competition from private alternatives. However, there are local authorities and county councils in Sweden which have adopted very ambitious programmes of competition. Both the city and county authorities of Stockholm are among these; by virtue of their size both in numbers of citizens affected and also in terms of the cost of the activities in question, the results of these programmes may have a considerable impact on the development of opinion in Sweden with regard to private alternatives in such spheres as old people's care. But it should be borne in mind that Stockholm is a large metropolis and that there are in fact only two similarly densely-populated regions in Sweden, viz the Gothenburg district and Scania, the southernmost province of Sweden.

The most usual change as regards alternative business forms in the care and treatment field is for the local authority to move away from an organisation consisting of budget-financed production units to an organisation with profit-centres and some form of buy-and-sell system. A buy-and-sell system can be designed in many ways, but its primary purpose is to separate and clarify the roles of customer and supplier. There is no previous experience to suggest that the introduction of a buy-and-sell system brings greater efficiency of itself. Fölster and others, for example, found that suppliers who only had responsibility for cost did not succeed in running the business more efficiently than when the traditional budget model for management of resources

---

22 Lokaldemokratikommittén (1992).
23 See, for instance, Brunsson (1972), McLean (1987), Lewin (1992).

was in force.[24] Suppliers with responsibility for profits, i e responsibility for both re-venue and costs, clearly did better but still not as well as if the business had been run on an entirely private basis. The study showed that competition rather than the private alternative itself was the most significant factor in providing the stimulus for a more efficient use of resources.

The buy-and-sell system with private entrepreneurs managing their businesses to the order of local authorities does not necessarily mean that the consumer, i e the pensioner and his or her relatives, immediately gets more influence. For this to happen the consumer himself has to be afforded the opportunity of choosing between different producers, private and public, and it has to be possible for the producer's financial profit-and-loss to be affected by these choices. A radical way of offering these possibilities is to introduce a system of vouchers (or service cheques) entitling their holders, with the help of public funds, to consume a certain type of service regardless of the individual's choice of producer (or at any rate as long as the individual selects one of the entrepreneurs recognised or licensed by the local authority). This solution has come under quite intense debate in Sweden but few local authorities have carried any form of voucher system into practice.[25] One notable exception is the local authority of Nacka in the Greater Stockholm region, which in the spring of 1992 introduced an "age-benefit", giving the recipient of home-help service a number of service cheques representing his or her entitlement at the rate of 200 *kronor* per home-help hour; cheques can be redeemed for service provided either by the local authority's own home-help service or by private or cooperative home-help firms.

Concluding remarks

There are three points in time during the twentieth century when the care of old people in Sweden can be seen to have struck out on new paths. Concerns over the preindustrial society's system of poor relief came to a head at the very beginning of the century, and the old people's home emerged as the ideal. Questions were raised about this ideology around the year 1950, and the "live-at-home" ideology flourished from that time on. The home-help service, originally "cheap", gradually became expensive, and it was this, along with growth in the number of very old people and difficulties in funding old people's care, that led to a realignment. The new ideology embodies a more balanced outlook on the care of old people. It also contains clear incentives so that efficient solutions can be arrived at.

The comprehensive responsibility of local authorities for the care and treatment of old people will mean that they experience the true costs of different alternatives. The relative costs, and a consumer charging structure based on these, will in all likelihood bring a revival of interest in old people's homes compared with residence at home supported by home-help service and nursing homes. These alternatives were of course favoured previously through the instrumentality of central government subsidies and low, regulated charges. It is also evident that old people's homes are enjoying a

---

24 Fölster and others (1993).
25 Kommunförbundet, undated.

renaissance in the field of Swedish old people's care.

Demographic developments, i e constantly-increasing numbers of the very old, and the financial straints of the public sector, suggest that consumer charges are going to rise. One effect of this will be that home-help service will assist the simpler care cases only to a limited degree (for example, cleaning and tidying only). This trend has been present since the 1980s, and in future the care of old people will probably be concentrated increasingly on the more serious cases.

The problem of senile dementia has attracted particular attention in recent years. At present the government is assisting the establishment of group dwellings. The growing number of senile persons will probably lead to the construction of group dwellings linked to old people's homes or nursing homes. In this way the benefits of coordination can be reaped, in contrast to those instances where group dwellings are integrated into ordinary residential districts.

Cost problems in the care of old people have led to a growth of interest on the part of local authorities in finding organisational forms that promote cost-consciousness. These include buy-and-sell systems, entrepreneurs and tendering as important ingredients. The move towards quasi-market systems has just begun in Sweden, so that clearly-defined experience is not available.

Relatives play an important role in the care of old people, but probably a smaller one in Sweden compared with other countries. The developments we can perceive in the case of Sweden will make growing demands on relatives. A factor which may generate tensions here is Sweden's female employment-frequency, which is very high in international terms. Perhaps new solutions, such as care allowances for looking after aged parents, may emerge in this high-tension field.

REFERENCES

Brunsson N (1972) Politik, ekonomi och rationalitet. Stockholm, SNS Förlag.

Ds 1989:27 Ansvaret om äldreomsorgen. Rapport från äldredelegationen. Stockholm, Allmänna Förlaget.

Ds 1992:7 Marknadsorientering av kommunal verksamhet: Konsekvenser och möjligheter. Stockholm, Allmänna Förlaget.

Ds 1992:108 Alternativa verksamhetsformer inom vård och omsorg. Stockholm, Allmänna Förlaget.

DsFi 1985:11 Sociala avgifter - problem och möjligheter inom färdtjänst och hemtjänst. Rapport till ESO. Stockholm, Allmänna Förlaget

DsFi 1987:6 Kvalitetsutvecklingen inom den kommunala äldreomsorgen 1970-1980. Rapport till ESO. Stockholm, Allmänna Förlaget

Edebalk PG (1990) Hemmaboendeideologins genombrott - åldringsvård och socialpolitik 1945-1965. Meddelanden från socialhögskolan 1990:4. Lund: Socialhögskolan

Edebalk PG (1991) Drömmen om ålderdomshemmet - åldringsvård och socialpolitik 1900-1952. Meddelanden från socialhögskolan 1991:5. Lund, Socialhögskolan.

Edebalk P G, Lindgren B, Persson U, Svensson M (1992) Individen, vårdinsatsen och ålderdomshemmets kostnader. Resultat från en enkätundersökning i tre kommuner. Studier i hälsoekonomi 1. Lund University,Departmentof Community Health Sciences (Malmö) and Institute of Economic Research.

Fölster S et al. (1993) Sveriges systemskifte i fara? Erfarenheter av privatisering, avreglering och decentralisering. Stockholm, Industriens Utredningsinstitut.

Lindgren B, Prütz C (1993) Ädelreformens samhällsekonomiska effekter. Förutsättningar för en utvärdering. Ädelutvärderingen 93:12. Stockholm, Socialstyrelsen.

Lewin L (1992) Samhället och de organiserade intressena. Stockholm, Nordsteds juridiska förlag.

Lokaldemokratikommittén (1992) Enkät till kommuner och landsting våren 1992. Stockholm, Allmänna Förlaget,

Lundh U (1992) Vård och omsorg i eget boende på äldre dar. Linköping Studies in Arts and Science No 73. University of Linköping: Department of Theme Research. (Thesis)

McLean I (1987) Public Choice. Oxford, Basil Blackwell.

Regeringsproposition 1990/91:14 Ansvar för service och vård till äldre. Stockholm, Allmänna Förlaget.

Regeringsproposition 1992/93:43: Ökad konkurrens i kommunal verksamhet. Stockholm, Allmänna Färlaget.

Socialstyrelsen (1993) Kommunernas avgiftssystem inom äldre- och handikappomsorgen. Socialstyrelsen redovisar 1993:5. Stockholm, Allmänna Förlaget.

SOU 1987:21 Äldreomsorg i utveckling. Betänkande av äldreberedningen. Stockholm, Allmänna Förlaget.

SOU 1991:110-111 Effektiva avgifter - resursstyrning och finansiering. Stockholm, Allmänna Förlaget.

SOU 1993:47 Konsekvenser av valmöjligheter inom skola, barnomsorg, äldreomsorg och primärvård. Rapport till Lokaldemokratikommittén. Stockholm, Allmänna Förlaget.

SOU 1993:48 Kommunala verksamheter i egen förvaltning och i kommunala aktiebolag. En jämförande studie. Stockholm, Allmänna Förlaget.

SOU 1993:49 Ett år med betalningsansvar. Stockholm, Allmänna Förlaget.

SOU 1993:73 Radikala organisationsförändringar i kommuner och landsting. Rapport till Lokaldemokratikommittén. Stockholm, Allmänna Förlaget.

Svenska Kommunförbundet Valfritt ... om alternativa driftformer inomäldre- och handikappomsorgen. Stockholm, Kommentus Förlag, undated

Svenska Kommunförbundet, Socialstyrelsen och Statistiska centralbyrån. Jämförelsetal för socialtjänsten. Stockholm, Svenska kommunförbundet,various years

Svensson M, Edebalk PG, Persson U (1991) Home services costs: the Swedish experience. Health Policy 1991(19):17-209

Chapter 8

Health Care and the Elderly
Per Broomé, Björn Lindgren, Carl Hampus Lyttkens and Rolf Ohlsson

A characteristic feature of Swedish health care is the dominant role played by the county councils. A county council (*landsting*) is an independent regional political organ which, like the municipalities (*kommuner*) at lower level, has the right to levy proportional income taxes on inhabitants within its geographical boundaries. There are 23 county councils in Sweden at the present time; three local authorities have opted to stay outside the county councils - in matters of health care these local authorities have the same responsibilities as county councils. In other words, Swedish health care is not a national system. To the extent that it is possible to speak of a system, it is a system which permits of many different variants. The fact that there are differences between county councils (including the three independent local authorities), for example with regard to organisation, resources, costs and taxes, is thus no cause for surprise. Although health care has been conducted according to a planned-economy model, it is not in the capital city of Stockholm that the plans have been drawn up but regionally, in each and every one of the county councils. There has been a deliberate political effort, even at the national political level, gradually to devolve former central-government responsibility for health care to the county councils. This circumstance makes it impossible to describe the Swedish model of health care. Different rules may apply to different county councils.

The county councils were established in 1862. The law does not state explicitly what areas the county councils are or are not responsible for, nor where the boundaries are drawn *vis-à-vis* the municipalities' and central government's respective areas of responsibility. Nevertheless health care was specified as a principal task from the very start. We shall briefly describe below the rise of the Swedish county council-based totally-integrated model of health care, but it is self-evident that there was some health care in Sweden prior to 1862. First of all, therefore, we shall look at Swedish health care in a more long-term historical perspective.

The health care provided for Swedes during the Middle Ages was administered mainly under the auspices of the then Catholic church at the monasteries and at certain charitable institutions. However, the Reformation in Sweden, king Gustaf I Vasa and the parliamentary resolution of 1527 known as the Västerås recess meant that the ecclesiastical estates and monasteries were confiscated by the Swedish Crown. The result of this was that health care began to be regarded as a state concern, distinct from care of the poor. However, it took a considerable time to translate this into a reality. It was decreed in 1605, during the reign of king Karl IX, that the sick should be cared for in "asylums", while paupers and the homeless were to live in almshouses (*sockenstugor*). These measures were implemented with great vigour by queen Kristina on the basis of her ordinance of 1642. However, administration of the asylums was for a long time governed by canon law.

As well as the humanitarian-based medical-care activities of the church, there was also commercial activity conducted by bath-women, barbers and barber-surgeons as well as by itinerant practitioners who treated cataracts, ruptures and gallstones. Their activities were unregulated save by their guild charters. However, towards the end of the seventeenth century the practice of medicine began to be organised. The Collegium Medicum was founded in 1663: it conducted examinations of physicians intending to practise in Stockholm. The College did not include surgeons, however. The latter had been associated in a guild, the "Barbers' Office" (*Barberarämbetet*) since 1496; the Office was renamed the "Surgeons' Society" (*Chirurgiska Societeten*) in 1685. From 1797 onwards surgeons (and dentists) were also obliged to be examined by the Collegium Medicum. The latter body was reorganised in 1813 as the College of Health (*Sundhetscollegium*), which became the National Board of Health (*Medicinalstyrelsen)* in 1878.

The first true hospital in the modern sense was opened in 1752. This was the Seraphim Hospital, whose activities were financed by various kinds of indirect taxes and donations. At first the management consisted only of Knights of the Order of the Seraphim, and there was no element of formal medical representation in the management. The hospital had eight beds, with room for two patients in each bed, and this was intended to meet the hospital care requirements of the entire Swedish population of the time, including those residing in Finland. In 1765 the Estates of the Realm agreed that funds donated locally could be retained in the county if the population wished to establish a hospital. By the 1860s just under 50 hospitals had been established with a total of about 3 000 sickbeds; most of the hospitals were small, with perhaps 10-30 beds each.

When hospitals began their activities, there was no such thing as out-patient care. Hospitals usually had but one doctor, their own. It was true that he held his own surgery, but this generally took place outside the hospital. By 1860 there were 472 doctors in Sweden, only 53 of whom were employed at the somatic hospitals and 9 at mental hospitals. Most health care at this time, obviously, took place beyond the confines of hospitals; for people living in the countryside medical attendance was provided by government-appointed district medical officers (*provinsialläkare*); towns employed their own municipal or city medical officers (*stadsläkare*); there were also private doctors conducting their own practices, but to a minor extent and mainly in the biggest towns. About 100 years later, however, hospital doctors formed about half of all doctors in Sweden, and they were responsible for a significant proportion of non-institutional treatment.

In other words it is worth noticing that Swedish health care contained significant elements of public-sector production and that it was the state which was primarily regarded as responsible for meeting the people's care requirements. Not until the establishment of the county councils in 1862 did health care begin to become a local or regional political affair, and for the first 90 years the transfer of duties from central government to county councils did not proceed with any particular celerity. During the 1860s, for example, only the state somatic hospitals went over to county council ownership. There was further delay - until 1928 - before the county councils became statutorily responsible for meeting the population's hospital treatment requirements, but only provided that the local authorities or central government did not already do so. The county councils' responsibility did not, for example, include mental health care, care of the mentally retarded, care of epileptics or care of the chronically sick.

During the 1950s the county councils became responsible for epileptic care and care of the chronically sick and for providing out-patient treatment at hospitals. During the 1960s, responsibility for treatment by district or municipal/city medical officers was transferred, along with mental health care, to the county councils. Since 1970 hospital doctors have been barred from holding private consultations in hospitals, and since 1980 it is individual county councils and not the central government which have responsibility for vaccination policy. The last two teaching hospitals still under state ownership, the Caroline (*Karolinska*) Hospital in Stockholm and the Academic (*Akademiska*) Hospital in Uppsala, were handed over to their respective county councils in 1982 and 1983 respectively. In this way all public-sector production of health care came under the control, in principle, of the county councils. The central government did nevertheless shoulder a part of the financial responsibility, and government subsidies still account for a significant portion of the the county councils' revenues.

Under the Swedish Health Care Act of 1982 (and subsequent amendments) the county councils have the principal responsibility for all planning of health care. The planning responsibility means for example that the county councils can determine in individual contracts the maximum number of patients a year a private doctor may have; in the absence of such a contract, consultations with a private doctor are not subsidised via social insurance - the patient pays the entire cost himself. In this way the county councils also regulate and control the market in private health care. Under the Health Care Act, the totally integrated Swedish county council-based health care model is complete. The county councils have become (a) representatives of the consumer, (b) health care producers, (c) financiers and (d) regulators of the health care market. By the end of the 1980s the county councils had attained their peak of economic and political importance. Since then their independent right of taxation has been increasingly called into question, and from 1 January 1992 onwards - for the first time in 130 years - a major reform was brought in which signified a diminution in the role of county councils; the functions of long-term care of the aged and handicapped were taken over by local authorities.

The effect of demographic factors on future costs of health care

At the beginning of the century, Swedish health care took up about one per cent of GNP and employed a virtually negligible proportion of the labour force. Ninety years later about half a million people are actively employed in health care, which consumes nine per cent of all goods and services produced in Sweden.

This expansion of health care was particularly intensive during the period 1960-1975. Massive investments were made at that time in new hospitals and new equipment. The numbers employed doubled. Political decisions guided an expansion in which, in principle, the only moderating factor was a chronic shortage of staff, especially doctors. Financial considerations aimed at economising resources, on the other hand, had a low priority.

In sharp contrast to this unparalleled growth during earlier periods, health care at the present time is faced with an accelerating relative diminution of resources. The current rapid technical progress in the medical field constitutes an important factor underlying this. Some of the innovations are cost-reducing, but often they represent a technique which both raises costs and widens the scope for medical treatment.

The relative contraction of resources is perhaps mainly the consequence of the generally low growth of the Swedish economy during recent years. This low growth has rendered it impossible to expand on the same scale as before, and the central government has tax-capped the county councils. This development has also resulted in an increased questioning of whether effective use is being made of resources in the health care field. Signs have not been lacking that there may be problems of low productivity in Swedish health care.[1]

The relative scarcity of resources has resulted in a number of new tendencies having made themselves apparent in Swedish health care since the second half of the 1980s (and in this Sweden is following the international trend towards health care reforms).[2] The general tendencies consist of decentralisation and the responsibility for results that goes with it. In addition, consideration is being given to prospective forms of payment, the use of DRG,[3] as it is called, market-style relationships and performance-based remuneration in in-patient treatment, while from 1994 onwards out-patient treatment in combination with the family doctor system will be characterised by a combination of remuneration by fee-for-service and capitation. It remains to be seen if and to what extent these reforms will relieve the county councils of their financial problems.

The growing relative shortage of resources must also be viewed in conjunction with the demographic factors. The most important of these factors is the sharp rise in the numbers of old people which has manifested itself during recent years, especially in the group aged 80 and above.

In other words, the outlook for the future of Swedish health care appears bleak in many ways. In fact, forecasts of the future trend of health care costs seem to be marred by great weaknesses and to have strong inbuilt elements of uncertainty. It is almost impossible today to produce reliable forecasts of the shape which the technology, productivity and organisation of health care will have assumed by the turn of the century. Forecasts of the relative magnitude of the resources which health care is going to require by the turn of the century are even more difficult to make, since such

---

1 Lindgren and Roos (1985).
2 See e g Anell (1990), Anell and Svarvar (1993) or Lyttkens and Borgquist (forthcoming a,b) for a summary and discussion of Swedish developments. For some international parallels, see e g Culyer, Maynard and Posnett (1990), Maynard and Hutton (1992), Saltman (1992), Saltman and von Otter (1992), and van de Ven (1990, 1991).
3 The DRG system (Diagnosis-Related Groups) usually means predetermined fixed payments for all patients with a given diagnosis. The system was originally developed for use in the Medicare system in the United States (publicly-financed care of the elderly).

forecasts must be based on guesses as to how economic growth will move in future. However, it is possible to predict developments with regard to one important variable with a fair degree of reliability, and that variable is the demographic. That this can be predicted so accurately results primarily from the fact that the vast majority of the people who will be living in Sweden at the end of the century have already been born.

In any study of Swedish health care and its future, therefore, it seems reasonable to take the importance of the demographic factors as a starting point. In this section we shall accordingly deal with the effect of these factors on health care costs.

The analytical instrument

A reasonable basis for an analysis of how the demographic factors will influence health care costs over the next few years is provided by data showing how health care costs are distributed between different age groups. In Diagram 1 we see such age-specific costs for 1983. For every one-year group, using all the available primary material and official statistics, each individual age group's health care costs have been calculated in six different areas: somatic short-term care, mental health care, out-patient care, pharmaceuticals, dental care and somatic long-term care. These areas in combination form health care as broadly defined in the Swedish national accounts for 1983, i e prior to the ÄDEL reform. It may be observed at this point that a detailed study of this sort has never been made before. The means for making one probably do not exist in any other country than Sweden.

In order to obtain the age-specific costs of short- and long-term somatic care and of mental health care we have used costs per hospital day at 429 different clinics in Sweden in combination with details of age and number of hospital days for all patients discharged from these clinics in 1983. A summation was then effected so as to produce cost figures covering the entire country. The age-specific costs of out-patient care, dental care and pharmaceuticals were ascertained on the basis of various selected studies, patient registers etc.[4]

Diagram 1 shows the costs per head at different ages, i e the total health care costs for a given age group in relation to the size of population comprised in the age group, expressed in 1000s of *kronor*. It is possible here to discern a positive and exponential correlation between costs per head and age.

The changes in costs per head across the age spectrum can be described in the following way: up to age twenty, costs per head are between 2 000 and 3 000 *kronor*.

4 This study was made through a collaborative effort by one of the authors, Rolf Ohlsson, and the Swedish Institute of Health Economics (Institutet för hälso- och sjukvårdsekonomi, IHE), Lund. The results are presented in Ohlsson (1991).

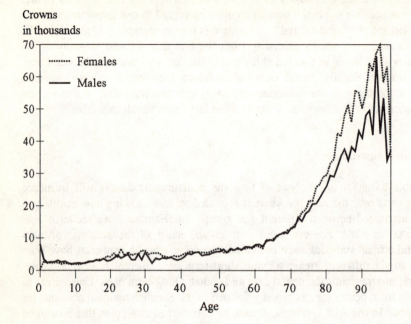

Diagram 1. Per Capita health care costs 1983.

The costs then rise gradually until 65 years of age, at which point they amount to about 8 000 *kronor*. There then seems to be a break-point around retirement which signals an acceleration of the rise in costs per head, measured in absolute figures, to reach about 30 000 *kronor* per individual per year at age 80-plus years. Costs at the highest ages, over 90 years, amount to over 50 000 *kronor*. The costs per head for the 90-plus group are thus 25 times higher than for children aged ten.

It is important to observe that we are dealing here with average costs per head for different age groups and that we do not touch at all upon the so-called heterogeneity problem, i e the fact that there are great differences between different individuals in a given age group. So it is entirely possible for equally high costs per head for two age groups to result from there being in the one case few people, but with high costs, charged to health care, while in the other case there are many people but with low costs per head.

An international comparison

An international comparison shows that a large proportion of resources in Swedish health care are expended on old people. Firstly, Sweden has the oldest population in the world. But even viewed on a per capita basis, more resources go to the elderly than in other countries. This is apparent from Table 1, which shows the average cost per head of the 75-plus age groups in relation to costs per head for the 0-64 years age groups in some selected countries. The wide disparity between France and West Germany on the one hand and Sweden on the other is especially worthy of remark. The cost per head of old people aged 75 and above in Sweden is nine times as high as for persons aged 0-64 years, but in France and West Germany it is only three times as high. Other studies too show clearly that Sweden has the most heavily age-weighted health care in the world, measured in costs per head. In combination with the fact that in addition, Sweden has the oldest population in the world, this means that in Sweden, older people take up a considerably larger proportion of total health care costs, compared with younger people, than in any other country.

Table 1. Average health care costs per head of the 75-plus age groups in relation to costs per head for the 0-64 years age groups in selected countries.

France	2.8
Germany	3.1
Ireland	6.0
The Netherlands	6.2
Great Britain	6.6
Sweden	9.2

Source: Hughues de Jonvenel, Europe's Ageing Population, Futures, 1989.

It is not possible here to make a detailed analysis of the reasons why health care in Sweden is more heavily age-weighted than in other countries, but any such model of explanation must undoubtedly pay regard to the way in which health care has been built up and organised historically; and in this the interaction with demographic events will be a particularly important factor. But other factors too, such as varying levels of income per head, differences in how health care is financed, differences in the definition of health care, different family patterns and cultural dissimilarities, are of importance in this respect.

Preliminary analysis

By way of introduction we shall here make a preliminary analysis of how demographic changes up to the year 2005 will influence the costs of health care, leaving a more detailed demographic analysis until later. We start off from a *ceteris paribus* assumption to the effect that everything except the demographic changes is regarded as unchanged. This means we assume that costs per head at different ages are unaltered from 1983 until 2005 and that the trend of total health care costs is determined wholly by how the numbers in different age groups will change during the period.

Obviously the assumption of unchanged costs per head is unrealistic. Neither do we claim here to be able to assess what the pattern of health care costs will be in the year 2005. But what we do assert is that the calculations we make approximate relatively closely to the demographic pressure on future health care costs. Furthermore, it is probably the case that the assumption of unchanged costs results in a lowest value for the impact of demographic changes on health care costs (cf. below).

An approximation of how total net health care costs will be changed during the period 1983-2005 is shown in Table 2. Here we have used the age-specific health care costs in one-year groups, with 1983 as the starting point and the population structure of the year 2005, also in one-year groups, in order to determine the health care costs of the latter year. Measured at 1983 prices, health care costs rise by about 11 thousand millions, from 58 to 69 thousand million *kronor*, which is equivalent to a rise of 18%, or an average of 0.8% per annum. The rise is considerably larger for women than for men - 21% and 15% respectively, or an average of 0.9% and 0.7% per annum respectively.

Table 2. Health care costs 1983-2005, due to demographic changes. Thousand millions *kronor*. 1983 year's prices.

	M	F	M+F
Total costs 1983	25.3	32.9	58.2
Total costs 2005	29.2	39.7	68.9
Net changes	3.1	6.7	10.7
% changes	15.4%	20.7%	18.4%
Average per year	0.7%	0.9%	0.8%

A more detailed analysis

Diagram 2 shows the difference between the number of persons in different age groups in 1983 and 2005, while Diagram 3 shows the corresponding difference in total health care costs. Diagram 2 shows in which age groups there will be more persons in the year 2005 than in 1983 (above the 0-line) and in which groups there will be fewer (below the 0-line). In similar fashion Diagram 3 shows in which age groups health care costs will rise and fall respectively.

The analysis is based on the five age-intervals where pronounced changes in numbers take place between 1983 and 2005: 1) born 1990-2005, 2) young people and the younger labour force born 1966-1989, 3) middle-aged and elderly labour force born 1939-1965, 4) younger pensioners, born 1925-1938 and 5) the oldest group, born prior to 1925. These groups are clearly distinguishable in that they belong to generations of different sizes. They therefore also have different values, different economic conditions and so on.

Born 1990-2005: Persons in this group will be between 0 and 15 years of age by the year 2005. Diagram 2 shows that the age group will be considerably larger in 2005 than it was in 1983. This results from a number of factors: low childbearing during the late 1970s and early 1980s, which caused the numbers aged 0-15 years to be small, along with Statistics Sweden's assumption that fertility will be relatively high during the period up to the year 2005. The most important reason why the group

Thousands

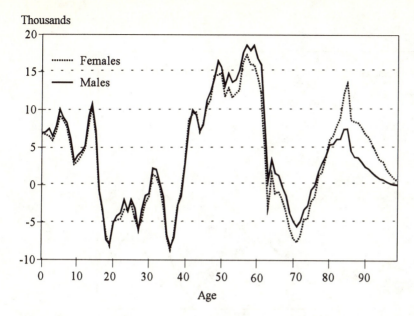

Diagram 2. The difference between the number of persons in different age groups in 2005 and 1983.

The larger number in the 0-15 years age group signifies that health care costs will rise for these ages. Because costs per head are relatively low, however, the rise in costs will be marginal compared with what happens in other age groups.

Born 1966-1989: Persons in this group will be between 16 and 39 years of age by the year 2005. Because of the sharply declining birth rate during the period 1966-1983, the number of young people coming on to the labour market will become smaller and smaller all through the 1990s and the early years of the 21st century. If in addition immigration turns out to be lower than is assumed by Statistics Sweden, which seems likely, the number of young people will decrease still further.

The diminishing youth generations signify falling health care costs for this group. Because costs per head are relatively low at these ages, however, the cost reduction viewed over the whole spectrum is marginal. In relative figures there is a fall of 6% from 1983 to 2005.

The consequences for health care of the diminution of the numbers aged 16-39 years will be primarily in the field of labour recruitment. The reduced labour market intake in combination with the constant fall in the number of young people will probably lead to a shortage of young workers, more or less perceptible depending on economic conditions but especially apparent at boom periods. The care sector will very likely be hard hit in terms of recruitment prospects, which will enforce great organisational changes in the sector.

Crowns
in 1 000 000

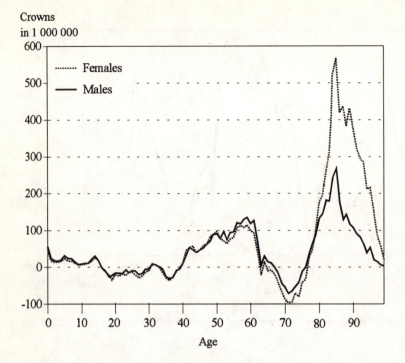

Diagram 3. The difference between health care costs in different age groups in 2005 and 1983.
Notes: Above 0 indicates that the health care costs will be higher in a specific age group 2005 than 1983.

Born 1939-65: Persons in this group will be aged 40-66 years by the year 2005. Sweden's biggest demographic change in absolute terms up to the year 2005 will consist of the massive increase in the numbers of middle-aged and elderly people in the labour force. Most notably there will be a substantial increase in the 50-60 years age group, resulting from the large numbers born during the 1940s who will then be coming up to this age.

It has been stated that the 1940s generation, by virtue of its size, has dominated the nation's development and values for a long time. We may cite as examples the education explosion during the 1950s and 1960s, the political radicalisation of the late 1960s, the expansion of day nurseries and the day-nurseries debate of the 1970s, the deregulation and income tax debate of the late 1980s. Because the 1940s generation is relatively large in numbers it has always been subject to strain, in terms both of its members' financial situation and of their career opportunities, which in turn, so it is alleged, has created social stress.

For self-evident reasons, health care costs will rise markedly because of the aging of the large 1940s generation. However, since the costs per head at ages 50-65 years are still relatively low there will be no dramatic increases in health care costs for this age group. In absolute figures, the age group's health care costs rise by 1 300 million *kronor*, which may be compared with the rise of 11 thousand million *kronor* in total health care costs.

It is possible that the social stress factors associated with the fact that the 1940s generation forms a large group will manifest themselves in rising costs per head compared with what was the case in 1983. But probably the 1940s generation's biggest influence on health care during the next few decades will be of an ideological nature: through their values and their impact on the public debate over health care.

Born 1925-1938: The persons in this group will be between 67 and 79 years of age by the year 2005. During the 1990s the group will contain the oldest segment of the labour force, and by 2005 all will have retired.

Diagram 2 shows that the number of persons in the age group will be appreciably lower in 2005 than in 1983, which results from heavily-falling birth rates in 1920-1935. If we assume that costs per head are unchanged, this signifies falling health care costs. Thus the health care costs for the age group will fall by about 7%.

However, we can assume that the age group's purchasing power will be considerably larger than that of earlier pensioner groups, provided that there are no fundamental changes in the pension system. The probable consequence of this will be a substantial impact on health care, home-help service and housing, mainly in the direction of improved quality.

Born prior to 1925: Everyone in this group will be over 80 years of age by the year 2005. The number of persons over 80 years of age will increase during the period 1983-2005 from about 290 000 to 480 000, i e by 190 000 or about 65%. Because there will probably be a more drastic decline in mortality than that assumed by Statistics Sweden in its forecast, the number in the age group will probably increase even more. At this point it may be observed that an important reason for the numbers in the age group to increase sharply is that many were born during the first two decades of the twentieth century. Even if mortality remains at the same level as now, which appears quite unrealistic, we should still get a sharp rise in the number of persons over 80 years of age until 2005.

If we take Statistics Sweden's prediction as a starting point, the health care costs of persons over 80 years of age during the period 1983-2005 go up by 75%. This is equivalent to an average cost increase of 2.6% per annum.

Some other figures which are relevant in this connection are as follows: In 1983, the 80-plus age group formed 3.5% of the total population. They accounted for 19% of health care costs in the same year. By the year 2005, the group will form 5% of the population and will then account for more than 27% of total health care costs.

Because costs per head are very high at ages above 80 years, a large part of the change which takes place in total health care costs will be determined in time to come by how many will be in the 80-plus age group. Relatively small changes in mortality, and thus in the numbers over 80 years of age, will entail great changes in health care costs.

Neutralising forces?

According to our diagnosis there is a strong demographic cost pressure on Swedish health care, primarily because the number of persons over 80 years of age is rising steeply. However, the possibility of neutralising forces cannot be ruled out. One such would be economic growth becoming high enough for health care to be provided with more resources. Another would be future technological advances assuming such a character as would ensue mainly in falling costs. A third would be the prevailing economic planning system becoming more efficient. Finally, it is possible that health care itself may become more efficient or may be furnished with larger resources through the application of market solutions. In the discussion below, however, it is our judgment that these forces will be unable to neutralise the strong demographic cost pressure on Swedish health care.

Economic growth

Rising health care costs occasioned by increase in the numbers of old people are by no means a new phenomenon. The proportion of old people in the Swedish population has increased in principle throughout the twentieth century, chiefly because the numbers born have fallen substantially. However, for a long time the cost increases ensuing from demographic developments could be absorbed relatively easily by means of an exceptional switching of resources into public health care. This shift of resources in turn was made possible by the extremely rapid growth of the Swedish economy, which viewed from an international perspective was unique. In such an economy, where health care costs were allowed to rise by up to 6% per year (which was usual for many years in the 1960s and 1970s), it was easy to remain passive, ignoring the fact that between a half and one per cent of this increase was occasioned by demographic changes.

In the latter part of the 1970s and during the 1980s, the situation has been quite different. Growth of production and productivity, in particular, has been low since 1985. Forecasts of the scale of resources which health care will require in future are difficult to make, because to a certain extent any such forecast must be based on guesswork as to the trend of economic growth in future. For a number of reasons, however, it would appear somewhat rash to express oneself too definitely on the subject of future economic developments. It suffices at this point to cite the uncertain effects on the Swedish economy of future possible membership of the European Union, to the difficulties of predicting international economic events, and to the challenges which confront Swedish business and industry in coping with the structural transformation currently under way.

However, most of the indications are that we can expect weak economic growth of the economy in the near future. Opinions among economic observers are divided on the subject of why Sweden will have weak economic growth. But the majority are agreed that future economic growth will be low.

Neither do political conditions exist at present for expecting there to be any major shift of resources into the public sector and into health care. The prevailing social climate scarcely gives scope for any major tax increases. Neither does it seem probable that within a foreseeable time there will be any revision of priorities with regard to the distribution of resources between health care and other public commitments.

That health care will be furnished with a substantial growth in new real resources, resulting from high economic growth or political decisions, therefore appears highly improbable. It will then not be possible to remain passive in face of a demographic pressure of 1 per cent per year.

Efficiency measures within the existing planning system

At present we are witnessing a clear trend in the direction of efficiency-improving measures in Swedish health care, the object being to increase cost-consciousness in health care and to exploit existing resources more effectively. We can point here to efforts to replace traditional budgetary control with specified targets in order to lessen detailed management and increase freedom of action of health care units. The move towards decentralised organisations with total cost responsibility is another example. The introduction of buyer-seller relations between different forms of health care units, population-based formulae for the allocation of resources, and new organisational forms are all further examples.

In other words, extensive efforts are being made to improve efficiency, but in our opinion these will lead to only limited positive results. This is because health care is a special good and there are such strong negative features in a planning system of the Swedish type. These negative features will probably become more and more noticeable when the demographic cost pressure increases and no new resources are provided.

* A planning system like the Swedish one is based on the price of health care services and consumers' incomes not being crucial in deciding who shall receive care. Because prices or costs are so low that the patient can wholly ignore them, there will usually be a high degree of over-demand.

* Available resources determine the entire consumption of health care. The county councils still act as producers and also finance health care; they have absolute power over what resources shall be allotted to health care in total. This leads to a sense of inability to control one's own situation and results in vociferous expressions of dissatisfaction with the way health care functions.

* The system has frequently created a self-generating cost spiral because the county councils are not compelled to determine priorities as between production of health care and other goods and services but only between refraining from funding more resources for health care and raising taxes. In many cases the county council finds itself in a dilemma and has difficulty in resisting arguments from the producer along the lines that: "If the clinic can't have this new piece of technical equipment Sven Andersson will die."

* The drawbacks of a planning system and the queues which exist in such a system are well known. People suffer as a result of having to wait a long time for medical treatment. Queues may also signify socioeconomic inefficiency. A six-month waiting period for a gallstone operation involves a loss of production which is considerably higher than the cost of the operation.

* In the planning system, the opportunities for increasing efficiency are few and frail, because there are no incentives in the system to obtain sufficient information about what different health care services cost, or about the effects which health care services have.

* The poor incentives for improving efficiency are associated in high degree with the fact that the Swedish system has traditionally been aligned towards expansion, in which the efficiency requirement was not a primary goal. However, when conditions change and it becomes necessary to economise the existing resources and revise the priorities for their use, it is difficult for the planning system to adapt itself to the new situation.

* In the existing planning system, moreover, there is little competition between producers, and this leads to a cost spiral. If the consumer's consumption is independent of price and he knows that a third party, i e central government, county council or local authority, is paying, then the consumer demands the highest-quality care available and therefore usually the dearest. The producer too is anxious to offer the best and therefore the most expensive care, since indirectly and in the long run this increases both his scale of activity and his influence as well as his income.

* In principle, the only external signal which the system gives to the producer as to where more resources are needed is the length of the queue. Moreover, it is the case that the production unit uses the length of the queue as an argument to get more resources from the county council.

* Furthermore, the weakness of the system is that the length of the queue reflects a demand which is difficult to define. The system also suffers from the weakness that it is chiefly those who have time and opportunity to queue, or who have vociferous deputies to represent them, who can influence how resources are shared out between those seeking care.

In sum: our verdict is that in the long run, the scope for efficiency-improving measures within a planning system is only limited, because of the special character of health care and the inherent weaknesses of the planning system.

Market solutions

There are two ways in which market solutions have been entering the health care sector: expansion of the private sector and introduction of quasi-markets in the public sector.

Since the middle of the 1980s, we have seen element of private market initiative being enlarged: flying weekend-operation teams, offers of private care for business leaders, the growth of private clinics, private care centres and nursing homes, and so forth. In other words we are seeing a trend towards the establishment of care markets based on direct patient influence in the buying process. It is possible that this could result in a certain amount of self-healing as a result of people's avoiding some of the planning system's weaknesses and making use instead of the market system's methods of improving efficiency and saving costs.

The pure market economy is a utopia, however. In point of fact the market economy needs strong safeguards in the form of legislation in order to be capable of surviving controlled competition. In reality, therefore, the majority of what we call free markets are more or less controlled. Examples of this are price agreements, cartelisation, limitation of entry and so on, all of which are justified on the ground sometimes of the advantages of large scale and sometimes of the desirability of certain social goals. In so-called market economies we often see the consequences of these imperfections in the form of inefficient production and over-consumption of certain goods and services. Even when efforts are made by the authorities to preserve the market, there are frequently strong neutralising forces. The Dutch and American examples in the health care field are illuminating in this respect. In the Netherlands, attempts have been made by the state to increase competition among health care producers and the insurance companies which usually pay for the financing of health care. However, the insurance companies endeavour to evade competition by means of various types of agreement. The American system, featuring relatively heavy government involvement, weak incentives for cost-effective solutions in the insurance system, a legal system which encourages over-consumption in the form of defensive medicine (excessive precautionary tests, etc.) to avoid liability claims and high court costs, is another example of a system which many would undeservedly call a free market, but in which there are strong market imperfections.

Another hindrance to the pure market economy is formed by the severe entry restrictions which exist in health care, for example arising from official accreditation requirements. But many would assert that there are no reasons for restrictions as severe as we currently have in the Swedish system, and that competition could be increased in this field.

The information requirement which the pure market economy presupposes may be met in various degrees. The more imperfect the information, the less efficient the production. Lack of information is one of the big problems in health care. This stems partly from the fact that it is hard for the consumer to judge the quality and effects of the care received. The consumer is always at a disadvantage in this respect *vis-à-vis* the producer. It has also been found difficult to devise procedures for improving the flow of information between consumer and producer in health care.

There is one special factor in health care which complicates the development of market solutions. In the simplest form of markets, all transactions take place between buyers and sellers. In health care, we seldom find this simple relationship. For good reasons, one of them being that illness strikes at random and may require expensive treatment, there is insurance cover in all health care systems. Insurance cover introduces a third party into the system, which complicates payment transactions and the purchasing process in health care. Third party financing means in principle that when a third party, the insurer, is paying the bill, patient and doctor can agree about treatment without considering the costs of treatment. The incentive existing in the market model to find the cheapest means of care has disappeared.

Nevertheless some slight element of cost-consciousness is beginning to creep into traditional health care. The debate today focuses primarily on how public-sector health care is to be made more efficient and how competition is to be sharpened within the public framework. Attempts are being made at market-style solutions in public health care (the family doctor reform, increased competition between hospitals, decentralisation). This will probably lead to improved thrift with existing resources and shorter queues. But there are many indications that this increased cost-consciousness can have only a limited impact on the system's intrinsic weaknesses (cf. also below). Probably the shortcomings of the planning system will become increasingly obvious when the demographic cost pressure grows and insignificant new resources are made available for health care. Hence the scope for increased efficiency and cost-reductions through increased application of market solutions within existing systems also appears limited.

Medical technology[5]

Forecasts of how technical progress will affect health care costs in future are likewise fraught with great weaknesses and have significant inbuilt elements of uncertainty.

Technical progress is commonly thought to mean primarily the ability to produce a given quantity of goods and services at lower cost. Rapid technical progress in medicine, however, has often had an entirely different character. Some innovations have been cost-reducing, but they have frequently represented a technique which has both raised costs and improved the possibilities of clinical treatment. The development of medical technology is often focused on product innovations rather than process innovations.[6]

At a general level the experiences of the most recent decades unequivocally suggest that on average new medical technology inflates cost. In 1960, health care costs were equivalent to 4.7% of GNP while the corresponding figure now is about 9.0% of (a considerably higher) GNP. This can hardly be interpreted solely as a function, for example, of a positive income elasticity for health care as a good.[7]

Health care costs are strongly dependent both on the application of existing medical technology and on the development of new technology. It is possible, but in our opinion not very likely, that developments in this field will solve the financial problems of health care managers. It is more probable that technical advances will be cost-inflating rather than cost-saving in their effects. This applies especially to a situation with an aging population.

Application of existing medical technology

Against the background of Sweden's demographic development, two aspects are particularly interesting as far as the application of existing medical technologies is concerned. The first is the general question of the circumstances in which it is deci-

---

5 "Medical technology" is used here in the narrower sense of care technology and accordingly does not primarily include aspects such as work organisation, administration or financing.
6 Cf. e g Zweifel (1992).
7 Cf. the similar discussion in Newhouse (1992). In international comparisons of aggregated health care expenditure one usually finds an "income elasticity" in the interval 1.0-1.5. See McGuire et al (1993) for a discussion of these results.

ded to exchange an old technique for a new. The other is that indications may be subject to change as time goes on, so that a given technology is applied to new patient groups. The latter has special significance for the health care costs of older people.

Decisions in health care are often considered to reflect what Victor Fuchs called a "technological imperative" - always to give patients the best care that is technically possible.[8] This effect can make itself felt both when a new medical technology is being introduced in Sweden and when a known technology is being applied to new patient groups. The technological imperative may manifest itself in a number of different ways.[9] In the first place it may be regarded as an imperative of the medical profession, with the implication that people should have all the care of which they can make use, i e the patient should receive care until its marginal productivity is very low. Such an interpretation of the doctor's role is close to the Hippocratic ideal and the traditional medical ethic of Western countries (to do good). It may also be a natural consequence of the fact that neither the individual patient nor the doctor has any reason to pay heed to the cost of care - a characteristic of many third party-financed health care systems (a "moral hazard" effect). Finally, doctors would rather demand more resources than decide that certain patients are not to receive any more care.[10]

In the second place, by seizing on the word "technological" it is possible to interpret the imperative as a tendency to overcapitalisation in health care production. The material prosperity of the Western world is intimately linked psychologically with "high technology", automation and the use of advanced equipment. This experience has formed people's "belief system", which influences their behaviour.[11] In the health care field it is therefore probable that high quality is associated with care which uses apparatus as new and advanced as possible. Such conceptions can be found among the medical profession,[12] and are at least equally possible among patients. The latter, as has been remarked, are badly informed concerning the value of different alternative treatments,[13] and can be expected to request hi-tech care.

In the third place, we may need to take a health imperative into account, so that there is a tendency always to opt for the alternative (the technology) which gives the patient the best health.

While the professional imperative implies a general and constant overconsumption of care, both overcapitalisation and the health imperative put a premium on the introduction of cost-raising new technologies. Appreciation of "high technology" probably leads people to opt for the technology which uses the most physical capital in absolute terms (rather than putting a premium on capital-intensive production for example). And the higher the costs involved in a given technical solution, the more likely it is that it consumes more physical capital than the alternatives, *ceteris*

---

8 Fuchs (1968).
9 See Lyttkens (1992) for a more detailed and formal analysis of the different imperatives.
10 Hernes (1975).
11 North (1993).
12 " ... there is no denying that physicians have been trained to favor sophisticated gadgetry" Harris (1977), p. 480).
13 The existence of asymmetrical information between doctors and patients concerning the quality of care and its value to the patient is one of the classic arguments in health economics. See e g Evans (1984), McGuire, Henderson and Mooney (1992), Weisbrod (1978).

paribus. With the health imperative on the other hand, an entire class of cost-diminishing new technologies is rejected, viz those which mean that the patient cannot expect to achieve the same condition of health as with the old treatment. Even such technologies could be regarded as welfare-raising provided the saving is sufficiently large in relation to the inferior health result. However, they are disqualified by the health imperative. They conflict both with the traditional medical ethic, with its concentration on the individual patient, and with the interests of the patients affected. Pressure groups consisting of doctors and patients can easily arise and neutralise the introduction of such technologies. The potential winners (the taxpayers), on the other hand, are often considerably more difficult to organise.[14]

For older groups of patients, it now becomes a question of their relatively weaker ability, because of age, to develop pressure groups compared with their growing numbers. New medical technology and new applications of technology already known will probably be focused on diseases of the elderly as the numbers of old people keep increasing. The prevailing values will make it hard to resist a technique that brings improvements in the form of increased lifespan for the many, even if the consequence is ever-spiralling costs.

Use of a medical technology is not infrequently limited to certain patient groups. These limits change as time goes on, which has effects on the future costs of care. Limitations to special patient groups can be justified in two main ways. Either there is uncertainty as to whether the treatment in question would form a welfare gain for other patients or else the limitation is occasioned by a shortage of resources. The latter opens interesting perspectives, because in all likelihood the professional imperative is not absolute but instead is connected with the sacrifices which have to be made in order to obtain further improvements in health. It means that with rising real incomes - and thus diminishing marginal utility of other consumption - the limit of least acceptable health effect will be shifted, so that the professional imperative will demand greater efforts on behalf of a given patient.[15] In other words we can expect the indication limit to be widened so that, for example, more individuals with "high" blood pressure or "high" cholesterol levels will be defined as needing treatment. This raises the per capita costs of health care.

It also seems probable that per capita costs will rise most among the elderly. Of course the incidence of health problems increases with age in many cases: stiffening of the joints, high blood pressure, brittle bones and so forth. An enlargement of the indications means that in such cases more old people, relatively speaking, will begin to be treated.[16]

An interesting special case in this context is that age itself sometimes functions as an indication. We know from experience that at a given point in time there are medical technologies where the treatment is not applied because the patient is "too old". In such cases it is often not a question of officially-established age limits but of the age limits forming a part of the informal rules structure applied at a given health care

---

14 Olson (1965).

15 Health care has positive income elasticity at the individual level, see e g Manning et al (1987).

16 However, it is not entirely certain that costs per head always increase more for the elderly. E g a one-off procedure may be carried out at increasingly early ages.

unit. Here too the underlying reason can be seen as shortage of resources and/or uncertainty as to the health or welfare gains for older patients.[17]

First let it be stated that if age constitutes the only visible indication not to treat a given patient, then this presents a strong challenge to change either the technology or the resource situation, that is, a strong latent pressure for expansion. This follows from the imperative, as well as from the ideal of justice in the care sector. "Equal access to health care" is embodied in the wording of the aims of most health care systems, including the Swedish,[18] and one of the ideas embraced in this is probably that patients with the same diagnosis should have access to the same type of treatment irrespective of whether they can be expected to derive different levels of benefit from it in terms of expected health effects. Age limits then imply disparity of access to care as between different age groups and also between geographical regions, since the informal rules can be expected to vary.

If the reason for the age limit is a general shortage of resources, it is not self-evident that it will be changed as time goes on, but the latent expansionary pressure means that any possible resource surplus in one part of the health care sector will immediately be eaten up; in other words there is an asymmetry between resource surplus and resource deficit. In such a case the effect of a cost-reducing technical advance will be that the technique will be applied further up the age scale. Therefore it can bring lower costs per head at lower ages and higher costs per head at higher ages. Total costs may be raised as well, especially with an aging population.

There may also exist a shortage of specific resources. The availability of specially-trained personnel may form a bottleneck. Such a shortage of resources probably comes to an end in time. It is true that the owner of the limited resource has monopoly rents to win, but in a health care system like the Swedish system it is more probable that the bureaucratic tendencies towards size- or budget-maximisation will carry the day and new specialists be trained (improved career openings, status etc.).

Finally we come to the possibility that the age limit results from uncertain health gains for older patients. A probable development, especially bearing in mind the above-cited imperative, is a gradual change in the technology so that health gains are guaranteed for older patients as well. Even without such a development occurring, however, a drift of the age limit is to be expected. In slightly simplified terms the situation can be said to arise either from the functioning of age as an indicator of the general state of health or from the expected lifespan after the treatment being too short to justify the trauma entailed in the procedure. In both cases, a parallel development in other sectors of medical knowledge can make the treatment of the older patients in question more attractive. Technological changes in other fields (the health imperative!) mean that the patients in question show better and better general condition and expected lifespan. The consequence is that treatment which was formerly of doubtful justification comes to be applied further up the age ladder. Whether this is

---

17 A third conceivable reason may sometimes be that a given technology is tried out initially on younger persons, so that clinical documentation for older patients is lacking. Here we would expect a continuous extension of the indications to include more and more older patients, for the same reasons as those which will be adduced in the discussion below.

18 See e g Lyttkens (1994), Mooney et al (1991), Steen (1993) and Wagstaff and van Doorslaer (1993).

cost-raising obviously depends on the treatment technology that is replaced. But experience suggests that active curative medical interventions are often dearer than caring.

In this way we can expect that in every time period a number of medical technologies originally reserved for younger patient groups will little by little come into use with older people as well. As suggested above, there are indications that the majority of these technologies will be cost-raising in their effect.

Active uremia treatment and open heart surgery provide illustrations of how informal age limits are shifted step by step without the necessity of entering at this point into the cause in the respective cases or discussing how they affected care costs. Of new admissions for active treatment of uremia in Sweden, 23% were over 65 years of age in 1982, which had risen to over 50% by 1992.[19] The growth of heart surgery is illustrated in Table 3 below.[20] These are two of our most expensive methods of treatment in absolute terms, which obviously says nothing about the productivity of the respective activity. The price per coronary artery by-pass grafting is around 100 000 *kronor*, and the health care cost for one patient with institutional dialysis is more than 400 000 *kronor* per year.

Table 3. Number of operations for acquired heart disease in Lund-Landskrona 1982 and 1992, age distribution (percentage in brackets)

	0-69	70-74	75-79	80+
1982	258 (90)	27 (9)	3 (1)	0
1992	948 (68)	262 (19)	151 (11)	28 (2)

Source: *Thoraxkirurgiska kliniken* (Thoracic surgery clinic), University Hospital, Lund.

A comparison with the trend of per capita costs of care of the elderly during earlier periods is instructive. Ulf Gerdtham and Bengt Jönsson have studied the changes in age-specific costs of health care during the period 1976-1985, using costs at relatively broad age-intervals.[21] Their findings show health care costs per person to have risen between 1976 and 1985 by 14.2% for ages 0-14 years and by 0.3% for ages 15-44 years. For ages 45-64 years, however, the cost per person fell by 3.8%, while for persons aged 65-74 years and 75-plus, health care costs per person went up by 16.7% and 54.3% respectively. In other words, over a ten-year period per capita costs rose by more than 50% in the case of the very oldest, while at the same time the per capita costs for middle-aged persons remained largely unchanged.[22]

---

19 *Aktiv uremivård*, p 22, and Schön, Staffan, secretary general of the Swedish National Registry of the Active Treatment of Uremia, personal communication.
20 The number of operations has increased over recent years as well, while at the same time other types of treatment are being developed (percutaneous transluminal coronary angioplasty (PTCA)) or being improved (medication).
21 Gerdtham and Jönsson (1991).
22 Barer et al. (1987) found similar results for Canada. During the period 1971-1982/3, for example, consumption of health care (hospital treatment) rose by 16% in the case of males aged 80 years and above while the average for all men fell by 14%; compared with the

We began by tracing the various imperatives back to medical ethics, to health care financing and remuneration systems, and to attitudes to "high technology". Of these, as already observed, the current financial and remuneration systems are in process of being changed. Quasi-markets, fee-for-service and capitation payments have begun to replace the traditional budget system with salaried doctors. In this way the doctor - who often has more influence on health care decisions than the patient - will begin to feel the economic consequences of treatment decisions. The capitation system, which is to be introduced into Swedish primary care, should exercise a restraining influence on the introduction of cost-raising medical technology, even though this system's cost-moderating effects in the American environment are chiefly a function of reduced hospital admissions in the Health Maintenance Organizations.[23] Because the object in today's situation is that primary care doctors should compete for patients, there is still an obvious possibility that people will prefer doctors who use "high technology" and that there will therefore be a cost-inflating competition between doctors. (They are not allowed to compete on price.) The introduction of DRG or similar payment systems may also have a cost-moderating effect, provided that cost-reductions represent the most effective strategy for producers compared, for example, with looking for gaps in the DRG system itself.[24] Fee-for-service elements will in fact probably have an encouraging effect on the introduction of new, expensive forms of treatment whose rate structure may be difficult for the finance-provider to penetrate. The effects of quasi-markets are more difficult to judge. With respect to internal markets in hospitals, for example, clinics have incentives to avoid buying-in services from laboratories, the cleaning unit, etc. At the same time, the clinics receive direct payment for what is produced, and this payment will probably be determined chiefly from the cost side.[25] As regards *competition* between health care producers, it is perfectly possible that quality- and cost-raising competition will arise,[26] while at the same time it has been shown that a well thought-out policy of *managed* competition may have a cost-moderating effect.[27]

To sum up: it appears possible but far from certain that new forms of financing and remuneration will have a restraining effect on the introduction of new, cost-raising medical technology. It seems less likely that they will change the fundamental logic of the system, with its imperatives of various kinds.

If the costs per head for every age group were to continue to change in the same way as during the period 1976-1985 and the number of old people were to rise in conformity with the forecast, then the total costs of health care during the period 1983-2005 would increase by almost 100% at 1983 money values. Such an explosive growth of health care costs is obviously an impossibility and will never be able to

---

average, the consumption of care rose by 35% among the oldest people. The effect was even greater in the case of women.

23 Manning et al (1984).

24 In the United States strategies such as "patient-shifting", "cost-shifting" and "DRG-creep" (change in classification practice) are reported.

25 Lyttkens (1993).

26 Cf Joskow (1983), Pope (1989), Robinson and Luft (1987 and 1988)) and for the Swedish situation Lyttkens (1993).

27 See e g Robinson and Luft (1988) and Melnick et al. (1992).

happen in practice. In all likelihood, costs per head over large areas of old people's care have reached a ceiling. But the figures still spotlight the great challenges - ethical and financial - which confront Swedish health care in the shape of an increased number of old people in combination with the fact that expensive medical methods are being used higher and higher up the age scale.

Development of new medical technology

In a number of works, Burton Weisbrod has used a classification of medical technology and knowledge in three categories with respect to the treatment of various ailments and their effects on costs.[28] The first category is termed "nontechnology" and consists of the treatment of ailments whose basic causes are unknown and whose symptoms cannot be dealt with effectively either. If any treatment is given at all, it consists of general and non-specific care and support along with help for the patient, and is relatively cheap. Historically, this type of treatment has predominated in the care of the sick. As examples of current ailments which are treated in this way we may cite strokes, cirrhosis of the liver and certain types of cancer. The second category is termed "halfway technology" and comprises treatment of the symptoms of certain ailments where knowledge of the basic causes is lacking. This technology adapts itself to the ailment and prolongs life but does not effect a cure. This also makes it very expensive. Examples which can be cited are transplants, most treatments of cancer and heart conditions. The third category is termed "high technology" and consists of measures to counteract the onset of, or to cure, a specific ailment, being the result of our having acquired understanding of the underlying causes. Such technology usually takes the form of vaccine or medicaments and is therefore cheap. Some examples are the modern treatment of tuberculosis, polio and diphtheria.

As Diagram 4 shows, the various technologies are usually associated with great differences in costs per patient. The total costs of health care at a given time then consist of the sum of costs for the treatment of different ailments, the treatment technology of which is at different stages.

According to Burton Weisbrod, we have gradually moved during the twentieth century from "nontechnology" to "halfway technology", and in his view this is an important explanation of the rising costs of health care. In the instances where we have moved from "halfway technology" to "high technology", which should then have a cost-reducing effect, these have often taken the form of becoming able to prevent or cure ailments which afflicted young people, such as tuberculosis, polio and diphtheria. The long-run consequence, however, has frequently been a move to "halfway technology". Instead of dying young, and cheaply in terms of health care, we now die, much later and expensively, of cancer or heart ailments. In other words the paradoxical consequence has ensued that the healthier we become and the longer we live, the more expensive for the health care system we become in the end.

---

28 See e g the outline article in the Journal of Economic Literature, Weisbrod (1991). The distinction goes back to Thomas (1975).

Costs per patient

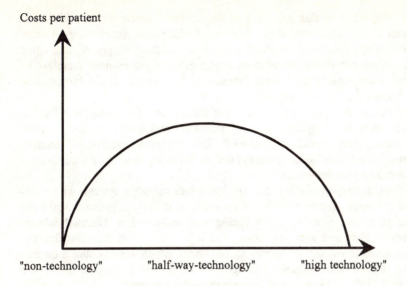

"non-technology"   "half-way-technology"   "high technology"

Diagram 4. Various technologies and costs per patient.
Source: Weisbrod (1991).

In assessing the future it is important to observe that technological advance is not a chance phenomenon. What new techniques are produced depends on the incentives in the organisations where research and development take place.[29] In part, incentives follow directly from what has been said above concerning the *application* of existing technologies. In all likelihood the production of new knowledge in the field of medical technology is governed to a large extent by which technologies have a good chance of being applied in practical health care. This is self-evidently true of private firms, pharmaceutical companies and others, which produce new technology for profit reasons. Much of the technological development carried out in non-profit environments, in practice usually by doctors, is probably also concentrated primarily on technologies which can be expected to achieve practical application. In this way the various imperatives and the choice between existing medical technologies have repercussions on long-term development of new technology, and we may expect more cost-raising than cost-reducing new technologies.

Technical development is also a long-term process. A new drug may take 15-20 years to develop from idea to finished product. Drugs represent the extreme case at present, but other technologies too require researchers to be trained, the research environment to be adapted, and other long-term factors allowed for. Today's medical technology is therefore a function of incentives which extend a long way back in time, and the technological development of the next 10-20 years is to some extent already focused on certain types of solutions.

---

29 Stoddart and Feeny (1986), Weisbrod (1991).

It is very important at this point not to forget that Sweden (as is indeed self-evident) forms only a small part of the total market for medical technology. Home-produced technology forms only a small part of the existing supply of alternative technologies. What sort of incentives there are in other countries must therefore be kept in mind, most notably the United States, which of course is the largest sub-market for modern medical technology.

Weisbrod has pointed out the significance of the fact that for a long time fee-for-service combined with retrospective cost-compensation was wholly dominant on the American market (and is still important).[30] The system is exceedingly tolerant towards cost-raising technological progress and so is largely lacking in incentives to produce cost-reducing technologies.

A supplementary aspect of this is that the incentives in budget systems with retrospective compensation may be regarded if anything as directly negative towards the development of certain types of cost-reducing new technologies. Doctors' salaries form a principal item in health care costs, and it is not easy to find anything but negative incentives in the sort of technological change which would entail a decreased need for doctors' time: shrinking budgets, fewer vacant posts, less favourable career prospects, difficulties in recruiting younger colleagues etc.

An important factor in confronting the future will be the way in which the remuneration of producers will be divided between retrospective and prospective payment (e g capitation) in different countries and how this will influence the propensity to choose (and therefore also develop) new cost-raising technologies. The main international trends here seem to be increased use of the capitation system and managed competition, which has already been discussed.

As mentioned above, capitation has shown itself to be cost-moderating in the American environment, but these effects remain to be proved in health care systems which are less cost-expansive at their starting point.[31] Competition is a more ambiguous phenomenon in terms of its effects on health care costs and the application of cost-raising medical technology. Firstly we lack empirical knowledge of the way in which the various competitive systems function, and secondly we can partly foresee that the effects will be dependent on the (often still obscure) details of their design.

A realistic judgment seems to be that the international market will put less of a premium than before on cost-raising innovations. It still remains to be seen, however, whether this will go far enough to achieve neutrality between cost-raising and cost-reducing technologies. Moreover, the health imperative suggests that among the available technologies the one that is always selected is the one which has the greatest effect on the patient's health, and the impact of this is cost-inflationary, as described above. Even if the international scientific community were to begin producing a larger proportion of cost-reducing innovations, therefore, the effect on cost increases might well be limited.

---

30 Weisbrod (1991).
31 Pedersen (1991).

Further complications?

In other words, it is our opinion that no sufficiently strong forces exist to be able to neutralise the demographic cost pressure. Instead we believe that complications are setting in which are closely linked with demographic developments.

There will be more old people than was previously thought

In the quantitative demographic diagnoses presented earlier we have made use of the forecast of Statistics Sweden. In order to ascertain the number of old people this forecast makes a straight-line projection to the turn of the century of the most recent years' mortality trends for different ages. It is assumed that the decline in mortality slackens after the turn of the century, the justification for this being that there are physiological, genetic and medical limits to the possibilities of prolonging life.

However, there are reasons suggesting that mortality will fall more than Statistics Sweden supposes. Intensive research is going on at present with a view to establishing the upper limit of human life. Most researchers disagree with earlier conceptions, believing that the maximum biological age for human life is about 120 years and that there is therefore much scope for a continued decline in mortality. There are also hypotheses of substantially reduced mortality in future ensuing from advances in medical techniques, improved welfare especially for the old, enhanced awareness concerning health questions (dietary habits, exercise, smoking etc), which now suggest that old people will become more numerous than has hitherto been believed.

If in addition the trend projection were to be made on the basis of mortality as it has evolved over a lengthy historical period, and especially if it were then based on mortality changes in the various birth cohorts (the so-called cohort method), then in all probability the result would be a forecast signalling a considerably steeper fall in mortality, and thus a larger number of old people, than indicated by the Statistics Sweden's forecast.

Sometimes it is suggested that calculations of how many old people there will be in future are irrelevant. According to this view, it is not age itself but the time-distance from death that is of significance for health care costs. Increased average lifespan and more old people would therefore not impose any extra strain on health care. On this interpretation the costs of health care would be the same irrespective of whether a person died when he was 75 or 80 years old. The majority of empirical studies tell against such an opinion. An increased average lifespan probably means both more years of health and more years of illness. For example, it takes a long time to die of Alzheimer's disease, but the tendency to be afflicted with this illness increases markedly with age. The costs of health care are therefore determined in high degree by how many older persons there are in a society.

In other words there is much to suggest that complications arise from the fact that the very oldest people are becoming more numerous than we had hitherto believed. How serious an impact these complications will have on health care as a whole is difficult to determine, however. A rough estimate based on an alternative forecast suggests that the numbers aged 80-plus will be at least 10% higher in the year 2005 than indicated by the Statistics Sweden's forecast. This alternative forecast is based on a long-term perspective, i e the trend of the death risk for persons over 80 years of age since the Second World War.

The number of lone old people is rising

That health care costs are high if there are many old people almost goes without saying. However, what is of equal significance for the nation's scale of health care costs is whether the elderly reside alone or cohabit. The need of lone persons for care via the public system is considerably higher than that of cohabitants.

There are no statistics or studies showing health care costs according to civil status and age. However, the differences in health care costs between lone persons and cohabitants can be illustrated indirectly by examining the differences in costs between the sexes. If we assume that the difference we observe between women's and men's costs per head reflect the fact that there are more lone women than lone men, it is relatively easy to demonstrate that the costs per head of lone persons in 1983 at 75 years of age and over were twice as high as those of cohabitants (35 900 *kronor* compared with 17 080 *kronor*).

Changes going on in the pattern of the family, and especially increased divorce frequencies and the prevailing disparities in mortality between men and women, will mean that it will be lone old people who increase in numbers up to the year 2005. A forecast of the civil status composition of the Swedish population up to the year 2050 has been made by Tommy Bengtsson and Agneta Kruse under the auspices of IIASA.[32] According to this forecast, the number of lone persons over 75 years of age will increase by about 150 000 during the period 1985-2005, while the numbers of old people cohabiting during the same period will increase by only 40 000.

The result of a detailed computation would probably show higher costs. In our opinion the significance of civil status has been entirely overlooked in discussions of the influence of old people on future health care costs.

Complications arising from the organisation of health care

In our opinion demographic developments will give rise to further complications occasioned by the organisation of health care. The inflexibility and rigidity which characterise this organisation mean that difficulties will present themselves in the redistribution of resources between different areas of health care.

In the demographic diagnosis adduced earlier a determination was made of the net changes in health care costs and how these will look until 2005. In a net calculation of this sort account it is assumed that a redistribution of resources is effected from age groups where costs fall to age groups where they rise. Having regard to the political reality in which we live and the inflexibility of the health care apparatus, such a

---

32 Bengtsson and Kruse (1992).

redistribution appears unrealistic. This is particularly so in the present situation with the ÄDEL reform, in which local authorities assume the main responsibility for the elderly (nursing homes, some aspects of long-term care etc). For example, it is difficult to imagine that psychiatric care, in which the demographic changes will bring reduced costs, will hand over resources to local authorities, whether voluntarily or by negotiation, in order to enable the latter to meet the increased needs of old people.

If we use as a measure of the demographic cost pressure not the net changes in health care costs but the sum of the surplus costs arising in the age groups which increase from 1983 to 2005 while ignoring the cost changes in the age groups which decline in numbers, the result this gives is a rise of 13.1 thousand million *kronor*, i e a rise of 22.5%. In our opinion this is a considerably more realistic and plausible measure of the demographic influence on future health care costs than net changes (10.7 thousand million *kronor*).

We have confined ourselves here to analysing the influence of demographic factors on health care, basing ourselves on the definition of health care made previously in the national accounts. However, the demographic developments will entail even greater strains on local authorities in terms of their costs and their assumption of responsibility for service housing, home-help service and concessionary travel. We have carried out here certain model calculations of local authorities' costs. It should be pointed out that the data in existence on the age-specific costs of old people's care are much inferior to the corresponding health care figures. But despite the shortcomings of the material it is possible to show that the age structure and cost structure by age of those who made use of old people's care services in 1983 were much the same as those pertaining to pensioners in long-term care.

If we base ourselves on the age-specific costs of old people's care in 1983 and assume that in real terms these will be the same in 2005, it is also possible to show that local authorities' costs will increase by about 50% up to the year 2005, depending on the changes in the age structure. This in turn can be compared with the demographic cost pressure of about 20% which we arrived at earlier for health care in general. Hence because of the ÄDEL reform, local authorities will take over and administer the elements of health care where the demographic cost pressure is most intense, i e nursing homes and certain aspects of long-term care.

In other words, the local authorities will be subjected to strong demographic cost pressure during the next 15 years. The county councils, on the other hand, which will retain mainly the activities in which demographic changes play a subordinate role in the trend of costs, only feel this cost pressure marginally. A model calculation shows that the county councils' costs will rise by 10% and the local authorities' by 50%, depending on the changes in the age structure.

Final verdict

In our original diagnosis the demographic rise in costs during the period 1983-2005 was established at 11 thousand million *kronor* in 1983 money values, which is equivalent to a rise of 18%. To maintain the same standard in 2005 as in 1983 will require extra resources equivalent to this amount to be switched into health care. Alternatively, efficiency would need to rise to enable the standard to be maintained at significantly lower costs.

In our judgment neither the one nor the other alternative will come to pass. Complications closely associated with demographic developments will supervene instead, making the need for resources and efficiency considerably greater than 11 thousand million.

In all probability the number of old people will rise by more than has been estimated in various forecasts. It is also easy to foresee that further complications will emerge by virtue of the fact that it is primarily the lone elderly who increase in numbers. Most of the signs also point to the inflexibility and rigidity of the health care apparatus persisting, which will bring complications by making the redistribution of resources in health care more difficult. Taken all in all these complications mean that health care costs will rise by at least 25% during the period 1983-2005. To this one should add the possible complications which can arise from the ÄDEL reform.

The most serious general problem seems to be that old people will go on increasing in numbers and that expensive medical methods will be used higher and higher up the age scale. If the trend which displayed itself during the period 1975-1985 should continue into the future as well - with sharply rising per capita costs for old people coinciding with increasing numbers of them - then health care costs will more or less double during the period 1983-2005.

However, it is considerably more difficult to arrive at a credible forecast of how future medical and technological developments will influence the costs for different age groups than it is to predict complications which are conditioned by demographic factors. A credible forecast has to be based on a well-founded theory. Our knowledge of the driving forces underlying medical and technical developments is very defective, however. Up to now, new techniques have been developed along two different lines. In some cases the consequences have been to make possible a reduction in costs, for example laparoscopic surgery which has resulted in substantial rationalisations. However, the predominant line of development has been that the scope for clinical treatment has been improved and that costs have risen. The medical technology seems to have been evolved mainly via its own inherent professional logic, often imported from outside, in which general economic principles seldom seem to have underlain the development or application of the new technique.

An obvious reason why it is difficult to predict future technical developments in medicine is that it is possible to influence them to a much greater extent than demographic developments. A degree of cost-consciousness is beginning to penetrate slowly into health care. In all likelihood this increased cost-consciousness in combination with limited resources must gradually also have some effect on technical developments, making it more and more possible that they may assume a cost-reducing bias.

To sum up: it is difficult to know anything about future medical and technological developments, but there are several reasons - prevailing values and the planning system which still wholly dominates the scene - which suggest that in the short term their effect will be to raise costs, while other reasons, mainly an increased cost-consciousness, suggest that in the long term they will reduce costs. It is difficult to say what the nature of this turn-round in the orientation of technological development will be or when it will occur. But to grasp the opportunities at hand in order to bring about such a turn-round, especially as regards the care of old people, indubitably presents the greatest challenge facing Swedish health care in time to come.

The authors thank Johan Brandt, Tore Lindholm, Staffan Schön and Kerstin Westman for their kind assistance in the assembling of material for this chapter.

REFERENCES

Bengtsson T, Kruse A (1992) Demographic Effects on the Swedish Pension System. Working Paper IIASA, May 1992.

Culyer A, Maynard A, Posnett JW (eds) (1990) Competition in Health Care. Reforming the NHS. London, MacMillan.

Lyttkens CH (1993) Avreglering av svensk sjukvård: seglats på öppna men stormiga hav? in Collin S, Hansson L (eds) Kommunal organisation i förändring. Lund, Studentlitteratur.

Manning WG et al. (1984) A controlled trial of the effect of prepaid group practice on the use of services. New England Journal of Medicine 310, 1505-1510.

Maynard A, Hutton J (1992) Health Care Reform: The Search for the Holy Grail (editorial), Health Economics 1, 1-3

Ohlsson R (1991) Sjukvårdskostnader och demografisk struktur (Health care costs and demographic structure). Lund, The Swedish Institute for Health Economics.

Saltman RB (1992) Recent Health Policy Initiatives in the Nordic Countries. Health Care Financing Review 13:4, 157-166.

Saltman RB von Otter C (1992) Planned Markets and Public Competition: Strategic Reform in Northern European Health Systems. London, Open University Press.

Thomas L (1975) The Lives of A Cell. New York, Bantam Books.

van de Ven W (1990) From Regulated Cartel to Regulated Competition in the Dutch Health Care System. European Economic Review 34, 632-645.

van de Ven W (1991) Perestrojka in the Dutch Health Care System. European Economic Review 35, 430-440.

Zweifel P (1992) Diffusion of hospital innovations in different institutional settings. Paper presented to the Colloque Européen, Paris, December 1992.

REFERENCES, continued

Aktiv uremivård. Socialstyrelsen redovisar 1983:11.

Anell A (1990) Från central planering till lokalt ansvar. Budgeteringens roll i landstingskommunal sjukvård. Lund Studies in Economics and Management, The Institute of Economic Research. Lund, Lund University Press.

Anell A, Svarvar P (1993) Reformerad landstingsmodell - En kartläggning och analys av pågående förnyelse. In Hälso- och sjukvården i framtiden, SOU 1993:38, 243-297.

Barer ML et al. (1987) Aging and Health Care Utilization: New Evidence on Old Fallacies. Social Science and Medicine 24, 851-862.

Evans R (1984) Strained Mercy. Toronto, Butterworth.

Fuchs VR (1968) The Growing Demand for Medical Care. The New England Journal of Medicine 279, 190-195.

Gerdtham U, Jönsson B (1990) Sjukvårdskostnader i framtiden - vad betyder ålders-faktorn? Rapport till Expertgruppen för studier i offentlig ekonomi, Ds 1990:39. Stockholm, Allmänna förlaget.

Harris JE (1977) The Internal Organisation of Hospitals: Some Economic Implications. The Bell Journal of Economics 8, 467-82.

Hernes G (1975) Makt og avmakt. Bergen, Universitetsforlaget.

Joskow PL (1983) Reimbursement Policy, Cost Containment and Non-price Competition. Journal of Health Economics 2, 167-174.

Lindgren B, Roos P (1985) Produktions-, kostnads- och produktivitetsutveckling inom offentligt bedriven hälso- och sjukvård 1960-1980. Rapport till Expertgrup-pen för studier i offentlig ekonomi, Ds Fi 1985:3. Stockholm, Liber Allmänna för-laget.

Lyttkens CH (1992) Imperatives in Health Care. Implications for Social Welfare and Medical Technology. Working Paper Series 16/1992, Department of Economics, Lund University.

Lyttkens CH (1994) Access, Need, Equity and Priorities in Health Care. In Wester-häll L, Phillips C (eds) Patient's Rights - Informed Consent, Access and Equality. Stockholm, Nerenius & Santérus Publishers, 155-169.

Lyttkens CH, Borgquist L (forthcoming, a) Swedish Health Care in the Late 1980s and Early 1990s - A Story of Institutional Change. In Alban A, Christiansen T (eds) New Initiatives in Health Care Systems. The Nordic Light. Odense Univer-sity Press.

Lyttkens CH, Borgquist L (forthcoming, b) Organisational Change in the Swedish Health Care Sector. In Alban A, Christiansen T (eds) New Initiatives in Health Care Systems. The Nordic Light. Odense University Press.

Manning WG et al. (1987) Health Insurance and the Demand for Medical Care: Evi-dence from a Randomized Experiment. American Economic Review 77, 251-77.

McGuire A, Henderson J, Mooney G (1992) The Economics of Health Care. London, Routledge.

McGuire A et al. (1993) Econometric Analyses of National Health Expenditures: Can Positive Economics Help to Answer Normative Questions? Health Economics 2, 113-126.

REFERENCES, continued

Melnick GA et al. (1992) The Effects of Market Structure and Bargaining Position on Hospital Prices. Journal of Health Economics 11, 217-233.

Mooney G et al. (1991) Utilisation as a Measure of Equity: Weighing Heat? Journal of Health Economics 10, 476-480.

Newhouse JP (1992) Medical Care Costs: How Much Welfare Loss? Journal of Economic Perspectives 6, 3-21.

North DC (1993) The Historical Evolution of Polities. Paper presented at the Arne Ryde Symposium on the Economic Analysis of Law, Department of Economics, Lund University.

Olson M (1965) The Logic of Collective Action. Cambridge, Mass.

Pedersen KM (1991) Health Maintenance Organisations. In Andersen P, Christiansen T (eds) Styring & regulering på udbudssiden i sundhedssektoren. Odense universitetsforlag, 114-135.

Pope GC (1989) Hospital Nonprice Competition and Medicare Reimbursement Policy. Journal of Health Economics 8, 147-172.

Robinson JC, Luft HS (1987) Competition and the Cost of Hospital Care, 1972 to 1982. The Journal of the American Medical Association 257, 3241-3245.

Robinson JC, Luft HS (1988) Competition, Regulation, and Hospital Costs, 1982 to 1986. The Journal of the American Medical Association 260, 2676-2681.

Steen K (1993) Equality of Access - Definitions and Implications. Paper presented at the Health Economists' Study Group Meeting, Glasgow, July 1993.

Stoddart G, Feeny D (1986) Policy Options for Health Care Technology. In Feeny D, Guyatt G, Tugwell P (eds) Health Care Technology: Effectiveness, Efficiency, and Public Policy. Montreal, The Institute for Research on Public Policy.

Wagstaff A, van Doorslaer E (1993) Equity in the Finance and Delivery of Health Care: Concepts and Definitions. In van Doorslaer E, Wagstaff A, Rutten f (eds) Equity in the Finance and Delivery of Health Care. New York, Oxford University Press, 7-19.

Weisbrod BA (1978) Comment on M.V. Pauly. In Greenberg W (ed) Competition in the Health Care Sector. Proceedings of a conference sponsored by the Bureau of Economics. Federal Trade Commission, Germanstown, Aspen systems.

Weisbrod BA (1991) The Health Care Quadrilemma: An Essay on Technological Change, Insurance, Quality of Care, and Cost Containement. Journal of Economic Literature 29, 523-552.

Springer-Verlag
and the Environment

We at Springer-Verlag firmly believe that an international science publisher has a special obligation to the environment, and our corporate policies consistently reflect this conviction.

We also expect our business partners – paper mills, printers, packaging manufacturers, etc. – to commit themselves to using environmentally friendly materials and production processes.

The paper in this book is made from low- or no-chlorine pulp and is acid free, in conformance with international standards for paper permanency.

Printing: Weihert-Druck GmbH, Darmstadt
Binding: Theo Gansert Buchbinderei GmbH, Weinheim